Exploring Strategic Change

Julia Balogun
Veronica Hope Hailey
with
Gerry Johnson and Kevan Scholes

Prentice Hall Europe
London New York Toronto Sydney Tokyo
Singapore Madrid Mexico City Munich Paris

First published 1999 by
Prentice Hall Europe
Campus 400, Maylands Avenue
Hemel Hempstead
Hertfordshire, HP2 7EZ
A division of
Simon & Schuster International Group

Typeset in 10 pt New Century Schoolbook
by Fakenham Photosetting Ltd, Fakenham, Norfolk

Printed and bound in Great Britain by T.J. International, Padstow

Library of Congress Cataloging-in-Publication Data

Available from the publisher

British Library Cataloguing in Publication Data

A catalogue record for this book is available from
the British Library

ISBN 0–13–263856–8

1 2 3 4 5   03 02 01 00 99

Contents

Figures and tables

Figures

Tables

Change in action – Illustrations

Preface

Exploring Corporate Strategy by Gerry Johnson and Kevan Scholes is
now established as the leading text in its field in Europe and beyond
with world-wide sales exceeding 300,000. It is a text provided for students and practising managers which aims to develop their conceptual
understanding of why and how organizations of many different types
develop and change their strategies. It does so within a practical context whilst drawing on best strategic management practice as
researchers, writers and practitioners understand it.

With so many managers and students now familiar with
Exploring Corporate Strategy we have responded to the requests for
material which takes the themes and concepts of strategic management further in a way which is not possible within the confines of a
broad textbook on the subject. Prentice Hall Europe have agreed to
publish a series of short practical books which build on the basic
framework of *Exploring Corporate Strategy*.

Exploring Corporate Strategy has always placed great emphasis
on the processes of strategic management and the problems and
importance of managing strategic change. *Exploring Strategic Change*
is the third of the books to be published in this series. The others are
*Exploring Techniques of Analysis and Evaluation in Strategic
Management* edited by Véronique Ambrosini and *Exploring Strategic
Financial Management* by Tony Grundy. Further books are in preparation. All of the books are developed under the editorial guidance of
Gerry Johnson and Kevan Scholes and have the following aims:

- to provide further depth on aspects of strategic management which
  should already be familiar to readers of *Exploring Corporate Strategy*;
- to do this in a practical and applied way whilst drawing on best practice from researchers, writers and practitioners.

Exploring Strategic Change addresses four main themes:

- that the task of managing change is context-specific and therefore an
  understanding of the organization's change context is essential;

- that analyzing the change context allows change agents to make design choices on the basis of 'best fit' for the organization;
- that once the change process has been designed the next task is to both design and manage the transition;
- that there are established levers and mechanisms for managing transition.

The first half of the book focuses on the design of the change process and the analysis of the change context within an organization. Chapter 2 addresses the subject of design choices by providing a menu of design options which are discussed within six overall groupings: change paths, change style, change targets, change roles, change start points and change levers and mechanisms. These are discussed at this point in the book in order that the reader is aware of the range of choices that are available to a change agent. Chapters 3 and 4 then examine the importance of determining contextual fit when selecting appropriate design choices. A diagnostic framework, the change kaleidoscope, is presented in Chapter 3 which helps identify the key contextual features in an organization. The kaleidoscope features are: time, scope, preservation, diversity, capability, capacity, readiness and power. Not only does analysis of these features allow the reader to make appropriate design choices, it prevents these features becoming barriers to change during the transition process itself. Both Chapters 3 and 4 illustrate how different features impact on different design choices. Chapter 4 demonstrates this through the use of five case studies of companies experiencing change and transition.

The second half of the book examines the transition process in depth. Chapter 5 explains the role of visioning in change and also introduces the idea of different stages of transition: unfreeze, move and sustain. Both Chapters 5 and 6 examine the various mechanisms that can be used for each stage of transition. These include both symbolic levers and human resource management processes. The importance of fit with context is highlighted throughout the discussion on levers and mechanisms. Chapter 7 explores the actual management of the transition process and puts forward ideas for evaluating change. The first and final chapters use a change flow chart to pull together the various stages of the change process that are detailed within all the chapters. Both chapters also put forward thoughts about the centrality of change capability as a competence for managers in the twenty-first century and the personal skills and attributes required of effective change agents. The appendices contain information on various diagnostic tools that can be used by a change agent when analyzing organizational contexts and making change judgements.

Acknowledgements

Many people have helped us in the process of writing this book. We would like to thank Jayne Ashley, Quaye Botchway and Tara Williams for their diligent, sympathetic and thorough approach in helping us to construct a manuscript fit for the publishers. Also thanks go to the many MBA students at Cranfield School of Management, both full-time and part-time, who offered important comments on the ideas presented in this book. Finally, we must thank our patient and understanding families who put up with our long periods at the word processors when we should really have been with them, and particularly to the many babies who were carried and delivered during the development of this book. This book is dedicated to all of them.

To Paul, Guy and Annys

and John, Helen, Mary, Frances, Joanna and Sarah Jane.

1

Exploring strategic change: an introduction

1.1 *Introduction*

Change management is fast becoming one of the most talked about topics in management circles. Discussions about organizational change often focus on how important it is for organizations or individual managers to possess a capability in this area. Few actually talk about how such a capability might be developed. Likewise, business school courses on strategic change stress that change competence is fast becoming a key promotion differentiator within a manager's toolbox. Yet few students are given concrete suggestions about how to develop that competence. This book aims to help managers and students alike to fill these gaps, by building on the concepts presented in its sister text, *Exploring Corporate Strategy* by Gerry Johnson and Kevan Scholes, also published by Prentice Hall.

Exploring Corporate Strategy introduces readers to the concepts of strategic management, and the different approaches to strategy development. The book explores various techniques for analyzing an organization's strategic environment, and considers strategic choice – the range of issues and options to be taken into account when developing an organization's future strategic direction. The final section of the book examines strategy implementation. The structure of the book is illustrated as a series of interlinked circles as shown in Figure 1.1.

One of the components of strategy implementation is labelled *managing strategic change*. This is the focus of this book. We are expecting readers to already have an understanding of strategic issues and the management of strategy from either *Exploring Corporate Strategy* or another text.

Exploring Corporate Strategy and *Exploring Strategic Change* share a common viewpoint. *Exploring Corporate Strategy* presents two views of the process of strategic management. One view is that strategy can, and indeed should, be managed through planning processes. As such, strategy is the outcome of careful, objective analysis and planning. The other view is that strategic management is not so much about formal planning, but more of a negotiated process, open to both managerial and cultural influences. This latter view recognizes that

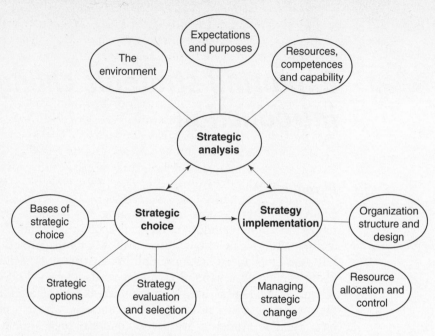

Figure 1.1   *A summary model of the elements of strategic management*
(Source: G. Johnson and K. Scholes, Exploring Corporate Strategy, 5th edn,
1999, Hemel Hempstead: Prentice Hall)

strategy develops within a context and is influenced by elements
within that context, whether they be managers' opinions, cultural
values or whatever. However good the plans may be, they will still be
subject to these influences.

This book argues that managing strategic change is also a
process. Change is not something that can be just mapped out in a
formal project plan in a manager's office. Change does not happen as
a result of a plan; it is more complex than that. In particular, this text
emphasizes that one reason change implementation is complex is
because successful change depends on the development of a context
sensitive approach. One of the distinguishing features of this book is
that it presents a framework – the change kaleidoscope – that can be
used to help make judgements about what approach to change is most
suited to a particular change context.

The text is aimed at both business students and practising managers. However, throughout the book, reference is made to the *change
agent*. The change agent is the person responsible for 'making the
change happen' in any organization. In reality these people are not formally given the label of change agent. Many different people can fulfil
this role. In some organizations it may be the Chief Executive, in

others the Human Resources Director, or even a selected team of people, who have responsibility for managing the change process. Whoever is appointed, formally or informally, into the position of heading up the management of change, this book refers to them as the 'change agent'.

There are two main sections to the book: the first section, Chapters 2 to 4, explores the role of context in developing appropriate approaches to change; the second section, Chapters 5 to 7, examines how to turn the chosen change approach into a reality to make change actually happen. However, it is first necessary to explain some of the assumptions underpinning this text. This is done in the rest of this introduction. Consideration is given to:

- The nature of organizational change and the philosophy behind this text.
- The need to develop a change approach which is suitable for the organization's specific context.
- The managerial and personal skills required by a successful change agent.
- The difference between the design of recipe-driven or formulaic approaches to change implementation and more context-specific approaches.

The chapter concludes with a flowchart which explains the structure and content of the book.

1.2 *The nature of organizational change*

Organizational change has three main components as shown in Figure 1.2: the change context, the change content and the change process:

- The change *context* is the *why* of change. *Outer context* refers to the social, economic, political and competitive environment in which the organization operates (Chapter 3, *Exploring Corporate Strategy*). The *inner context* is the culture, structure and capabilities of the organization, and also includes the political context (Chapters 4 and 5, *Exploring Corporate Strategy*).
- The change *content* is the *what* of change, and refers to choices that need to be made about an organization's product range, the markets in which it competes, how it competes, how it should be structured, and so on (Chapter 6 onwards, *Exploring Corporate Strategy*). Any of these may need to change because of changes in the organization's context.
- The last point of the triangle, the change *process*, is the *how* of change, the things done to deliver change, and is the focus of this book.

Exploring Strategic Change is therefore concerned with how organizations change. However, when people talk about organizations

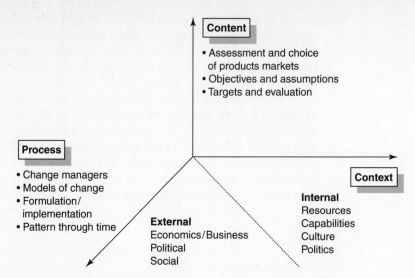

Figure 1.2   *Three components of change*
(Source: *A. Pettigrew and R. Whipp,* Managing Change for Competitive Success, *1991, Oxford: Blackwell Publishers. © A. Pettigrew and R. Whipp, 1991)*

changing, what they really mean is that people must change. Of course buildings, technology and products can all be changed, but if an organization is to really change, then the people within that organization also need to change the way they behave. This principle affects the way this book approaches change. People are not seen as objects who change because a plan or office memo says they should. They have minds of their own and can decide to react in any way that they choose. Managing change and achieving change in individuals is therefore a challenging undertaking for any manager.

In addition, because change involves people and people react in different and sometimes unpredictable ways, change is more than the development of a plan. A failure to appreciate this can lead to two fatal flaws within many change plans that are otherwise very impressive in their detail and scheduling – the assumption that employee reactions to the plans can be controlled; and no provision within the plan for managing the process of change.

Chapter 2 of *Exploring Corporate Strategy* discusses this in some depth, with particular reference to the impact of culture and politics on the way strategic change develops in organizations. Suffice to say this text explicitly acknowledges that changing organizations is about changing people and that any implementation approach has to work within the cultural, political and social nature of organizations.

One extension of this line of argument is that the nature of organizations and organizational change is so complex, that it is virtually impossible to manage change. Whilst we accept that people are unpredictable and can react to change in many different ways, we take the view that the process of change can be managed. Furthermore, given the way some organizations operate, that change can be better managed in some organizations than in others. This means that the management of change is a competence that can be developed by practitioners, and an exciting area for study and research. This book contributes to both of these areas by giving practitioners practical advice which they can implement within their workplace, to enable them to develop their change management competence. At the same time, the book aims to add some new thoughts and concepts to the broad base of academic literature associated with the management of change.

1.3 Context-specific change

Although the management of change is a managerial competence that can be learnt over time, this book does not advocate 'one best way to change'. Instead it is argued that change needs to be context-specific. The determination of the design and management of any change process should be dependent on the specific situation of each organization.

One of the dangers with prescriptive books on change management is that the writers try to advocate an ideal or best practice approach to managing change. Their ideal way may be derived from consultancy, research or practitioner experience, but it is often obtained from just a few case studies of organizational change. The danger lies in extending lessons from the specific into general prescriptions. Cases can be very important for illustrating what is possible. However, a limited number of cases, particularly when repeatedly cited, may imply that the formula that works for these organizations is generally applicable, when this may not be so (1). This is particularly true when the cases studied represent certain contexts, such as, for example, companies starting afresh at new sites (greenfield sites), or high technology companies.

The 'best practice' models put forward by many texts on change management frequently suggest that there are universal formulae that can be applied to any organization that needs to undergo change. The sort of best practice rhetoric that is often heard in the change literature is 'you must get senior management support before attempting to manage change'. This may be true for many change situations – but perhaps for certain organizations senior management support may not be necessary, or may take too long to acquire. For instance, if the senior management are themselves major blocks to the implementation of change, the change agent may need to start with some other intervention and hope to gain senior support later on in the change process. Yet how can this be determined without analyzing the context of each organization?

What this means for change agents is that instead of identifying 'best practice' solutions, they need to start looking for 'best questions'. Just as *Exploring Corporate Strategy* explains that a contextual analysis is important in determining how strategy should shift, this book argues that the internal and external context of the organization should be examined in order to determine the appropriate change process. Some of the features considered in this analysis may be the same as for a strategic analysis, for example, power relationships, whilst others will be very specific to change management rather than strategy, such as readiness for change and change capacity and capability.

However, understanding an organization's change context requires the change agent to develop certain managerial and personal skills. These are discussed next.

1.4   *Managerial skills for the change agent: analysis, judgement and action*

Change agents need to develop their *analytical*, *judgemental* and *implementation* skills. All three of these are important. Without analysis the temptation is to draw upon ready-made change recipes; without judgement, after contextual analysis, change agents can miss the most critical aspect of the change context; and without action, the process can remain a planning exercise which never tackles the reality of change within the organization.

Therefore, change agents need to possess *analytical* abilities, rather than to know the '10 best ways to run a change programme'. They need to be able to dig deep into an organization, to understand its culture and the motivations of its staff, to develop a full and holistic picture of the organization concerned. This is discussed in Chapter 3.

However, equally, the practitioner needs to be wary of the old danger of falling into 'paralysis by analysis'. It is easy to become overwhelmed by a detailed analysis. So an additional skill is being able to *judge* which are the most critical features that are revealed by the contextual analysis. To take a medical analogy, a doctor giving a patient an examination following an accident might reveal that the patient has cracked ribs, but also lymphatic cancer. The ribs can be treated immediately, but clearly the most critical condition, requiring longer-term and more intensive care, is the cancer. Similarly, the change agent has to prioritize or weight the organizational features she or he uncovers in terms of how critical they are to the change process. The key skill for a change agent is being able to recognize what is critical in the particular change context. This idea is examined further in Chapter 4 through a series of change case studies.

Finally, a change agent needs to develop the ability to manage the *implementation* of change. Management is practice not just analysis – it is about making things happen. Two key aspects of implementation that have to be addressed are which interventions to make in a change situation, and in what order to apply them. The change agent may recognize that a reward system must be changed within an organization along with changes to the production system and job redesign. Yet to avoid confusing the employees with too many simultaneous change initiatives, the agent has to decide which initiative should be carried out first and which one can wait until later. This sounds like common-sense. In practice, these decisions can vex managers as change situations are usually very complex. Choosing and sequencing change interventions are discussed in Chapters 5 and 6 of this book.

1.5 *Personal skills for change agents*

In addition to the managerial skills of judgement, analysis and action, change agents also need certain personal skills, including the ability to handle *complexity*, *sensitivity* and *self-awareness*.

1.5.1 *Complexity and sensitivity*

The ability to deal with complexity and sensitivity are relevant for the initial design stage of a change process – the analytical and judgemental parts of the intervention – and are interrelated. Change agents need to be able to 'see the big picture' yet also have the maturity to appreciate the need for deep analysis of the big picture. It is easy for managers to be impatient with what they see as easily identifiable malfunctions. They often fail to understand that organizations are complex systems, and that it is therefore difficult to make changes in one area without having repercussions in others. To use a medical analogy again, there is a tendency to treat the symptoms rather than to identify and treat the root cause.

However, sensitivity is not just about appreciation of context, it is also about appreciation of the impact of action. Organizations and their reorganization affect people's lives. Euphemisms for making staff redundant (downsizing, rightsizing etc.) screen us from the potential impact of that action on the lives of employees. Families and children are affected by decisions in the workplace: houses can be repossessed, families split up geographically and individuals personally shocked or traumatized by changes in the workplace. Although hard business decisions will always have to be made, they should never be made lightly or without adequate analysis because of their potential influence on the personal lives of staff.

As an extension of the need for change agents to handle complexity and be sensitive to context and the impact of actions, change agents also require *influencing skills* to help them to sell the change process to those around them. They also need well-honed political skills to help them manage the power relations in any change situation. Change often involves winners and losers. A change agent needs to be able to deal with the fall-out from change!

1.5.2   Self-awareness

Self-awareness is the capacity to understand one's own prejudices, preferences and experience. The way people view organizations affects the type of approach they are likely to take to change. Individuals view organizations in fundamentally different ways. Without realizing it, change agents often allow their personal philosophy and style to influence the change interventions they choose. As a result, they often give limited consideration, if any, to the actual change context and its needs. Just as the idea of organizational paradigms (2) was introduced through the framework of the cultural web in *Exploring Corporate Strategy*, *personal paradigms* can also exist at an individual level. They act as a filter or lens through which individuals view, discuss and judge change.

It is important for change agents to recognize the existence of personal paradigms for two reasons:

- Designers of change should be driven more by the needs of the organization than by their own perceptions or prejudices of what has constituted 'good' change management in the past. This requires an awareness of their own biases.
- It may be easier for change agents to understand other people's prejudices, paradigms or biases if they are armed with a certain degree of self-awareness. This is vital for working with others within the organization and for persuading them of the wisdom of a particular change approach.

There are many complex explanations of the different ways in which individuals may view organizations – whole books are written on this subject alone. What follows highlights only a few key differences in order to illustrate how a change agent's 'world-view' can affect the change choices they make.

Words like 'objective' and 'subjective' are encountered in everyday use. When asked to define objective as opposed to subjective, individuals may make the following sorts of distinctions:

- Objective: rational, logical, analytical, facts, data, hard, quantitative.
- Subjective: intuitive, experience, moral, feelings, emotions, soft, qualitative.

Objective assessments are seen as hard and measurable. Decisions are made on the basis of tangible facts and figures. Subjective assessments are seen to be based on something less tangible, more intuitive than data driven.

Managers with a preference for either objectivity or subjectivity might describe organizations and their approach to change in a similar way to the respondents in Illustration 1.1. A manager taking an objective view of organizations may conceive change in terms of reconstruction not necessarily perceiving a need to tackle underlying beliefs and assumptions. This sort of change agent may feel more comfortable

Change in action

Illustration 1.1
An objective versus a subjective world-view

An objective perspective

'Organizations are physical and tangible. Things are done according to rules and regulations which are written down ... there is something tangible and measurable about organizations ... I'm very tool oriented ... my inclination is to state very clearly what the objective is, to chart the process and assume that others working with me have sufficient rationality to see it similarly to myself.'

A subjective perspective

'Organizations should not be thought of as physical entities which can be controlled and modelled ... An organization is a social entity, something that is socially constructed by the people within it. I see an organization in terms of its meaning systems rather than its physical aspects ... This concept of organization does have implications for the way I view change. For a start we have to be careful not to impose an objective mindset on what we see as an organization and assume it is something we can control ... An organization includes people's attitudes and views, and for change to occur these have to change too. This is not to say that if you force people to change their behaviour by imposing new control systems and ways of behaving on them, they will not also change their attitudes. But you have no guarantee that they will change their attitudes in the way you want or anticipated, you cannot control the type of meaning change that occurs ... If you take my view of organizations to an extreme, it in fact suggests you cannot control or manage change at all. As such all you can do is to facilitate change.'

with a directive change approach which involves little participation: they may not see a need to understand a wide variety of views at different levels of the organization. In an extreme form, the rational approach may involve the development of change plans by senior managers, which are then issued as edicts to be implemented by others.

In contrast, managers with a more subjective orientation may be more likely to perceive of change in terms of evolution. They therefore rely on a more participative approach, which allows for greater involvement from all levels of the organization. Such managers are more likely to assume that any change approach will need to allow for the existence of differing perspectives within the organization, and will therefore want to work hard at fostering consensus. There is likely to be a greater emphasis on softer interventions such as communication.

This presents the subjective and objective perspectives as opposite ends of a spectrum, whereas there are many shades of grey in between. The point is, that for any change agent, an awareness of which perspective predominates within their own mind will make them aware of how they will view change. The skill is for the change agent to check that their perspective is not in danger of becoming a prejudice. If an organization is not in crisis and there is little readiness for change, a more objective manager should not automatically dismiss the option of extensive communication to generate some degree of readiness, even if it is not her/his preferred way of working. Likewise, if an organization is in real crisis, a more subjective manager may have to accept that there is insufficient time for extensive consultation with all staff members, however much it goes against their personal philosophy.

This attribute of self-awareness is an important ability for change agents, and its existence within any manager illustrates a maturity of understanding of change, organizations and self.

1.6   *A formulaic approach to change design: a dangerous route*

The first half of this chapter has explained how the text meshes with its sister text, *Exploring Corporate Strategy*, with its view of change as a process, and in its emphasis on the importance of contextual analysis. It has also discussed some of the attributes required of change agents. The second half of the chapter expands on the structure of the argument followed in the book, and explains how this argument differs from many other approaches to change. In particular, it emphasizes the importance of context and draws attention to the danger of formulaic change.

In an approach which uses pre-existing best practice models for managing change, the change agent would go through the stages illustrated in Figure 1.3.

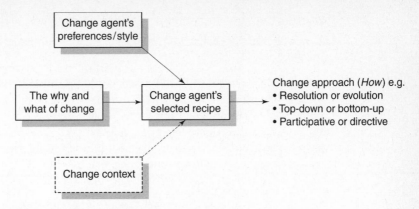

Figure 1.3   A formulaic approach to change design

- *Step 1*: Consideration is given to the why and what of strategy development. The internal and external *context* of the organization is analyzed in order to gain an understanding of *why* change is necessary. In addition the strategists decide on the *content* of change, in *what* areas it is essential to achieve change. In terms of Figure 1.4, strategists analyze the current situation of the organization (A); identify what the new organization should look like (B); and then they ask the change agent(s) to devise a change process (C) to shift the organization from A to B (3).
- *Step 2*: The change agent designs the change process. What many change agents do at this stage is to turn to a number of existing change solutions. They then derive the design of the change process from these predetermined change formulae. There are various sources for these existing solutions (see Figure 1.5).

  Unfortunately, what can then happen is that the change agent picks existing solutions without assessing the appropriateness of the solutions to the current organization's change context. This is not to

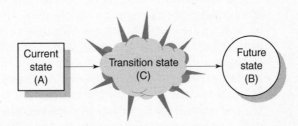

Figure 1.4   Three change states

Change agents can choose from a range of existing formulaic approaches to change:

- The past experience of the change agent within previous organizations.
  'In XKX Tea Manufacturers we did it this way and it worked really well.'

- Previous experiences of change within the organization:
  'Well in 1988 we had to change to launch a new division and the way we did it then was like this – it worked really well.'

- Organizational consultants:
  'Buy our proven approach to change. Twenty other companies have followed our 10 point plan and it has worked for them!'

- Books or articles on change:
  'Follow the rules for change set out in this book and you will achieve organizational breakthrough and beat the competition!!!'

- Dominant CEOs or other senior directors:
  'Bruce – I'm delegating the design of the whole of the change process to you. You have complete autonomy but I'd like to see it done this way!!!!! Change always happens when you follow these procedures – trust me ...'

Figure 1.5   *Source of existing change approaches*

denigrate the value of past experience or previous learning. They are important and valuable. However, the past must also be analyzed with reference to the current context. When reflecting on the past, a change agent needs to ask her/himself questions such as: 'Why did that work well for that organization then? What was it about the culture at that time, or the structure, or the external marketplace, that made that change process so right for that situation? What are the differences between that organization's context then, and this organization now?'

Pulling down existing solutions is by far the easiest way of going about designing change. The problem is that if the design selected is inappropriate for the current organization's change context, it will only emerge later as the change process fails to deliver the required changes and after much wasted time and effort. This text argues that a more appropriate way to go about designing the change approach is to use the organization's context to guide the approach selected. A contextual analysis may reveal that an existing change approach is workable in the current situation; on the other hand, it will also guard against the use of inappropriate solutions.

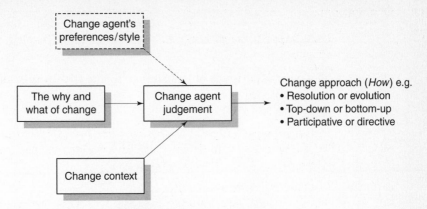

Figure 1.6   *A context-sensitive approach to change design*

1.7   *Context-sensitive change: a safer route?*

A context-sensitive approach to change sees the stages in the design process as shown in Figure 1.6.

- *Step 1*: As above, the strategists decide on the *content* of change, and in *what* areas it is essential to achieve change.
- *Step 2*: The change agent carries out an *analysis* of the change *context*, which examines the organizational features pertinent to the change situation, such as the scope of change required, the time frame, the power of the change agent to effect change, the diversity within the workforce and the capability for change within the organization.
- *Step 3*: The change agent *judges* which are the most *critical* features of the current change situation. In any organization, the contextual features do not carry equal weighting – some will be more important than others. So, for instance, in some organizations the existence of strong professional groups may create diversity among the workforce. Professionals, such as hospital consultants, will often identify more readily with the values and aims of their professional association rather than with their employing organization. It would be difficult to design a successful change process within a hospital without taking this in to account. However, in organizations which employ few professionals this feature may not be so critical.
- *Step 4*: The change agent selects the appropriate *design choices*. Information derived from the contextual analysis in steps 2 and 3 will start to make some design options seem unworkable and others either possible or essential. For instance, if the organization has only a small amount of money to invest in change, some of the more expensive, educative styles of change, using expensive management development options, may not be feasible.

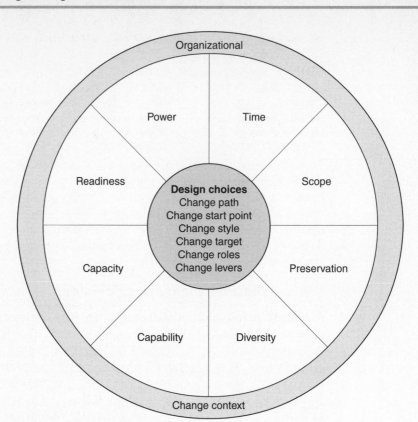

Figure 1.7   The change kaleidoscope

This text uses a diagnostic framework, the *change kaleidoscope*, shown in Figure 1.7, to help with steps 2–4.

The kaleidoscope contains an outer ring concerned with the organizational strategic context, a middle ring concerned with the features of the change context, and an inner ring which contains the menu of design choices open to change agents:

- The *strategic context* refers to the fact-finding exercise carried out in step 1 that determines why the organization should change and what it should change to. This analysis is the focus of *Exploring Corporate Strategy*.

- The organizational *change contextual features* are aspects of the organization to do with its culture, competences and current situation, which change agents should consider before selecting the change approach. These features can be extracted from the broader organizational strategic context, and can be used by change agents to help determine the appropriateness of any change approach for a particular context. It is these features that are examined as part of steps 2 and 3, and they are explored in depth in Chapter 3.

- The *design choices* are the range of options a change agent needs to choose from when selecting an appropriate change approach. For example, what type of change path is best here? Do we need to do something radical and fast? Or would it be more effective in the long term if it were a staged change process, planned over time? Where should the change start point be? Should the change be organized so that it cascades down from the senior management, or would it be better if it was piloted on the edges of the organization first? Who should lead this change – the CEO or external consultants? These are the questions that need to be considered in step 4 and the answer to them should be determined by the analysis of the change contextual features from steps 2 and 3. The range of choices open to a change agent are explored in detail in Chapter 2.

As explained under step 3, the contextual features in the change kaleidoscope do not carry equal weighting in all organizations – some will be more important than others in different organizational change contexts. This is why the diagnostic framework is called a kaleidoscope as its configurations of features will constantly shift according to the organization being analyzed. This aspect of judging the relative criticality of organizational features is examined in more depth in Chapter 4.

However, although the change agent has now selected a change approach, this is not the end of the story. One of the key managerial skills is *action*; the change agent now has to design the levers and mechanisms that will deliver the selected approach and also manage the process of implementation. This is why the change process in Figure 1.4 above is referred to as the *transition state*. It is the phase of change when a series of change interventions are put in place to effect a transition from the current organization state, to the future desired organization state.

1.8 *The transition state: design and management*

Implementation is often conceived of in terms of the planning for change, with scant attention to managing the transition process itself. In fact, the transition state is not like either the current or future state. Specific attention is required to both the design and management of the transition state.

The issues that need to be considered in designing the transition fall out of the design choices made. For instance, as a result of the design choice phase it may have been decided to focus on realigning employee behaviours as a means of achieving change. In order to achieve that behavioural change, the change agent will need to deploy a series of levers and mechanisms, such as new reward systems and training. However, the identification of the primary levers and mechanisms is only the beginning. If the new reward system is to be effective, other things may need to be changed, such as the appraisal mechanism. Existing practices that could obstruct the new required behaviours also need to be identified and removed. There are also issues about timing. Are new rewards and training to be introduced simultaneously, or are new rewards introduced to reinforce the training? There are also likely to be other changes such as alterations to the payroll system, that have to be scheduled. All these different interventions need to be sequenced during the transition along with other change interventions such as communication of the need for change, and the form of the changes. Effecting transitions is therefore a complex business.

Chapter 5 addresses this issue. It introduces the idea that transitions have three phases – *unfreeze, move* and *sustain* – and considers the various activities that are necessary to take an organization through all three phases. It also explains how any organizational change process is underpinned by the personal transitions of individuals within that organization.

Since the implementation of change involves people, it can be an unpredictable process. Change agents may plan each aspect of the implementation carefully, but they can never anticipate all human reactions or, for that matter, the impact of events outside the organization. Chapters 6 and 7 discuss transition management techniques such as communication and resistance management that can make transition through the change process more effective for the organization and more acceptable to employees.

1.9   Putting the jigsaw together: a change flow chart

For change to be successful, managers charged with the responsibility of managing this activity need to address the complexities of both context and process. However, the very complexity can be off-putting. Figure 1.8 presents a flow chart of the steps this text is advocating to inject some clarity into the process. It shows which questions have to be addressed at different stages of the change process.

Stages 1, 2 and 3 are addressed within *Exploring Corporate Strategy*, although this text will discuss the development of the desired future state in more detail in Chapter 5. Stages 4 and 5, analyzing the change context and identifying the critical change features, are presented through a fuller account of the change kaleidoscope in Chapters 3 and 4. Stage 6, determining the design choices, follows on from stage 5, but this text discusses the design choices in Chapter 2, before the contextual features are described, since it is easier to appreciate how

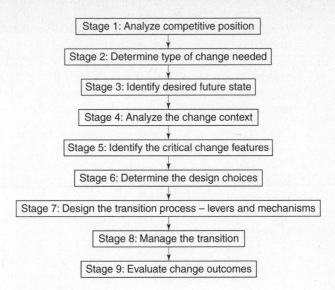

Figure 1.8   *The change flow chart*

the contextual features impact on the design choices once the range of design choices is understood. Chapters 5 and 6 consider the design of the transition through exploring the different stages of transition, the use of different change levers and mechanisms and the overriding importance of appropriate communication at all stages. Chapter 7 discusses how to monitor the success of the change process and resourcing issues for the transition.

1.10   *Summary*

This opening chapter has established the links that exist between this book and its sister text *Exploring Corporate Strategy*. It has also introduced the role of the *change agent*, and highlighted the fact that change is distinct from strategy in so far as change is about moving an organization from its current position to a future condition in order that a change in strategy might be achieved. In particular the chapter has introduced several central concepts that underpin the philosophy of the whole book:

- The view that change is manageable if not controllable.
- That all change design must be context-specific, which requires change agents to possess managerial skills of analysis, judgement and implementation; and personal skills such as appreciation of complexity, sensitivity and self-awareness.
- The difference between formulaic and context-specific approaches to change implementation.

- Transition as a stage in change which demands that attention is given to both its design and management
- A general change flow chart, which identifies different decision-making points in the strategic change process and sets out the overall way this text recommends a change agent should approach the management of strategic change.

These central concepts underpin the rest of the chapters of the book. *Exploring Strategic Change* aims to provide an intelligent guide to managing change in today's complex organizational environments. It is hoped that readers will gain worthwhile insight into the challenging subject of change.

Notes and references

(1)   This is discussed by D. Guest, 'Human Resource Management and the American Dream', *Journal of Management Studies,* 27, 2, 1990, pp. 377–97. Also see J. Storey (ed.), *New Perspectives on Human Resource Management,* London: Routledge, 1989, and P. Blyton and P. Turnbull (eds), *Reassessing Human Resource Management*, London: Sage, 1992.

(2)   Paradigm is a term used by a number of writers, but in *Exploring Corporate Strategy*, Chapter 2, organizational paradigms are defined as the taken-for-granted assumptions and beliefs that become shared among an organization's members about the nature of the organization and its environment. The paradigm is the result of collective experience and enables the members of an organization to work cohesively together without the need to constantly reinvent new ways of doing things. It acts like an invisible lens through which the organization's members view the world, affecting the way they see things and therefore react to them. The paradigm is also the central component of the cultural analysis framework used in *Exploring Corporate Strategy*, the cultural web, which is also used in this text and is explained in Appendix 1.

(3)   The concept of change as three states – the present, the future and the transition – is advanced by R. Beckhard and R.T. Harris, *Organizational Transitions: Managing Complex Change,* 2nd edition, Addison Wesley, 1987.

2 *Understanding implementation choices: the options to consider*

2.1 *Introduction*

Chapter 1 introduces the concept of the change kaleidoscope (see Figure 2.1). It shows that a change agent faces a bewildering array of implementation decisions – the *design choices* – that need to be made about how change should be implemented within her or his particular context. This chapter explains these different design choices, and the options within each choice. The design choices from the change kaleidoscope are explained in detail before the contextual features. It is then simpler to explain the contextual features and how they link to the choices that need to be made.

The change kaleidoscope separates the array of choices that need to be made on any implementation approach into six categories, within which there are a range of alternatives. The six categories are:

- *Change path*: The type of change to be undertaken in terms of the nature of the change and the desired end result. This category is referred to as change path as distinct from change type, as in some circumstances it is necessary to undertake an enabling phase of change before it is possible to undertake the actual changes required.
- *Change start point*: Where the change is initiated and developed, which could be summarized simplistically as top-down or bottom-up, but there are other choices.
- *Change style*: The management style of the implementation, such as highly collaborative or more directive.
- *Change target*: The target of the change interventions, in terms of people's attitudes and values, behaviours or outputs.
- *Change roles*: Who is to take responsibility for leading and implementing the changes.
- *Change levers*: The range of levers and mechanisms to be deployed.

This chapter discusses each one of these choices in more detail. The choices should always be considered separately for each change initiat-

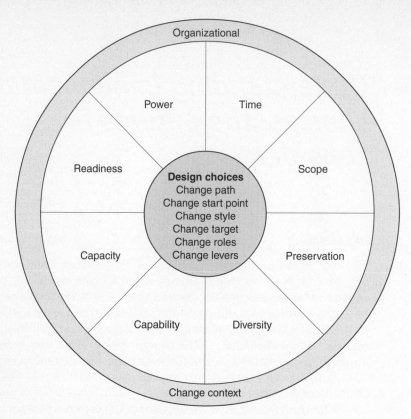

Figure 2.1   The change kaleidoscope

ive to avoid the use of change recipes involving particular combinations of choices in inappropriate situations.

2.2   *Change path*

There are four main types of change illustrated in Figure 2.2. These four types are defined in terms of two dimensions – the *end result of change* and the *nature of change*. The end result is about the extent of change desired. Change can involve a *transformation* of the organization or a *realignment*. Transformation is explained in *Exploring Corporate Strategy*, Chapter 11, as 'change which cannot be handled within the existing paradigm (1) and organizational routines; it entails a change in the taken-for-granted assumptions and "the way of doing things around here"'. It is a fundamental change within the organization.

As an example, in the late 1990s, Shell, the world's second

End result

Transformation   Realignment

	Transformation	Realignment
Incremental	**Evolution**	**Adaptation**
Big bang	**Revolution**	**Reconstruction**

Nature

Figure 2.2   *Types of change*

biggest company, embarked on an intended transformational change
driven by the need to remain competitive in the face of better performance by its rivals. This transformation was to involve a culture
change to the traditional bureaucratic way of working at Shell, which
underpinned a slow, although consensual, decision-making process,
and put predictability, order and stability above all else. Faster
decision making, greater creativity, unconventional thinking, flexibility and nimbleness in the way business was conducted was wanted.
The historical emphasis on technical competence, rather than on commercial businessmen, was to be challenged with the intent to create
market- and customer-focused businesses. There was also an intent to
increase the diversification of the senior management team through a
larger number of women and greater ethnic diversity (2).

Realignment is a change to the way of doing things that does not
involve a fundamental reappraisal of the central assumptions and
beliefs within the organization. It may still involve a substantial
change like a major restructuring. Electronic Data Systems (EDS), the
international information, communication and computing technology
company, grew very rapidly in Europe, often by acquiring new teams
of people. This created diversity among the business practices in use.
By 1994 there was a need to harmonize the way EDS did business in
Europe. A pan-European re-engineering effort was put in place, the
implementation of which continued into the late 1990s (3).

The nature of change is the way change is implemented, either in
an all-at-once, big bang fashion, or in a more step-by-step, stage-by-
stage incremental fashion. These two dimensions – the end result of
change and the nature of change – provide the explanation for the four
different types of change.

Evolution

Evolution is transformational change implemented gradually through different stages and interrelated initiatives. It is likely to be planned, proactive transformation, in which change is undertaken by managers in response to their anticipation of the need for future change. Illustration 2.1 discusses such an evolution that took place in the AIB Group, the largest bank in Ireland, from the late 1980s and into the early 1990s. The change process involved transformation, since the aim was to differentiate the bank by better customer service. This required staff to be marketing professionals rather than 'bankers'. The intent from the outset was for change to be implemented as a series of initiatives over a period of years.

Evolution can result from forced transformation. Although the organization's competitive environment may require rapid change, it could be that other aspects of the organization, such as the need to preserve some aspects of the organization's culture, for example, employee loyalty, mitigate against the feasibility of revolution.

Change in action

Illustration 2.1

Evolutionary change at the AIB Group

The AIB Group is the largest bank in Ireland. Formerly known as Allied Irish Banks, it was formed in 1966 with the merger of three long-established clearing banks. During the 1970s and early 1980s, the AIB Group went through a period of structural transformation, evolving into a national financial services organization with sizeable international interests. Despite this success, the Group had an entrenched clearing bank culture which inhibited change. The emphasis was on systems rather than customers. Employees were not customer focused. The bank needed to undergo a cultural change to become a market-focused organization, a process which started with the arrival of a new chief executive in 1984 and continued into the 1990s.

A new structure was introduced in 1986, and revised in 1989, aimed at achieving differentiation through better customer service. A new vision statement was also developed to support the new structure. However, to differentiate the bank through the provision of a superior service required an innovative and flexible approach to customers. Employees had to change from bankers to marketing professionals. It was recognized that this would take time so a phased approach was used. A Marketing Action Programme was developed which brought together initiatives including new marketing strategies, information systems and technology, as well as a change in employee attitudes.

The first step was to make sure the changes were understood by the employees. To create an awareness of the need for change and the commit-

Chapter 4 discusses such an example at WH Smith News in some depth.

Evolution can also occur in a more emergent manner. Xerox, the global company best known for their manufacture of photocopiers, decided in 1983 that they were not competitive in terms of quality, cost and delivery. A Leadership Through Quality scheme was implemented which involved the training of all staff in quality practices. A move was also made to team-based working. However, the traditional structure obstructed cross-functional team working, so a second change phase was introduced. Teams became responsible for business processes, and concentrated on error reduction, cycle time reduction, and customer satisfaction improvements for these processes. This led to another change initiative towards the end of the 1980s to do with the simplification of business processes to enable better empowerment and performance improvement. In 1993, a third phase of the cultural revolution, the Xerox 2000 vision, was launched to continue the momentum of change (4).

Illustration 2.1 continued

ment of all employees, the programme was launched through meetings, videos and briefings in early 1987. Seminars were also run for executives, followed by marketing workshops. In 1988 the Management Effectiveness Programme was launched to discover the values appropriate to the new market-focused AIB, and the management practices that would support them. Once the values and supporting practices were identified, all managers attended a training course to enable them to adopt these practices. The training was supported by personal action plans and feedback from each manager's staff. Another initiative called 'Superthought' was launched to elicit ideas from staff on appropriate changes. Over one thousand ideas from this scheme were implemented.

The second phase involved making customers aware of the changes. A corporate television and press advertising campaign was launched in 1988 in Ireland, emphasizing the bank's new focus on customer service. A new corporate identity was also needed. The name 'Allied Irish Bank' was replaced by AIB, and a new logo was adopted. The new corporate identity was launched in January 1990 by a televised gala event at AIB headquarters.

AIB's commitment to continuous change was reaffirmed in late 1992, when the results of an extensive review of the group's direction for the rest of the decade were communicated to all employees along with the organization's vision for the year 2000. The appointment of a new chief executive in 1993 has enabled further fine-tuning.

(Adapted from: K.J. Bourke, 'Corporate Culture, Identity and Design: AIB Group', *Irish Marketing Review*, 7, 1994, pp. 100–9. Prepared by Quaye Botchway, Cranfield School of Management.)

Revolution

Revolution is fundamental, transformational change that occurs by using simultaneous initiatives on many fronts, and often in a relatively short space of time. It is more likely be a forced, reactive transformation, due to the changing competitive conditions the organization is facing. If an organization's strategy is still rooted in the ways of behaving that used to lead to success, then the mismatch between the strategy being pursued and the new strategies required may be great enough to force fundamental change in a short space of time if the organization is to survive. An organization may also need to implement planned transformation rapidly, because, for example, the organization sees the need to pre-empt fast competitor response, or realizes that rapid change is necessary to meet changing customer needs.

Stanton, a British manufacturer of pipeline systems for water, gas and sewage, implemented fundamental, pre-emptive, revolutionary change in the mid-1990s. The company went through a cultural transformation, in which it changed rapidly from an internally cost-focused organization into a customer-focused organization, through many simultaneous initiatives. A new customer services manager was recruited in 1993, who changed half of the employees in the customer services department and brought some of the first women into a male-dominated industry. In 1994 the company put its 1,200 workers through a customer awareness programme, and launched a performance initiative called S4 to provide greatly improved customer service and support. S4 stood for system, stock, support and speed. Stanton also used advertising to encourage customers to challenge them on their performance. Production rates virtually doubled between 1993 and 1996, and schemes that used to require 18 months to complete are now being completed in 12 to 16 weeks. When in 1996 sales of pipes increased dramatically due to the effect of the nationwide drought on water companies and political pressure to reduce leakage from pipes, Stanton was able to respond. Employees willingly postponed their holidays to meet demand (5).

Adaptation and reconstruction

Adaptation is less fundamental change implemented slowly through more staged initiatives, and reconstruction is change undertaken to realign the way the organization operates, but in a more dramatic manner. A large number of change attempts fit within this latter category, for example, many turnarounds and business re-engineering initiatives. Many such change programmes are significant and important to the longer-term survival of an organization. Many, particularly turnaround initiatives, are also highly successful. However, these change initiatives are about reconstruction rather than transformation, since they are about making organizations more efficient, or better at what they already do. Unless the changes are also accompanied by an effort to significantly alter an organization's culture, they are not transformational change. Furthermore, to highlight the complexity and uncertainty of change, it is fair to say that some change initiatives that start out with the intention of delivering revolution often end up delivering reconstruction because the underlying cultural and attitudinal shift which is desired is hard to achieve and does not occur.

Paths of change

The last point of the above paragraph is important as it emphasizes why this book talks about paths of change as opposed to types of change. The eventual aim of an organization may be to achieve transformation, possibly as part of a turnaround, but the organization may lack the resources, skills, or finance to achieve transformation. Alternatively, the organization may be in a crisis, and losing a lot of money, and therefore needs to stop the rot before any longer-term change can be undertaken.

To give a well known and popular example first, British Airways (BA) in the 1980s effected a much cited cultural transformation. However, the cultural transformation followed a financial turnaround of the airline. In 1981 BA was loss making, requiring extensive government subsidies. Lord King was appointed chairman of the board to effect a turnaround, so that BA could be privatized. The first phase of the turnaround, from 1981 to 1982, involved a significant and dramatic downsizing of the workforce, particularly at the middle management level. There was also a pay freeze, route closures, the halt of cargo-only services, and cuts to offices, administration and staff clubs. Only then, in autumn 1982, was attention turned to changing the airline's image and culture from an organization more about transportation to one focused on customer service (6). Thus the actual path of change at BA was reconstruction followed by evolution (see Figure 2.3). The reconstruction resolved the financial crisis at the airline, and provided both money and time for the culture change. It also shook staff out of their complacency and into a recognition of the need for change.

A second example is of the transformational changes at General Electric (GE), the international corporation with businesses as diverse as financial services, aircraft engines and lighting. Change was initiated at GE by Jack Welch in the early 1980s, following his appointment as CEO. However, up until 1988, the changes had arguably been mainly to do with reconstruction, such as altering the

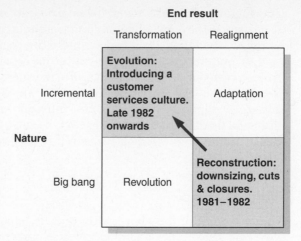

Figure 2.3   Paths of change

GE infrastructure, working practices and political make-up (7). However, by 1988, if a genuine transformation was to be achieved, culture change was also needed. Therefore, the initial change effort was extended into the 1990s by a ten-year programme called 'Work-Out' (see Illustration 2.2). However, it would not have been possible to put Work-Out in place had GE not already been through a change which left it in a financially sound position and created a desire and commitment for change.

Therefore, existing examples of change suggest that, dependent on the context of the organization, it may be necessary to undertake an enabling realignment phase before embarking on a longer-term transformation. Alternatively, having undertaken a transformational change, it may then be necessary to move to adaptation, to ensure that the changes are embedded throughout the organization (8), to sustain competitiveness. However, there are many aspects of the change context represented within the change kaleidoscope that need to be taken into account when making choices about the type of change and the change path. This book will discuss how to decide on an appropriate change path in Chapters 3 and 4.

2.3   Change start point

Change start point refers to where the change is initiated and developed, or rather the locus of control and influence. There are three main approaches – top-down, bottom-up or by using prototypes/pilot sites. A fourth approach is through pockets of good practice.

Change in action

Illustration 2.2

The GE Work-Out programme

Nearly eight years after Welch had become CEO, he knew that far too many GE managers still weren't 'walking the talk' ... Progress was visible almost anywhere you looked, resistance had become rare – and yet they lingered, these unimaginative, frightened bosses from hell, the ones who demanded that fewer people do everything that once had been done by many more. These were the managers or supervisors who snored through the videos of Welch's speeches, then pushed their subordinates to work weekends and nights often under intolerable pressure, with no end in sight, often to accomplish tasks that seemed irrelevant, senseless or worse.

The GE Work-Out programme was designed to be a ten-year programme aimed at changing the behaviour and attitudes of GE employees throughout the organization. It was designed to enable Jack Welch, the CEO of GE, to reach past the middle managers who had so far resisted his change initiatives to the work-force beneath them.

The Work-Out programme was about large-scale employee involvement. By 1992, over two-thirds of the GE workforce had attended a Work-Out session. The programme involves employees working in groups, initially of 30–100, with a facilitator for three days at an off-site location, with a brief to identify par-ticular problems they are experiencing and to find solutions to them. Line man-agers are not allowed to be present for the group discussions so employees can feel free to speak out, but they have to return to hear the group's recommen-dations and are expected to make a decision on these recommendations immediately. Even recommendations requiring further study need to have a decision within a month. The original goals of the programme were to build trust, to empower employees and encourage them to accept greater responsi-bility, to eliminate unnecessary work, and to change the paradigm to create a 'boundaryless' organization. However, the programme also exposes managers who are resistant to Welch's changes.

By the early 1990s, the Work-Out sessions were being incorporated into the everyday way of working for staff. It became a technique for solving prob-lems. Work-Out also moved into a third phase in 1992, under the name of the Change Acceleration Programme (CAP). CAP aims to develop a new type of GE manager, with the skills of a professional change agent.

(From *Control Your Destiny or Someone Else Will,* by Noel M. Tichy and Stratford Sherman. Copyright © 1993 by Noel M. Tichy and Stratford Sherman. Used by permission of Doubleday, a division of Bantam Doubleday Dell Publishing Group, Inc.)

2.3.1   Top-down change

Much of the prescriptive change literature has emphasized a top-down approach, in which the direction, control and initiation of the changes come from the strategic apex of the organization. It usually involves a programme of change determined and implemented by the top management or their representatives.

However, although top-down change is clearly driven by the top executives, this does not mean that a top-down change approach is never collaborative or participative – although this is the way some people interpret it and it is often portrayed. In top-down change initiatives the plans developed can be achieved with the collaboration of senior managers, and a wider group of individuals within the organization (see Illustration 2.5 on change at UNHCR below). Similarly, part of the selling of the plans can be to use employee participation in workshops to work out some of the details of implementation. The programme might also include a comprehensive programme of staff involvement through roadshows or workshops.

Top-down change may have to be imposed in a directive or coercive manner. In a crisis or turnaround situation there may be no alternative but to impose the change throughout the organization. For example, when Tim Parker took over at Clarks, the British shoe manufacturer, as chief executive in 1995, he sacked 10 per cent of the workforce and closed five factories shortly after his arrival, as part of a longer-term change strategy to revitalize the organization (9). Arthur Martinez took over the merchandizing group at Sears, the international retail group, in 1992, the year when Sears' losses amounted to close to $3.9 billion of which almost $3 billion came from the merchandizing group. Martinez had to carry out directive, rapid and radical surgery on the organization, including store closures, and the withdrawal of the heavily loss-making 101-year-old Sears catalogue (10).

This directive form of top-down change design has the advantage of being speedy to implement. Staff can also feel that there is a clarity in the nature of the change, which can be an advantage at a time of uncertainty.

2.3.2   Bottom-up change

Emergent or bottom-up change has a very different starting point and logic to top-down change. This is partly because the assumption here is that responsibility for change should not just lie with the senior managers, but also because in certain change contexts, a top-down approach may not encourage the needed ownership and commitment to the required changes. Illustration 2.3 describes a

Change in action

Illustration 2.3

A bottom-up approach to change at the OU

In 1993, the Open University (OU) launched a change programme called 'New Directions', to encourage the development of self-organization and networking, in support of the university's strategic plan. The programme started as a consultation exercise, but evolved into a self-sustaining organization development and change programme. The human resources department played a key role, helping the volunteers whose enthusiasm kept the programme going.

The university's training and development staff initially organized six two-day workshops. The workshops were designed to involve staff from many different functions, departments and levels of the organization. In each of the workshops, the participants worked in small groups on 'visioning the OU of the future'. Key themes raised by the groups were identified, and the groups then had to develop action plans for each of the key themes. By summer 1993, the workshops had gained their own momentum with other employees volunteering to attend. The ideas that came out of the workshops were added into the strategic plan. The staff paper, *Open House,* regularly included articles on the workshops.

In 1994, the focus of the workshops was switched to the development of action plans for the key workshop themes from 1993, for example, internal communications, and the technology strategy. The change programme also gathered momentum in other ways. In 1994, a group of volunteers from the 1993 workshops organized a one-day conference on the OU's achievements so far. An outcome from the conference was that the organizers formed themselves into a planning team to ensure follow-up on the conference ideas. They organized lunchtime briefings and additional workshops. The conference also led to the completion of a staff survey on the university, which had been agreed to two years earlier, but had never been undertaken. Other initiatives included a cartoon competition on 'the OU of the future', the winning entries from which were published in a New Directions 1995 staff calendar. The competition was run again in 1995.

New Directions continued into 1995 and 1996 with the formation of a New Directions action group, launched by a one-day workshop in January 1995. More ideas came out of this workshop, such as asking students for their views on the university and facilitating the development of a culture which encouraged staff to learn from mistakes. Yet again, these ideas were taken forward through workshops. Other events included a discussion on 'academic staff renewal' and workshops on communications.

(Adapted from C. Russell and E. Parsons, 'Putting theory to the test at the OU', *People Management*, 11 January 1996, pp. 30–2.)

bottom-up change process undertaken at the Open University (OU) in the 1990s. This highly collaborative approach to change gradually led to ownership of the change process by employees, and became self-generating.

There are some drawbacks to a bottom-up approach:

- Bottom-up change is an emergent process, therefore it can be much slower to mature.
- Bottom-up change is much more unpredictable in its consequences as it is subject to interpretation and negotiation by the very staff who put the changes in place. Senior management have far less control over the process, since by the very nature of bottom-up change it has to be more participative and collaborative.

It is possible to combine a top-down approach with a bottom-up approach (11). Advocates of this sort of approach argue that certain activities, such as mobilizing support for change, may need to be done in a top-down way, whereas others, such as creating a vision for change, can be more participative. In particular, creating revitalization throughout a business unit may be a more bottom-up and emergent process. The leader of a change effort may be directive about the fact that the departments within the business unit must change to meet the aspirations of the vision. However, the leader then allows each department or section to *choose* the way in which they want to implement that vision, to ensure ownership and commitment. The changes that emerge within each department, and the new behaviours these changes engender, then need to be institutionalized and supported in the organization through top-down actions, such as changes to organization-wide systems and structures.

2.3.3   Prototypes

A third approach to change is to use a prototype or pilot site as the start point. This may involve implementing change in just one department, or it may be by using a new start-up site. Prototyping is an approach that can be used for implementing technical change involving new information systems or equipment, but new processes and working practices can also be implemented initially at a pilot site, or as a prototype, before being introduced elsewhere. New sites, sometimes with completely new staff, are also used by organizations to set up businesses that need to work in a very different manner to existing businesses. When the express rail link from central London to Heathrow airport, Heathrow Express, was set up in the late 1990s, the company looked for employees from the customer service sector, such as airlines and retailers, rather than those who had worked for British Rail. It was felt that guards, drivers and ticket office staff already working in the railway industry had not developed an appropriate customer service orientation (12).

The advantages of prototypes are many:

- It is possible to test out the impact of the new systems and procedures, and iron out any unforeseen faults or problems before the changes are made throughout the organization. It is also possible to identify and rectify potential and actual problems and weaknesses with the accompanying change management interventions, such as training and communication.
- A successful pilot can be used to mobilize awareness of the need for change and support for the changes in an environment where change awareness is low.
- Prototypes followed by a gradual roll-out programme reduce the amount of change management expertise needed at any one time.
- Prototypes can reduce the complexity of change. Illustration 2.4 describes why and how prototyping was used at Kingston Hospital for just these sorts of reasons.

However, there are also disadvantages to prototypes:

- Each site and department involved in an implementation may be different. Changes made to the implementation approach to mitigate against the problems identified in one site may not be suitable for another site.
- The time period it takes to run a prototype may give opponents of change more time to build their resistance, particularly if there is not a strong and powerful backer of the changes. Managers resistant to change can continue to pay lip service to the changes, and then become obstructive when attempts are made to implement the pilot concepts into their departments.
- The use of pilot sites and prototypes creates a prolonged period of change, and therefore uncertainty for staff, and the need for the use of parallel systems and processes for the organization.
- Organizations have found it difficult to transfer changes made at new sites to existing sites and departments.

2.3.4 Pockets of good practice

The fourth approach, pockets of good practice, is less well known. Change is initiated in various units or departments, by an individual within that department at that individual's instigation. The changes made are more piecemeal and fragmented, since they are not orchestrated from any central point. These changes may involve leading projects or running pilot schemes to enhance organizational performance, changing the interpersonal dynamics and culture within teams and

Change in action

Illustration 2.4

A prototype approach to change: Kingston Hospital

In 1991, Kingston Hospital, London, was given independent trust status as were many other National Health Service hospitals. This required the hospital to generate revenue by bidding competitively with other hospitals for health care provision to health authorities and general practitioners. Faced with an increasingly competitive market, and more demanding patient needs, the newly recruited CEO, John Langan, decided to try to implement Patient Focused Care (PFC). PFC was an innovative technique from the USA which aimed to provide superior quality care to patients through flexibly skilled, multidisciplinary teams. A team of consultants first investigated the feasibility of such a programme at Kingston, and recommended that the hospital would benefit from a re-engineering programme similar to PFC, to reduce the inefficiencies derived from stagnant processes that had become part of daily life in the hospital.

A steering group was formed to take the project forward. Once they had obtained the go-ahead for the project in 1992, a Patient Focused Care Team was recruited. However, it was decided that the only feasible way to radically re-engineer the hospital was to split the task. Attention was therefore initially focused on one floor of acute medical wards. The reasons given for this prototype approach were that all the medical acute wards were located on the same floor, the clinical consultants there already worked well as a team, and PFC had not been fully applied to such wards before.

The design for the re-engineering project was completed in the summer of 1992, and was followed rapidly by a phased implementation. As part of the re-engineering project the four wards were merged, but only two of them were refurbished at a time. When the patients moved into the newly converted care areas, they were immediately attended to by newly formed and trained cross-functional care teams, made up of both qualified and unqualified carers capable between them of the full range of required activities. An essential element of the re-engineering process was the focus on communication to and among staff. For example, the PFC team ran weekly surgeries for about 14 staff members at a time. A bulletin board, placed at strategic locations and updated regularly, was used by the team to communicate progress and the rationale for the programme to all staff. A newsletter was also launched for all staff, including those as yet not affected by the changes.

By October 1993, the first floor was operationally completed with the new refurbishment, layout, diagnostic facilities, care teams and IT networks. The PFC approach was next introduced into the maternity ward.

(Adapted from: 'Case on Kingston Hospital' in Nick Obolensky, *Practical Business Re-Engineering*, 1994, London: Kogan Page. Prepared by Quaye Botchway, Cranfield School of Management.)

departments, or even working with managers in another department to improve communications and interdepartmental working practices (13).

This type of change will lead to further organizational change, only if the practices established by the individuals concerned are then copied by others. Change occurs in an evolutionary manner as working procedures and management styles evolve in particular departments, in line with good managerial practices the individuals who initiate the changes have encountered in others, or on training courses. However, such an approach does have its limitations. Unless these individual attempts are harnessed into some collective initiative for the organization, they will lead to limited change. Furthermore, unless sanctioned and supported from the top of the organization, it is unlikely that such initiatives will deliver any change other than adaptation, as the scope of individual initiatives will be limited.

2.4   Change style

The style of change is to do with issues about how the process of change is managed. There are many classifications of management styles during change, but this text uses a classification of five styles (see Table 2.1).

2.4.1   Education and communication

Education and communication involves convincing employees of the need for change, and gaining their commitment and support for change. This may involve more than just talking to employees. It could involve, for example, sending them on benchmarking visits to other organizations to learn how things could be done better. Scottish Power decided prior to privatization in 1991 to use benchmarking to help introduce changes that would enable the company to be more efficient. Each business conducted a benchmarking exercise against other utilities identified as performing well. Power Systems, the distribution and transmission business, sent employees to Australia, Japan and the USA. This business saved £20 million through changes introduced as a result of these benchmarking visits (14).

This change style is easily confused with participation. However, communication and education is more to do with equipping employees with an understanding which enables them to undertake personal change that is supportive of the organizational change goals. When the CEO of Eisai, a Japanese pharmaceutical company, wanted to change the focus of the company from manufacturing drugs, to improving the quality of life for elderly sick people, he put his managers through a training programme to encourage them to become more innovative

Table 2.1   *Styles of managing change*

Style	Description	Advantages	Disadvantages
Education and communication	Use small group briefings to discuss things with people and explain things to them. The aim is to gain support for change by generating understanding and commitment.	Spreads support for change. Also ensures a wide base of understanding.	Takes a long time. If radical change is needed, fact-based argument and logic may not be enough to convince others of need for change. Easy to voice support, then walk away and do nothing.
Collaboration	Widespread involvement of the employees on decisions about what and how to change.	Spreads not only support but ownership of change by increasing levels of involvement.	Time consuming. Little control over decisions made. May lead to change within paradigm.
Participation/ intervention	Consultation of employees about how to deliver the desired changes. May also include limited collaboration over aspects of the 'how to' of change as opposed to the 'what' of change.	Again, spreads ownership and support for change, but within a more controlled framework. Easier to shape decisions.	Can be perceived as manipulation.
Direction	Change leaders make the majority of decisions about what to change and how. Use of authority to direct change.	Less time consuming. Provides a clear change of direction and focus.	Potentially less support and commitment, and therefore proposed changes may be resisted.
Coercion	Use of power to impose change.	Allows for prompt action.	Unlikely to achieve buy-in without a crisis.

and develop new products and services in line with his strategic intent for the organization. The programme examined health care trends and organizational change. Managers also spent time in health-care organizations assisting with the nursing to help them understand better the needs of the elderly. These managers were then expected to use their learning to propose and implement new products and services (15).

There are problems with this style of leading change:

- It can be difficult to generate commitment to action from it. Workshops and seminars can be seen as an interesting exercise, and fun to do, but change will only occur if a series of explicit actions are identified and carried out.

- It can be necessary to inject some energy, emotion and direction into the process. Otherwise, an awareness of the need for change may be developed, but this awareness will not translate into a commitment to doing something about it, especially if there is no onus on senior managers to take note of ideas that arise and act on them.
- It can be very time consuming and costly if there are large numbers of employees to be convinced. A multinational company operating in many different countries with possibly thousands of employees could find such an approach difficult to undertake.

2.4.2 Collaboration

In collaboration, there is widespread involvement of employees in both what to change, and how to deliver the needed changes. Employees are asked to contribute to both the goals set for change and the means of achieving those goals. This may be through workshops or focus groups, or any other type of participative face-to-face meeting. The principle behind collaboration is that the more employees are involved, the more likely they are to support and be committed to the changes that they have helped design, and the more likely they also are to sell those changes to others in the organization. Furthermore, collaboration can be used to not only determine what to change and how, but also to create an awareness of the need for change by challenging complacency within the organization.

One form of collaboration is the workshop, where consultants introduce participants to analytical tools and frameworks and get them to apply these frameworks to their businesses to get new insights. The difference here from more general educational interventions is that the workshops would be focused on identifying and addressing critical change issues, and would also end with explicit consideration of actions to be taken, and by who. However, collaboration does not have to involve face-to-face situations. In organizations where employees are widespread this is difficult to achieve. Illustration 2.5 describes how the UNHCR, the international aid organization, used a collaborative technique called Project Delphi to get involvement in change from a broad group of staff.

Collaboration can be a good management style to use when dealing with professionals, such as hospital clinicians, or even academics, who value the freedom and autonomy they normally have in their work. Such groups of people are likely to rebel against more directive interventions, which they perceive to be limiting their autonomy and their right to have a say in their future. However:

- Collaboration can be time consuming, and is therefore not a technique to use in a crisis situation.

Change in action

Illustration 2.5

Achieving change at UNHCR

UNHCR, the Office of the United Nations High Commissioner for Refugees, has undergone rapid growth in recent years, fuelled by events such as the Gulf War and the exodus of the Kurds in 1991. UNHCR's expenditure has also risen sharply (to $1.3 billion in 1995), against a backdrop of greater competition for donor community funds. The organization needed to be seen to be efficient, well managed and effective to maintain levels of funding. Head office needed to become less bureaucratic and more responsive to the needs of the field.

The change agent, Lynn Wallis, led many change initiatives following her appointment in 1992. The major change initiative was Project Delphi, a highly collaborative initiative to review the UNHCR operations, spearheaded by the Change Management Group (CMG) created by Wallis. The Delphi process involved staff in thinking through the organization's problems themselves. Via *Delphi News*, a newsletter launched in 1996, staff were introduced to the Delphi Process. The Delphi concepts were to do with improving efficiency and effectiveness. Staff everywhere were asked to hold a Delphi Day to brainstorm in small groups about how their work could be changed to improve the way UNHCR worked. Ideas were to be sent to the CMG (anonymously if wished) before 1 March 1996.

2,200 ideas were collected from 100 Delphi groups in over 118 country offices and fed back to staff. The CMG then devised a list of actions and needs arising from these ideas, through consultation with staff world-wide. The next phase of Delphi was to be the implementation of these ideas by a project team supervised by the High Commissioner of UNHCR herself.

(Adapted from 'The UNHCR Case – Achieving the Impossible', I. Sayers and G. Johnson in *Exploring Corporate Strategy*: *Text and Cases*, 5th edition, 1999, Hemel Hempstead: Prentice Hall.)

- Employees may not come up with the suggestions or ideas wanted by senior managers, so there is a loss of control.
- If employees are consulted and then ignored, this will do more harm than good, as it can raise expectations about what it is possible to achieve. The employees will feel devalued, and perceive the senior managers to be practising tokenism in respect of collaboration.
- The ideas offered by existing employees could be within the existing way of thinking, or the existing organizational paradigm, and the existing way of working within the organization. This could stifle creativity and transformational change. Some organizations use external facilitators and consultants to challenge ideas and thinking in order to overcome this problem.

2.4.3   Participation/intervention

Participation is limited collaboration. The principle that involvement will equal greater commitment still underpins this approach to change. However, it is more about consultation than complete collaboration. Employees are allowed limited involvement in certain areas of change, such as *how* the desired changes can be achieved. For example, employees may be told of the overall vision and change goals for a firm, such as to achieve greater efficiency, greater productivity, and to eliminate waste. They can then be asked to think about what they need to do differently if they are going to help to deliver that vision. The GE Work-Out programme described in Illustration 2.2 provides an example of this type of participation. Alternatively, employees may be asked to contribute to the design and delivery of specific tasks which will assist the overall change process. A series of working parties may be set up to address issues, from new working practices to communications.

Obviously, this management style enables the change leaders to retain greater control over the outcome of the change process, as they are setting the overall goals if not the means of achieving the goals. Unfortunately, it may be seen by employees as a type of manipulation, an attempt to pay lip service to employee involvement, particularly if participation is limited, or employees are told what outcome is expected from a workshop, or whatever type of forum is used to achieve their participation. Indeed, participation can be used in a manipulative manner, to encourage buy-in, agreement and consent through limited involvement. Decision-making power may only be devolved to others in areas where the decisions made are not considered to have a significant impact by the change agent. As such, participation, and at times collaboration, can be politically motivated change styles. Participation can also be a time-consuming way of delivering change, although less so than collaboration.

2.4.4   Direction

When those leading change make the majority of decisions about what to change and how, and use their authority to direct the achievement of change, this is a management style of direction. This approach effectively separates the thinkers from the doers. The thinkers come up with the change ideas and 'sell' them to the doers, who are then supposed to implement the plans and the ideas developed by the doers. There may still be an attempt to sell the changes to the employees, to encourage them to buy-in to the changes and support them. There can still be an extensive communication effort in which employees are involved in workshops to debate the implications of change for themselves. However, employees are not invited to contribute to the goals or means of change, except in a limited way. Many turnarounds involve this style of change.

The advantages of this approach are that it is easier to retain control over the direction and content of change, and decision making is faster than it would be under a style which involves consultation. The disadvantages are that:

- The lack of employee consultation and involvement might create more resistance to the proposed changes. As a change style it is more likely to be suitable in an organization which is either in crisis, or in which there is a widespread awareness of the need for change. In such a situation, despite the lack of participation by employees, they are more likely to support the proposed changes.
- The success of a directive management style may be limited by the change outcomes to be achieved by the change process itself. Imposed change may work in the opposite way to the values it is trying to achieve. For instance, in the early 1990s organizations emphasized the value of empowered staff and often tried to impose a policy of empowerment upon the organization. However, where directive communication and bureaucratic controls are used as part of that change process, the implementation itself may counteract any motivation on the part of staff to feel empowered. To be told that you are going to be 'empowered' or you are to become more 'innovative' is quite different from feeling empowered. Staff are more likely to believe in such rhetoric if it is supported by a participative management style that allows staff some degree of autonomy and say over what happens.
- An imposed change process may result in impressive rhetoric within an organization, with little change in actual behaviour or job and ultimately organizational performance. Staff may find it easy to repeat the language of the change process without really embracing the change at an emotional or behavioural level. Staff recite the rhetoric, rather than internalizing the goals of change and changing their attitudes and behaviours appropriately (16).

2.4.5   Coercion

Coercion is an extension of direction. Here change is imposed on staff, rather than staff having the idea of change sold to them. It is a way of achieving rapid change, but as with direction, it may lead to greater resistance. Given the lack of effort devoted to explaining the need for change to staff, or to encouraging buy-in for the changes, this approach is unlikely to work unless there is a very *real* crisis that is felt by most staff within the organization. However, unless the coercion is such that all aspects of behavioural change can be enforced in some way, the result may still be lip service to the changes rather than actual change.

2.4.6   Examples of change styles

KPMG, the large international firm of accountants and consultants, initiated a change in 1992, to differentiate themselves from the other accountancy firms. Illustration 2.6 describes how Colin Sharman, the partner in charge of the south-east region, created a recognition of the need for change in an organization in which there was no crisis. As one of the partners at KPMG, Sharman had no power to *impose* change. He could only put in place interventions to trigger questioning and challenging of the status quo. A number of interventions were used, such as workshops, conferences and feedback. However, the style of change was different for different groups of staff. For the partners, Sharman put in place extensive *collaboration*. For the senior managers, their opinions were sought, but at a later stage, so for them, the style was more like *participation*. Those below senior manager level were never really consulted at all. They were informed of the decisions, and as such, the change style for them was *direction*. This illustrates that the context determines the type of style that is likely to be effective, and that the approach may be different for different groups of staff. However, some observers would question whether it was right to not involve staff below the senior manager level in the workshops. Would they have had more commitment to the changes and the firm if they had been involved in a more participative change experience?

The description of the different change styles suggests a contingency approach to selecting the appropriate style – what matters is matching the style to the internal and external context of the firm. This is the recommendation most change texts make (8). Indeed, this is also what this text recommends through use of the change kaleidoscope.

2.5   Change target

An important design choice requiring consideration is the different organizational levels at which to intervene. Some change processes concentrate on attempting to change the values of employees, others emphasize behavioural change, whilst others may only seek to change the performance objectives or outputs of employees.

2.5.1   Employee values

Interest in values as a lever for change was particularly strong in the 1980s, associated as it was with developments in human resource

Change in action

Illustration 2.6

Initiating strategic change at KPMG

KPMG is a large international firm of accountants and consultants. Like many other such organizations, traditionally the primary interface to the market had been discipline-based practice units (audit, tax, consultancy). At the beginning of the 1990s Colin Sharman, partner in charge of the south-east region, perceived the need to change the firm into a client-focused organization. Although the firm was increasingly run along corporate lines, each partner of the firm is, in effect, an owner-manager and has to agree, or at least not disagree, with any change. Given this partnership structure, and the fact that the firm was very successful in its existing form, Sharman had no mandate or authority to impose change. He initiated change in a way designed to obtain the support needed from a critical mass of partners.

As a first step a series of partner workshops were run, at which the partners considered the firm's strategy, the blockages to change and the actions needed. Sharman attended debriefing sessions at the end of each workshop, but did not direct the outcomes from the workshops. Subsequently, Sharman held evening feedback sessions attended by most of the partners, which were focused on building consensus on the need for change and what should be done. The Senior Managers' Conference was also used as a way of getting those below the level of partner involved. The senior managers were asked to work through a similar process to that undertaken at the workshops by the partners. This was followed by more briefing meetings for partners and senior managers.

In 1992, a special partners' conference was called where the '20:20 Vision', the blueprint for change, was presented to give impetus to the change process. Similar events were held for both senior and junior managers. Change was also communicated in a variety of other ways, including videos, glossy brochures, the personal repetition by Colin Sharman, and later on publicly through the financial media.

The decision-making context within the firm meant that strategic change was a lengthy process. Formulating the new strategy and getting partners to buy-in to it culminated in the launch of '20:20 Vision' in mid-1992. The actual processes of change continued throughout the following year and is still continuing.

(Adapted from the case studies on KPMG within *Exploring Corporate Strategy: Text and Cases*, 5th edition, G. Johnson and K. Scholes, 1999, Hemel Hempstead: Prentice Hall.)

management and the increasing popularity of culture change programmes (17). In the 1980s, the belief was that if employees could be made to adhere to a predetermined set of corporate values, they could then be given licence to innovate freely. In other words, by prescribing shared values, appropriate employee behaviour would emerge in such a way that there would be less need for bureaucratic rules and regulations. Appropriate values would drive appropriate behaviour, reducing the need for other types of managerial controls on employees.

Some organizations and individuals feel that the dividing line between organizational values and individual values is hard to define. They therefore feel uncomfortable with this level of intervention, and question the legitimacy of trying to alter something as personal to an individual as their set of values. Other organizations, such as churches, charities, pressure groups and voluntary organizations, might expect to find a close alignment between their values and that of their employees. They might expect their staff to share a common set of values which are directly aligned to the aims of the organization. Such organizational contexts may seem ideal for managing through shared values.

However, the evidence shows that this approach can be fraught with difficulty in certain organizational contexts:

- Many espoused value statements are devalued in employee eyes if these are not reflected in changed behaviours, particularly from senior managers. So values such as 'individuality' or 'people are our greatest asset' quickly became relegated to meaningless slogans in many companies (17).
- An emphasis on managing values may lead to staff feeling manipulated or brainwashed, which can result in cynicism about the values themselves.
- The acknowledgement of all kinds of diversity within organizations may undermine the attainment of a common set of values. In hospitals, for example, there are consultants, nurses and managers, each with their own professional allegiances, and different professional values, identities and motivations. Can common values be achieved across such diverse professional and occupational groups, or for that matter, different national cultures or business divisions (18)?

Yet, if an organization needs to achieve fundamental, transformational change, this by its very nature requires a change in the assumptions and beliefs shared by the organization's employees. Therefore, there are circumstances where targeting values in an effort to effect change in the shared assumptions and beliefs is appropriate, although value change can take a long while to achieve. Lloyd's of London, the insurance market, needed to undergo a culture change in the mid-1990s which involved focusing on the customer more, in order to meet the changing environmental circumstances in which it was operating, and help maintain profitability. Illustration 2.7 describes how new values were used as the driving force for the culture change process.

Change in action

Illustration 2.7

Value change at Lloyd's of London

Lloyd's of London, one of the oldest financial institutions, was in crisis in 1992, due to a number of huge losses from a series of disasters ranging from hurricanes to oil rig catastrophes. However, Lloyd's did not just need to find new sources of capital, it also needed to reduce its cost base, restructure itself and undertake a culture change. Staff needed to be encouraged to behave in a way that would sustain commercial success, which involved focusing on customer satisfaction, learning from mistakes rather than seeking scapegoats, and being less command and control oriented.

Initially, in 1993, job structure and performance management were addressed. The number of job grades were reduced, pay was linked to performance, and a redundancy programme reduced the workforce by 15 per cent. Then attention was focused on the culture change. External consultants were appointed to help the HR team. The HR team had identified ten core values for the new management culture. Focus groups were put in place to test the new values. The focus groups revealed cultural issues that had to be addressed, such as little concept of service, not enough consultation or delegation from managers, lengthy decision making and a sense of 'them and us' between managers and staff.

With the help of the consultants, two-day workshops for all employees were subsequently organized, with the intention of making each of the 2,000 employees a change agent. These participative workshops took place over nine months between 1994 and 1995, and aimed to improve awareness of the business plan and the core values, and ensure everyone understood their role in the changes. As part of the workshops, the focus group findings were also reported, as evidence of management support for the new values, such as open communication.

Each individual took an action plan away from the workshops. Employee suggestions were passed to appropriate departments and monitored by the personnel team. To better equip managers for their role in the change process, leadership workshops were also organized for the most senior managers.

Employee opinion surveys in 1994 and 1996 showed improvements in most areas. Feedback from underwriters showed that they had noticed a greater interest by staff in them as 'customers'. By 1997, the Corporation of Lloyd's was restructuring to meet its commercial challenges with the culture change well underway.

(Adapted from J. Clarke and J. Nicholson, 'Reversal of Fortune', *People Management*, 20 March 1997, pp. 22–9.)

2.5.2   Behaviours

Others argue that instead of focusing at the level of values, and believing that over time behaviours will change as an individual's values change, organizations should focus primarily on enforcing new behav-

Programmatic change	Task alignment
Problems in behaviour result from individual knowledge, attitudes and beliefs.	Individual attitudes and beliefs are shaped by recurring patterns of behavioural interactions.
The primary change target should be attitudes – actual behaviour should be secondary.	The primary change target should be behaviour – attitudes should be secondary.
Behaviour can be isolated and changed individually.	Behavioural problems come from the roles individuals are in – the impact of the organizational system on the individual are greater than the impact of the individual on the system.
Therefore ...	
The change target should be at an individual level.	The change target should be at the organizational level – changing roles, responsibilities and relationships.

Figure 2.4   *Programmatic change versus task alignment*
(Source: Adapted and reprinted by permission of Harvard Business Review. *An Exhibit from 'Contrasting Assumptions About Change' from M. Beer, R.A. Eisenstat and B. Spector, 'Why Change Programs Don't Produce Change', November–December 1990. Copyright © 1990 by the President and Fellows of Harvard College; all rights reserved)*

iours. Those that support this view argue that the individual can only change if the organizational system in which the individual operates is changed. Figure 2.4 summarizes this argument.

Programmatic change targets individual attitude change to effect behaviour change. Yet individual behaviour is constrained by the organizational system in which individuals work. Roles and responsibilities, and existing ways of working, force particular behaviours on to individuals if they are to function effectively in an organization. If individuals learn new attitudes, but are then returned to the old organizational system, they will not be able to practice the new ways of behaving that accompany their new attitudes. If instead the organizational system is changed, as proposed by task alignment, and individuals are placed in job roles with different responsibilities and different relationships to their peers, subordinates and superiors, then this forces them to behave differently, and ultimately to think differently.

A focus on work-based behaviours can therefore be used to effect behavioural and accompanying attitude change and perhaps, ultimately, value change. A target of behaviours may also be used for other reasons:

- Behaviours are an appropriate target in changes involving reconstruction or realignment, which require some degree of behavioural change without a fundamental change in the shared organizational values or beliefs.
- Behavioural interventions are felt by some people to be a less intrusive intervention than prescribing a person's value system. Behaviours can also be seen as more task related and therefore as a legitimate area for intervention at work.
- The prescription of behaviours may be useful in service outlets such as McDonalds where routinized procedures ensure quality of delivery or product.
- In a crisis situation where there is little time, the enforcement of behavioural change may be an appropriate initial intervention, since value change can take a long while to develop.
- Behaviours are an appropriate intervention level in situations where the employees concerned are all involved in the same core business or the same management function, because the intervention is aimed at a homogeneous group of employees with similar values and motivations. This is particularly true if the changes do not require a change in the shared organizational values. For example, the Nationwide Building Society decided to introduce self-managed teamworking into the mortgage and insurance customer service department in 1995, to help develop multiskilling and support a flatter structure. The teams, each consisting of 9 to 18 members of staff, manage and organize their own workload. As such this was more a behavioural intervention than it was about altering shared organizational values. To enable the change to teamworking, training was provided for the staff on working in self-managed teams, decision making, conflict management, team building and giving and receiving feedback (19).

2.5.3   Outputs

A third level of intervention for change is to focus on changing the nature of outputs or performance objectives to in turn trigger a change in behaviours. The point of managerial control then becomes not replicable behavioural patterns, but the achievement of managerially determined outputs or objectives. The target is the *outcome* of what people do, for example, profit margins, hourly sales levels, levels of customer response. This usually involves the redesign of performance measures, such as rewards and control systems.

A focus on outputs is useful when high levels of autonomy are required. Individual, national or functional business divisions may require a degree of independence from the parent corporation in order to manage the change in a way that is appropriate to their specific country's context or the nature of their staff. Alternatively, autonomy may be required by individual staff themselves as in the case of doctors or consultants or city traders. Such groups of people may see an attempt to overtly manage their values, or even their behaviours, as an attack on their personal autonomy or their latitude of discretion within their jobs. For example, an investment bank will employ many traders to make their financial deals for them. These traders are usually highly self-motivated and skilled, valuing the independence and autonomy in their jobs. Their primary motivation, and performance measure, is the achievement of their commercial targets and the high financial bonuses this earns them. Therefore, in any change situation, changing these measures and rewards is likely to be a more suitable target and effective intervention, than any attempt to prescribe their behaviours. The traders would not feel their autonomy was under threat.

However, care needs to be taken when using outputs as an intervention level. For example, a telesales operation requiring better customer service may impose new performance measures such as answering the phone within a certain number of rings. This may encourage staff to provide worse customer service, as they will be more concerned with dealing with customers as quickly as possible in order to answer the next call. Similarly, if the need is to encourage staff to sell more services to customers, paying greater commission on sales, or measuring sales revenue per staff member, may encourage staff to sell inappropriate services to customers, leading to a decline in customer satisfaction. A more appropriate approach may be to train staff in which additional services are suitable for which types of customers.

2.6   *Change roles*

Change is only likely to succeed if someone is responsible for leading that change, although it is also accepted that this responsibility may not reside with just one person. A change agent needs to be supported by additional change agents. Increasingly less faith is placed in one charismatic and heroic figure (20), since it is now recognized that change is complex and requires consideration and management of many different tasks. One individual could not hope to manage a major change effort entirely on her or his own. This is not to say that the role of leadership has been trivialized in anyway. Major change efforts in particular are likely to require a champion who shows tremendous commitment to, and enthusiasm for, the vision she or he wants to see implemented in the organization.

However, there are a number of different ways change can be managed, although none of them are mutually exclusive. The primary change agent roles are:

- *Leadership*: The success of the change programme is based on a key, pivotal figure. The 'leader' may be the CEO, the MD, another senior manager acting as the internal change agent, or another director such as the HR Director. Tim Parker at Clarks, or Jack Welch at GE, both mentioned in previous examples in this chapter, are good examples of leadership during change. If the individual championing change is not the CEO or the MD, then they may need to gain the support of more powerful individuals within the organization if they are to push change through.
- *External facilitation*: External consultants may be appointed and play a pivotal role in the change process. This may be in the form of advice or more active participation (see Illustration 2.7 above on change at Lloyd's).
- *Change action team*: A team of people within the organization may be appointed to lead the changes, this may be in the form of a steering committee. If this team does not consist of senior and influential people, the team is likely to need the support of a more powerful individual or group of individuals in major change efforts.
- *Functional delegation*: Change responsibility may be assigned to a particular function such as HR, quality, or operations management. This may be appropriate when implementing change limited to a particular function or if the skills needed to manage the change reside within a particular department. For example, in the bottom-up change at the Open University described above, the HR department played a key role, as it did in the change process at Lloyd's. In major change efforts, unless the function head is endowed with a large amount of authority, or is able to gain the support of other powerful backers, the individual is also likely to need the backing of a more powerful figure.

The choices made are likely to be affected by the scope and time-frame of the changes, the extent of change management skills possessed by the organization's managers, and the availability of organizational personnel that are either knowledgeable about, or can be trained to be knowledgeable about, change. Transition management is a time-consuming activity, and there may be a trade-off to be made between the amount of time managers need to devote to keeping the business going, and the amount of time they have to act as a change resource. For example, an organization's MD may decide to lead the change, supported by a change team of other senior managers, but also appoint external consultants to provide advice and assistance, and additional resources when needed.

Illustration 2.8 gives an example of how the Natural History

Museum combined change roles of leadership, external facilitation and a change team. The public relations manager worked with a steering group that she herself established, to improve internal communications at the museum. External consultants were also used to facilitate the change process.

One of the major choices that is likely to be made is whether or not to use external consultants. There is evidence (21) that external consultants may be more effective at persuading senior managers in an organization of the need for change, and what type of change, than other senior managers. They can challenge more effectively. They can also offer advice on the design of change in terms of tools, techniques, mechanisms and approaches, provide facilitation and possibly training

Change in action

Illustration 2.8

Leading change at the Natural History Museum

Founded in the eighteenth century, the Natural History Museum had a traditional system of isolated, semi-autonomous, hierarchical departments. The need for cost containment and a concentration on the museum's strengths led to the start of a major restructuring programme in 1990. Jane Bevan was appointed in 1992 as the first public relations manager to help enhance the museum's image. She soon realized that she also needed to address internal communications.

Bevan started with an employee attitude survey, and hired consultants to help her carry it out. Subsequently, in 1995, she formed a steering group of junior managers from across the business to tackle the problems identified. The group targeted four areas – a staff newsletter, team briefing, the staff suggestion scheme and the need for information 'hotspots'.

The demand for the newsletter has led to a popular 12-page bimonthly magazine *Waterhouse Times*. A better team briefing system was secured through the help of other consultants brought in by Bevan to run communication workshops for managers. The existing staff suggestion scheme needed to be explained and better publicized; this was done in *Waterhouse Times*. Information 'hotspots' were implemented via a museum-wide network of information points where employees can access specific information.

Other initiatives included 'Talk back', staff forums on issues of interest, an expansion of the use of the museum's intranet by staff, and a compilation of an internal business directory which lists what people are working on and other skills that might be useful.

(Adapted from: Ruth Prickett, 'Alive and Kicking', *People Management*, 15 May 1997, pp. 28–30. Prepared by Quaye Botchway, Cranfield School of Management.)

too. External consultants may also be employed throughout change to act as mentors and coaches for those senior managers leading the change effort. However, they are unlikely to be effective at leading the implementation of change, as this is not normally something that can be delegated to an outsider. Employees are less likely to perceive the organization as owning change led by outsiders.

2.7   *Change levers*

One of the issues facing any change agent is the range of levers and mechanisms to use. Organizations are composed of a number of inter-connected and interdependent parts or subsystems, and are most effective when the major components are in alignment with each other (22), just like a car engine. Given the interdependency of these sub-systems, it is difficult to change one part in isolation. Either other parts of the organization with which the changed part interconnects will counteract the effect of the change, or the change made will force domino change effects, perhaps unforeseen, in the other parts of the organization.

Readers who have read *Exploring Corporate Strategy* will be familiar with one tool based on these principles – the cultural web shown in Figure 2.5, although there are others (22). The cultural web suggests that organizations consist of a number of interlinked and inter-dependent subsystems to do with organization structures, power

Figure 2.5   *The cultural web of an organization*
(Source: *Adapted from G. Johnson and K. Scholes,* Exploring Corporate Strategy, *5th edn, 1999, Hemel Hempstead: Prentice Hall)*

structures, control systems, symbols, stories and myths, and routines and rituals, all interconnected with the paradigm.

For those not familiar with the web, how to use it is explained briefly in Appendix 1. As with other such frameworks, it is suggested that to achieve effective change it is necessary to use interventions in all parts of the web. Transformational change initiatives, requiring a change in the shared assumptions and beliefs, in particular, are more likely to fail if change practitioners apply a change recipe which concentrates on the use of a range of levers and mechanisms from just one or two of the subsystems that make up the whole. This will be particularly true if these changes are introduced in isolation without considering how they link together to form a coherent change strategy (22). Consideration should be given to both hard aspects, such as structures and systems, and the softer aspects, such as symbolism and communication (23).

Illustration 2.9 shows the extent of change that occurred at Baxi Heating, the UK's leading gas domestic heating appliance manufacturer and the core business within the Baxi Partnership group of companies, during a change process designed to make the organization more competitive and profitable during the late 1980s and early 1990s. The new paradigm shows that the changes involved a transformation from a solid, slow, manufacturing organization, to a more dynamic, market-focused organization. In order to support this transformation, the organization structure and control systems have been changed, but also new ways of working and managing have been introduced (rituals and routines), and new symbols and stories more to do with success and change rather than the organization's history have replaced the old ones. How this transition was achieved at Baxi will be discussed in more detail in Chapter 5.

Not all changes require a fundamental realignment of all subsystems. A change that only involves adaptation, or possibly even reconstruction, will not necessitate a fundamental shift in employee values, or the paradigm. It is also likely that earlier decisions will determine what range of levers should be used. There is a link between the range of levers and mechanisms to use and the change target, as illustrated in Figure 2.6:

- If the target is *change outcomes* then it is likely that this can be achieved by changing rewards and performance measures and targets, since this is only likely to be an appropriate intervention target if existing values remain appropriate.
- If the target is *change behaviours* then this is about putting in place interventions to do with organization structure (particularly roles and responsibilities), performance management, control systems to support and measure the behavioural changes occurring, and supportive

Change in action

Illustration 2.9

Baxi Partnership

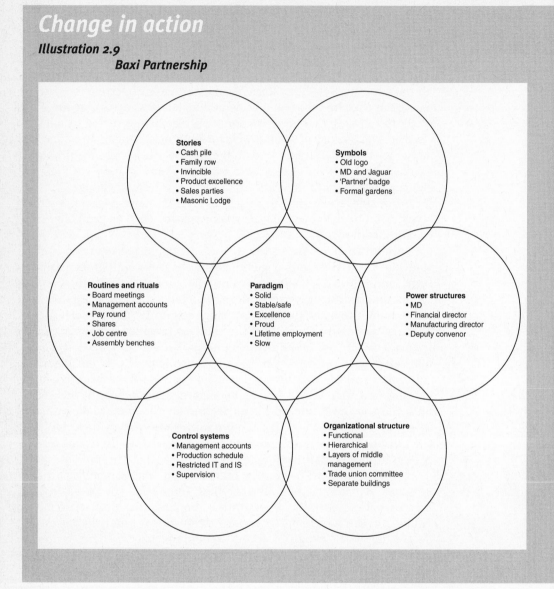

Stories
- Cash pile
- Family row
- Invincible
- Product excellence
- Sales parties
- Masonic Lodge

Symbols
- Old logo
- MD and Jaguar
- 'Partner' badge
- Formal gardens

Routines and rituals
- Board meetings
- Management accounts
- Pay round
- Shares
- Job centre
- Assembly benches

Paradigm
- Solid
- Stable/safe
- Excellence
- Proud
- Lifetime employment
- Slow

Power structures
- MD
- Financial director
- Manufacturing director
- Deputy convenor

Control systems
- Management accounts
- Production schedule
- Restricted IT and IS
- Supervision

Organizational structure
- Functional
- Hierarchical
- Layers of middle management
- Trade union committee
- Separate buildings

training. For example, see the Nationwide Building Society example cited above on changing behaviours. However, mutually supportive and consistent changes may be needed in all organizational subsystems, including symbols and routines, to ensure there are no contradictory messages sent to staff. Many organizations have undergone change through a mixture of restructuring, downsizing and business process re-engineering initiatives in the early 1990s in a response to

Illustration 2.9 continued

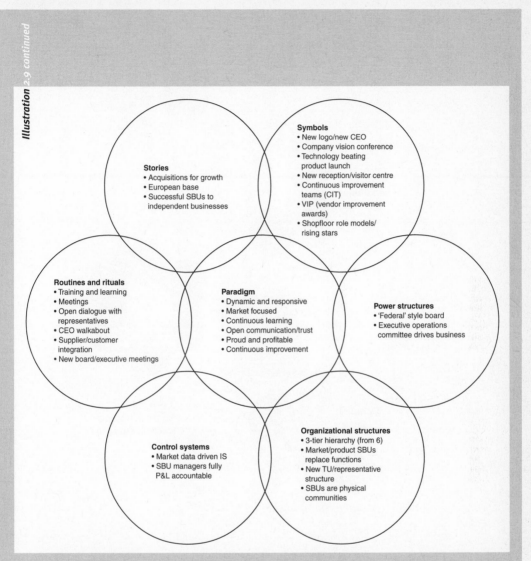

Stories
• Acquisitions for growth
• European base
• Successful SBUs to
  independent businesses

Symbols
• New logo/new CEO
• Company vision conference
• Technology beating
  product launch
• New reception/visitor centre
• Continuous improvement
  teams (CIT)
• VIP (vendor improvement
  awards)
• Shopfloor role models/
  rising stars

Routines and rituals
• Training and learning
• Meetings
• Open dialogue with
  representatives
• CEO walkabout
• Supplier/customer
  integration
• New board/executive meetings

Paradigm
• Dynamic and responsive
• Market focused
• Continuous learning
• Open communication/trust
• Proud and profitable
• Continuous improvement

Power structures
• 'Federal' style board
• Executive operations
  committee drives business

Control systems
• Market data driven IS
• SBU managers fully
  P&L accountable

Organizational structures
• 3-tier hierarchy (from 6)
• Market/product SBUs
  replace functions
• New TU/representative
  structure
• SBUs are physical
  communities

(Prepared by Simon Carter, Transition Strategies Limited, former CEO of Baxi, 1992.)

increasing competition. A common complaint is that employees receive mixed messages about the intent of change. Managers talk of innovation, quality and teamwork, but continue to use old routine ways of behaving to punish mistakes, cut costs and reward individual performance.

• If the target is *change values* (or *change behaviours* with the ultimate intent of driving in new *values*), then the range of interventions to use

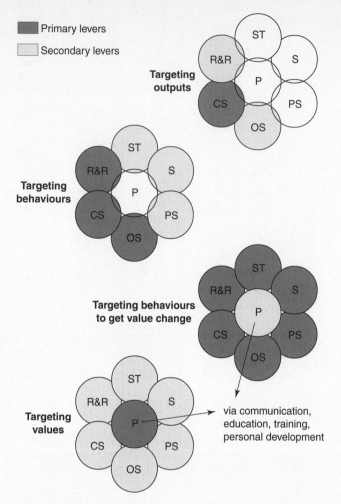

Figure 2.6   *Linking change target and change levers*

is wider than just the levers and mechanisms in the web. Many communication, education, training and personal development interventions will be required to help employees understand exactly what is expected of them in the new culture. These interventions will need to be supported by changes to all aspects of the web, to create a mutually supportive and consistent organizational system, which will enable and reinforce behaviours appropriate to the new values (see Figure 2.4 above).

However, which change levers to use when is a complicated topic and will be revisited in Chapters 4, 5 and 6.

2.8 Summary

A key issue when planning for change implementation is to decide which design choices to take. This chapter has explained that there are six main design choices a change agent needs to examine – the change path, the change style, the change start point, the change target, the key change roles, and the range of levers and mechanisms. All of these choices need consideration with relation to the context of change, to avoid the application of simplistic change recipes.

However, choosing which options to take is not straightforward. Within each of the choices there is a number of options, which creates a wide variety of possible permutations:

- The *change path* may involve more than one type of change, for example an enabling phase of realignment or reconstruction, followed by evolution or revolution.
- The *change start point* options include not just top-down or bottom-up change, but also prototyping, pockets of good practice, or some combination of these options.
- The *change style* may vary from highly collaborative to coercive, and is not necessarily dictated by the change start point. Top-down change, for example, can still be collaborative. The change style may also vary by staff level or occupational groupings.
- The *target of change interventions* may be attitudes and values, behaviours or outputs. However, outputs are normally used indirectly to achieve behaviour change, and behaviour change may be used to effect value change.
- The *change roles* are often some combination of leadership, functional delegation, the use of external consultants and change action teams.
- The *range of change levers* is likely to be affected by other choices, such as the change target and style. The range of levers and mechanisms that can be used includes not just structural and systems interventions, but also softer interventions such as symbols and routines, and interpersonal interventions to do with communication, education, training and personal development.

The temptation for change agents is to simplify the decision-making process by basing their choices on popular change recipes they have seen used successfully elsewhere, or on their personal preferences, rather than the context in which they are currently operating. This may lead to the use of an inappropriate change approach. Therefore, it is necessary to use the features of the change context shown in the change kaleidoscope to help make judgements about the appropriate choices. This ensures the development of a context-sensitive approach to change. Chapters 4 and 5 explain how to do this.

Notes and references

(1) The concept of the paradigm is discussed extensively in *Exploring Corporate Strategy*, Chapters 2 and 5. An organization's paradigm is the shared, although often taken-for-granted, assumptions and beliefs of the organization that shapes the way things are done in an organization. Also see Appendix 1, on the cultural web.

(2) For details on the planned transformation at Shell see Robert Corzine, *The Financial Times*, Inside Track, 'Shell discovers time and tide wait for no man', 10 March 1998, p. 17; 'Thunder signals a rumpus on Olympus', 26 March 1998, p. 24; 'Oiling the group's wheels of change', 31 March 1998, p. 20.

(3) See J. Pendlebury, B. Grouard and F. Meston. 'Case Study on Catalysing: Electronic Data Systems (EDS) Corporation', *Successful Change Management,* 1998, Wiley.

(4) See G. Bounds and F. Hewitt, 'Xerox: Envisioning a Corporate Transformation', *Journal of Strategic Change*, 4, 1995, pp. 3–17.

(5) See J. Lawless, 'The Enterprise Network', *The Sunday Times,* 22 February 1998.

(6) There are many sources of information for the change process undertaken at British Airways in the 1980s. Two good sources are L.D. Goodstein and W.W. Burke, 'Creating Successful Organization Change', *Organizational Dynamics,* 19, 4, 1991, pp. 5–17; and J. Leahey and J.P. Kotter, 'Changing the Culture at British Airways', Harvard Business School, 1990, case number 9-491-009.

(7) The story of the transformation at General Electric led by Jack Welch is told in N.M. Tichy and S. Sherman, *Control Your Destiny, or Someone Else Will*, 1993, New York: Doubleday. Also by same authors a summary of the Work-Out programme, 'Walking the Talk at GE', *Training and Development*, June 1993, pp. 26–35.

(8) For a discussion of change paths and an example of a contingency approach to change style, see for example, D.A. Stace, 'Dominant Ideologies, Strategic Change and Sustained Performance', *Human Relations*, 49, 5, 1996, pp. 553–70.

(9) See M. Lynn, 'Parker kicks Clarks into shape', *The Sunday Times*, 12 April 1998, p. 7.

(10) See A.J. Rucci, S.P. Kirn and R.T. Quinn, 'The Employee–Customer Profit Chain at Sears', *Harvard Business Review*, 1998, January–February, pp. 82–97.

(11) For a fuller description of how to combine a top-down approach to change with a more bottom-up approach, see M. Beer, R.A. Eisenstat and B. Spector, *The Critical Path to Corporate Renewal*, 1990, Harvard Business School Press.

(12) See 'Right, pay attention new chaps. This is a train', *The Times*, 18 December 1997.

(13) D. Butcher, P. Harvey and S. Atkinson, *Developing Businesses*

through Developing Individuals, Cranfield School of Management, 1997.

(14) See A. Murdoch, 'Lateral Benchmarking or … What Formula One Taught an Airline', *Management Today*, November 1997, pp. 64–7.

(15) See P. Strebel, 'Why do Employees Resist Change', *Harvard Business Review*, May–June 1996, pp. 86–92.

(16) For a discussion of imposed change see H. Willmott, 'Strength is Ignorance: Slavery is Freedom: Managing Culture in Modern Organizations', *Journal of Management Studies,* 30, 4, 1993, pp. 515–52.

(17) For a discussion of the role of values in change see V. Hope and J. Hendry, 'Corporate Cultural Change – Is it relevant for the Organizations of the 1990s', *Human Resource Management Journal,* 5, 4, 1995, pp. 61–73.

(18) For a discussion of the impact of diversity see P.R. Lawrence and J.W. Lorsch, *Organization and Environment,* Boston: Harvard, 1967. Also J. Purcell, 'The Impact of Corporate Strategy on Human Resource Management', in J. Storey (ed.), *New Perspectives on Human Resource Management,* 1989, London: Routledge.

(19) See W. Scott and H. Harrison, 'Full Team Ahead', *People Management*, 9 October 1997, pp. 48–50.

(20) For a discussion of leadership during change see A.M. Pettigrew and R. Whipp, *Managing Change for Competitive Success*, 1991, Oxford: Blackwell Publishers. Also D.A. Nadler and M.L. Tushman, 'Organizational Frame Bending: Principles for Managing Reorientation', *The Academy of Management Executive*, III, 3, 1989, pp. 194–204.

(21) For a comparison of internal and external change agency roles see A. Ginsberg and E. Abrahamson, 'Champions of Change and Strategic Shifts: The Role of Internal and External Change Advocates', *Journal of Management Studies*, 28, 2, 1991, pp. 173–99.

(22) For an alternative way of analyzing organizations and designing levers and mechanisms to achieve the desired future organization in terms of three subsystems (technical, political and cultural), see N.M. Tichy, *Managing Strategic Change: Technical, Political and Cultural Dynamics*, 1983, John Wiley. Also N.M. Tichy, 'The Essentials of Strategic Change Management', *The Journal of Business Strategy,* 3, 1983, pp. 55–67.

(23) Tichy as in n. 22 above, and also see M. Orgland and G. Von Krugh, 'Initiating, Managing and Sustaining Corporate Transformation', *European Management Journal*, 16, 1, 1983.

3 Analyzing the change context: the change kaleidoscope

3.1 Introduction

Chapter 1 stressed the importance of understanding the strategic change context when designing an appropriate change approach for an organization by using the change kaleidoscope. Chapter 2 built on this by discussing the range of design choices open to a change agent. This chapter:

- reminds the reader of the perils of formulaic change and the importance of taking the change context into account when designing change;
- introduces and explains the contextual features in the change kaleidoscope – scope, time, preservation, diversity, capability, capacity, readiness for change and power;
- discusses the implications of each of the kaleidoscope features for the design of change.

Successful change, by its very nature, depends heavily on context and circumstance. The aim of this chapter is to not only examine each contextual feature of the kaleidoscope in depth, but also to give examples of the implications of each of these features for the design of change.

3.2 The perils of formulaic change

The lack of a universal change formula and the complexity of the change task has led to a number of different descriptive change models. These models are designed to improve our understanding of change. They appear to make the highly complex business of change simpler and more manageable. Chapter 1 described how it is therefore tempting for managers to use one of these 'off the shelf' solutions in order to cope with the complexity of change. However, Chapter 1 also discussed the potential dangers of this. Companies cannot necessarily apply approaches that have worked in one organizational context to their different organizational context. It has to be appreciated that even organizations that seem very similar are in reality very different. The two International Non-Governmental Organizations (INGOs) discussed in Illustration 3.1 highlight how organizations can appear very similar in terms of certain aspects such as size, income and mission, yet they can have fundamentally different cultures, which also means that suitable change approaches for the two organizations would need to be very different.

The use of past experience when designing change approaches can also be dangerous. What worked well in one context may be a poor indicator of what will work well in the current context. This is not to say that previous experience is irrelevant. However, for a change agent it is important to remember what was unique about a specific change situation and what was generalizable or replicable in other organizations. Similarly, it is important to appreciate and acknowledge what is unique and specific about the current context in which he or she is working. *Contextual judgement* becomes the competence required of a change agent rather than knowledge of the ten best change recipes from other organizations.

Change in action

Illustration 3.1

Two international organizations – Plan International and World Vision

Plan International and World Vision are both International Non-Governmental Organizations (INGOs). Their roots lie in the United States of America. They are both child sponsorship charities – they raise money for aid through asking people to sponsor children in some of the world's poorest regions. They are well established and operate over wide geographic areas. They employ similar numbers of staff. To someone who is unaccustomed to the INGO sector these organizations may appear very similar in purpose.

However, there is a contextual difference between these two organizations which is absolutely key. World Vision is a Christian foundation which sees its organization and delivery of aid as a form of Christian ministry. This permeates the organization at a strategic level in terms of defining its mission statement and also at a micro level in terms of defining everyday behaviour between staff. There are formal times allotted for prayer during the working day at World Vision. All documents refer to their commitment to Christian ministry. The result is a very strong culture built around the Christian religion. It is impossible to describe World Vision without referring to its Christian basis. Plan International does not have any form of religion as a declared culture value and its culture is therefore very different. Like World Vision it is task focused, concerned with the effective delivery of aid to the world's poorest communities, but it does not have this strong Christian culture.

3.3   *The change kaleidoscope*

Chapter 1 has already explained the components of the change kaleidoscope shown in Figure 3.1. It is a *diagnostic framework* which enables change agents to pin-point the key contextual features of their change context.

This book is not concerned with the outer ring of the kaleidoscope, the organizational strategic change context. As Chapter 1 explained, this is to do with the analysis to determine the why and what of change, and is dealt with in *Exploring Corporate Strategy*. However, the contextual features of any change situation, the middle ring of the kaleidoscope, are extracted from the broader strategic context. Explaining what these contextual features are, and how they can be derived and used, is the focus of this chapter. Table 3.1 briefly explains each feature.

There are two parts to the examination of the contextual features. The first part is the detailed analysis of each feature, which this

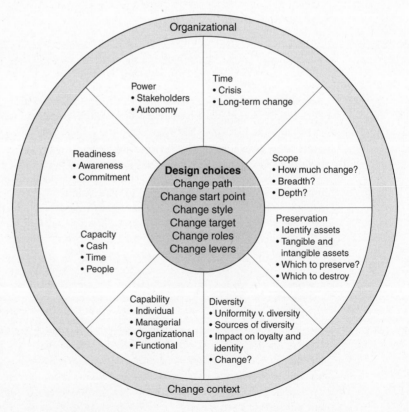

Figure 3.1   The change kaleidoscope

Table 3.1   *Short definitions of the change context features*

Time	How much time does the organization have to achieve this change? Is it in crisis or is it concerned with long-term strategic development? Are stakeholders, such as the stockmarket, expecting short-term results from the change?
Scope	Is the required outcome realignment or transformation? Does the change affect the whole organization, or is it only concerned with a particular division or department perhaps?
Preservation	To what extent is it essential to maintain continuity in certain practices or preserve specific assets? Do these practices and/or assets constitute invaluable resources, or do they contribute towards a valued stability or identity within an organization?
Diversity	Is the staff group concerned diverse or relatively homogeneous in terms of its values, norms, attitudes? Are there many subcultures or national cultures within the group? Are there different departments or divisions or is it one particular staff group? With whom or what in the organization do different staff groups identify – their team, job, department, division or the whole organization? Are there professionals who identify more with their profession or vocation than their employing organization?
Capability	How capable or competent is the organization at managing change and how widespread throughout the organization is this capability? How much change has the organization and its individual staff experienced in the past? Is there an expertise at an individual level for handling change?
Capacity	How much cash or spare human resource is there to divert towards the change?
Readiness for change	Are staff aware of the need for change? If they are, how willing and motivated are they towards the change? How much support generally is there for the change? How much understanding is there of the scope needed?
Power	Where is power vested within the organization? For this change to be successful who are the major stakeholders within and outside the organization whose support must be canvassed? How much latitude of discretion does the unit needing to change possess? Is it part of a larger group or is it relatively autonomous?

chapter deals with. The second part is the determination of which of the features are most critical in any particular organizational context, and how this affects the design choices made. This is the focus of Chapter 4. The range of design choices open to change agents have already been explained in Chapter 2.

The reason for calling this framework a kaleidoscope is important. The *Oxford English Dictionary* definition of a kaleidoscope is '*a constantly changing group* of bright objects; a tube through which are seen symmetrical figures produced by reflections of pieces of coloured glass and *varied by rotation of the tube'*. The kaleidoscope does not give predictable configurations that lead to more formulaic change recipes. Instead the pieces of coloured glass, the eight contextual features, remain the same but are *constantly reconfigured* to produce different pictures for each organizational change situation they are used to assess. Therefore, the change designs will also vary. Certain features infer certain design choices, but the potential permutations are endless. This chapter can only give a few examples for each feature.

3.4   Time

Time is to do with how long an organization has to achieve change. Is the organization in crisis or is it concerned with long-term strategic development? Time can also be affected by stakeholder attitudes, such as, are stakeholders like the stockmarket expecting short-term results from change (see Figure 3.2)?

3.4.1   Assessing time

How much time an organization has to deliver change should have been determined by the strategic analysis. It may be that an organization is in a crisis situation, with rapidly declining market share and profitability, and therefore in need of a reactive rapid turnaround and recovery change process. This may be due to a change in the competi-

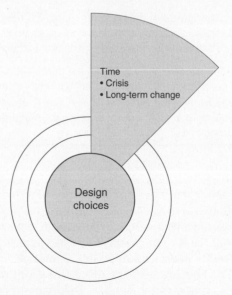

Figure 3.2   Contextual features for time

tive conditions the organization is facing, such as the arrival of new competitors and/or the development by competitors of different products and services. Alternatively it could be that an organization has become complacent and failed to keep up with the trends in its marketplace, continuing instead to pursue strategies still rooted in the ways of behaving that used to lead to success, placing the organization in an uncompetitive position. The examples given of organizations in this sort of position in Chapter 2 include British Airways in the early 1980s, and Sears merchandising in the 1990s.

An organization may also need to implement proactive change rapidly, either to pre-empt fast competitor imitation, or to meet changing customer needs. Illustration 3.2 describes the way in which Pearl

Change in action

Illustration 3.2

Pearl Assurance

In 1995 Pearl Assurance was in crisis. Market share was falling, costs were rising, the product range was overly complicated, the regulators were unhappy and the best of the salesforce were leaving. Pearl Assurance's new Managing Director, Richard Surface, decided that rapid change was needed. He later declared: 'Pearl did not have the luxury of time on its side . . .' He also believed that the faster the pain the quicker the gain.

Surface focused on a number of solutions: overhauling senior management, cutting costs, halving the product range and reforming the salesforce. The plan was to replace individual sales agents with teams of three covering larger areas. These teams would comprise an area manager and two agents. The plan meant that 1,000 jobs would be lost. Agents who were promoted to area manager posts received pay cuts as their jobs now carried less responsibility.

McKinsey, the consultants employed by Surface, wanted to test out this plan by piloting it in different geographic areas. However, the MD insisted on implementing it wholesale across the company starting in the last few months of 1995 and finishing the process in early 1996. In so doing he went over the heads of both the unions and the management consultants. Surface's reasons for this were that he felt the salesforce were already demoralized, and that prolonging the uncertainty would only increase their negative feelings.

Reflecting on this choice of speed Surface believes it also meant they didn't have to deal with the problem of dissent: 'Going too fast can be a good thing . . . it enables you to get round the difficult people rather than being held up by them . . .'. This passion for speed seems to have paid off. Operating costs for Pearl Assurance were down from £411 million in 1995 to £265 million in 1998. Over the same period market share rose from 1.5 to 2.2 per cent.

(Adapted from the *Financial Times*, Inside Track, 28 May 1998.)

Assurance's Managing Director pushed through rapid change in the mid-1990s against the advice of his own management consultants. He believed that Pearl Assurance did not have the luxury of time. Stockmarket and shareholder pressures may also lead to the need for rapid change.

An organization that is implementing change in a pre-emptive manner, before the organization is showing many visible signs of decline in competitiveness, may have the luxury of time on its side. The AIB banking group in Ireland (see Chapter 2) undertook change to turn its employees into marketers rather than bankers, not because it was unsuccessful, but to ensure continued success. Other organizations may undertake change on an ongoing incremental basis, in an attempt to avoid the need to have to undertake more fundamental change due to a lack of competitiveness in a short space of time. Such organizations usually possess a capability for continuous incremental change, that is built into their management systems. How these types of organizations operate is discussed in more depth below when considering organizational capability for change.

It would be easy to assume that a situation where change is not necessary in the immediate future is a more desirable context than one where crisis is looming. On the other hand, when senior managers anticipate change far in advance of any crisis, they are then faced with the problem of communicating to their staff the need for change. The example of KPMG in Chapter 2 illustrates this. Staff and other stakeholders may be perfectly happy with the current way of working and the current profit levels and results. Why engage in something as risky and painful as change when there is no obvious need? These sorts of issues have an impact on the design choices made and explain why some texts on change advocate the exploitation of, or the creation of, a crisis to trigger change.

3.4.2   Time and design choices

If there is limited time available to the change agent, particularly if the organization is in a crisis for whatever reason, then some design choices become automatic. Initial change initiatives are likely to involve some type of *realignment*, probably through *big-bang reconstruction* as at Pearl Assurance, as opposed to a more *incremental* approach, since the immediate need is to stem the decline in the organization's competitive position. This then places an organization in a position where it can embark on longer-term and more fundamental transformation if this is needed. Chapter 2 describes how this type of path was taken by both British Airways and General Electric, although General Electric was not in the crisis situation of British Airways. If there is money available, possibly from a parent group or other stakeholders such as national governments who are prepared to invest in the turnaround process, it may be possible to opt for more of a revolutionary approach from the start. This was the approach taken at Scandinavian Airline Systems by Jan Carlzon at a similar time to the changes at British Airways (1).

Such big-bang approaches, whether reconstruction or revolution, are also likely to be more top-down and directive in approach, and supported by a leadership change role. This is partly because there is not the time for more participative approaches, but also because the crisis legitimizes the action and there is likely to be a greater willingness among staff to follow top management edicts. However, it may be that if an organization needs to change rapidly, but there is not a felt need for change within the organization, that the change agent needs to force change in order to trigger the realization among staff of the inevitability of change. The change target, particularly with reconstruction where the aim is not an immediate shift in values, will be behaviours, or even outputs to effect rapid change. Change will therefore be delivered by means of harder interventions to do with structures and control systems, which may include new rewards to incentivize different behaviours.

However, a big-bang approach may also involve the use of symbolic levers such as the closure of certain parts of the business, or the closure of executive dining rooms and the removal of subsidized staff activities, to indicate that times are hard and things must be done differently if the organization is to survive. Illustration 3.3 describes the approach taken to change at Burton Group, the retailers, by three different Chief Executives between the 1970s and the 1990s. All pursued a top-down and directive change approach. However, in the late 1970s Ralph Halpern needed to deliver a fundamental shift in the focus of the core menswear business from manufacturing to fashion retailing. He had neither time nor money on his side, although there was arguably a recognition of the need for change among staff in the shops. To deliver a revolution he utilized a mixture of structural and symbolic interventions through a change style which verged on the coercive. This was followed by ongoing realignment using more incremental adaptation.

If organizations have the luxury of time then this enlarges the design choices available to the change agent. For instance, they can choose to map a particular change path whereby the organization starts with one form of change, which over time develops into another type of change. Organizations can start with adaptation aimed at increasing the organizational and individual capability for change, and then move into more fundamental and transformational evolution. Similarly, when time is not an issue it is possible to consider change processes which are educative, participative or collaborative in

Change in action

Illustration 3.3

Directive change at the Burton Group

During the early 1970s, Ladislas Rice, the then CEO of Burton, took many initiatives to revitalize the flagging business. Burton was a manufacturer of made-
to-measure menswear, with many shops which functioned as order points. In
response to the changing requirements throughout the 1960s of the increasingly fashion conscious young man who wanted ready-to-wear clothes, Rice
attempted to do two things – reposition Burtons as a group of retail divisions
by means of many acquisitions, and switch the manufacturing focus of the core
menswear business to a retailing focus.

The initiatives taken to change the focus of the menswear division
included the recruitment of new executives with retailing experience, the split
of manufacturing and retailing into two separate divisions, the creation of new
planning and remuneration systems at group level, cost control measures, and
the refurbishment of some shops. Manufacturing capacity was rationalized, but
the Burton family who retained control of the company were reluctant to
enforce redundancies in the factories. The financial performance of the
company continued to decline.

In 1976, the year the Burton Group experienced a trading loss for the first
time, Cyril Spencer took over as CEO, and Ralph Halpern assumed responsibility for the menswear retailing division within the group. Halpern took many
rapid and symbolic moves to turn menswear into a retailer of ready-to-wear
clothes. The merchandising team was moved to London from Leeds, and manufacturing was cut by a third. The closure of the Hudson Mills factory in Leeds
was seen by Halpern as a destruction of a symbolic totem of the past, since it
was a 'feudal castle' at which the Burton family administered 'the rites'. Money

style. Highly participative or collaborative change processes take time
to cascade through an organization. Furthermore, if there is no obvious need for change, such participative approaches may be needed to
gain a recognition of the need for, and a buy-in to, change.

Decisions about the change start point can work either way. If
awareness of the need for change is low, then getting the change
process started may still require a top-down approach. The choice is
also affected by other contextual features. If there is a low capability
for change among staff, then the approach may have to be directive in
style as well. On the other hand, there may be parts of the organization that are more ready for change, or have senior managers more
willing to embrace change than some other managers, enabling change
to be initiated by means of pilot sites. Alternatively, the time for
change and the capability for change among staff may allow for the
creation of awareness of the need for change, and the development of

Illustration 3.3 continued

was also invested in the shops – they were completely gutted and refitted. Finally, there was a switch in emphasis to fashion retailing of both men's and women's clothes, with different shops focusing on different market segments. By 1979 the Group was profitable as were all retailing divisions.

Halpern became Chairman and Chief Executive of Burtons in 1981 and the Group continued to go from strength to strength. In 1985 Burtons acquired Debenhams, the department store chain. However, by 1990 with the advent of a retailing recession among other problems, Halpern and Burtons were suffering from a credibility problem. Pressure mounted in the city for Halpern to resign, which he did in November 1990. The legacy of the 1980s for the group in the early 1990s was a number of middle to downmarket retail chains, occupying too much space. There was also competition between different brands in the group.

Despite cost-cutting exercises put in place by Halpern's successor, Burtons went into the red again in 1992. Thus when John Hoerner, the Chief Executive of Debenhams, took over as CEO of the Burton Group in 1992, he faced a very different set of circumstances to those faced by Halpern in the 1970s. The need was not to force a fundamental shift in the business focus, but a repositioning of the businesses within the Group. This was achieved through directive and top-down reconstruction which involved extensive rationalization, a reappraisal of target markets for the different brands, modernization of shops, the introduction of group-wide systems based on best practice within the group, a large number of redundancies, and new reward and assessment systems.

(Adapted from the Burton A, B and C cases by G. Johnson and J. Gush in G. Johnson and K. Scholes, *Exploring Corporate Strategy: Texts and Cases,* 5th edition, 1999, Hemel Hempstead: Prentice Hall.)

what should be changed, through a more bottom-up approach. Staff diversity also has an impact here. Even in circumstances where there is a low readiness for change, staff groups that value their autonomy may need to be involved through a more participative approach if they are to buy-in to change.

In terms of change targets, when there is more time available and transformation is required, then it may be possible to target values. This in turn impacts on the change levers. Longer-term change interventions, particularly those where the intention is to aid value change, include communication, management development programmes and personal development initiatives such as coaching or mentoring.

Time also affects the choice of change roles. Change agents need to ask whether there is sufficient time to establish and develop a change action team. Also the potential champions of the change – be it the chief executive, the HR director, or another change agent – need to be screened for competence and capability. If they require a great deal of coaching in change leadership, yet there is no time to develop this, then support may be needed from external consultants or champions. If time is available then teams can be established to spread the vision and required changes throughout the organization.

3.5   Scope

Scope is the required outcome of the change, varying from realignment through to more radical change aimed at transformation of an organization. Scope is also affected by whether the whole organization needs to change, or just one division or department of it (see Figure 3.3).

3.5.1   Assessing scope

The scope of the change determines just how much change is necessary. There are two aspects to scope – the depth of the change required in an organization and the physical spread of change across the organization.

The depth of change required is equivalent to the extent of change discussed in Chapter 2 when considering the types of change to be undertaken and the change path to be followed. As such, it is one of the key determinants of the type of change, although by no means the only one. It also impacts on design choices other than the type and path of change. When considering the depth of change, it is therefore necessary to consider whether the desired change involves a trans-formation, a change which cannot be handled within the existing par-

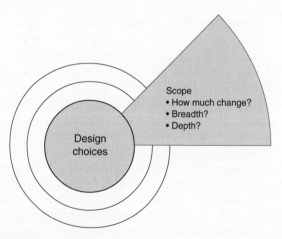

Figure 3.3   Contextual features for scope

adigm and organizational routines and entails a change in the taken-for-granted assumptions and 'the way of doing things around here'; or a realignment, a change to the way of doing things that does not involve a fundamental reappraisal of the central assumptions and beliefs within the organization.

Chapter 2 illustrates the difference between transformation and realignment by reference to change at Shell, and EDS (Electronic Data Systems) in Europe. The changes wanted at Shell included a shift from a technical and consensual organization, to one characterized by faster decision making, greater creativity and a stronger customer focus. Whereas the aim at EDS was more to do with harmonization of business practices. Organizations can also pass through phases of realignment, followed by transformation. Consider the example of the retail banking industry in the UK. The banking industry until the late 1990s had undergone several forms of change but in retrospect these changes had all fundamentally been forms of realignment. This is because the changes never altered the fundamental purpose of the banks – banking. The new entrants into the marketplace in the 1990s, in the form of direct telephone banking and the supermarkets, coupled with growing customer sophistication and demand, required the banks to respond in a more fundamental fashion. The banks had to switch from being bankers to being retailers of financial services. This necessitated a shift in the fundamental beliefs and assumptions of these organizations.

A useful framework that can be used to help assess the scope of change required is the cultural web. This framework has already been introduced in Chapter 2 as a way of considering the range of levers and mechanisms that need to be used to effect change, and is explained in more detail in Appendix 1, and in *Exploring Corporate Strategy*. By drawing up a current cultural web for an organization, and then drawing up an outline web of the sort of organization needed if the desired changes are to become a reality, the extent of required change can be determined, since the two webs provide a picture of how different the future organization will need to be to the current one. If the changes also impact on what sits in the paradigm, then the change is likely to be transformational in nature (see Illustration 2.9 on Baxi). To return to the banking example, the changes carried out by retail banks in the 1980s and into the 1990s, did little to shift the internally-focused, conservative, risk averse nature of the banks. Whereas, if a move to a retailer of financial products is to be successful, this requires a change in the assumptions and beliefs to ones which support the notion of a responsive, customer-focused organization.

The questions about the physical spread of the change process concern formal structures rather than informal cultures. Is change limited to a small department, or a particular national division, or a particular layer of management? Or, alternatively, is it a change process that should affect the whole organization? There is no formal tool that can assess the physical spread of change, but the strategic analysis already conducted should have determined the factor.

3.5.2   Scope and design choices

The depth or extent of change obviously impacts on the type of change required in terms of *adaptation, reconstruction, evolution* or *revolution*, and therefore the choice of change path. However, the change path is also affected by other contextual features, such as time, capacity and capability. If the scope of change suggests a need for realignment rather than transformation, the other main factor is likely to be time. A short timescale points to reconstruction with the associated design choices described above under time. A longer timescale suggests adaptation, which brings with it a wider range of design choices – again see time above.

If the scope of change points to transformation, then the choice of change path is more complex. The discussion above on the impact of time on design choices explains how when in a crisis, an organization has little time to effect change, and probably a low capacity in terms of cash to invest in the change process, and therefore may need initially to undertake reconstruction, even if the ultimate aim of the change process is transformation rather than realignment. The implications of this for the other design choices are also explained above and will not be repeated here. However, once the reconstruction has been delivered, the organization then needs to consider how it delivers the transformation that is still required.

An example is the transformation undertaken at ASDA, the supermarket group, by Archie Norman in the 1990s (see Illustration 3.4). It was necessary to return ASDA to a financially viable position, and then drive in transformational change. The approach selected involved much initial restructuring, followed by the use of a wide variety of levers and mechanisms, ranging from structures and systems, to the more symbolic, to drive in changes to the way of thinking at ASDA through behavioural change.

If the organization has more time to effect a transformation, or has carried out a reconstruction which has in turn gained the organization more time, then there is a wider range of design choices to pick from. These have also been discussed above. However, when needing to carry out a transformation, with or without time on its side, an organization can still be constrained from revolution or evolution, by aspects such as a lack of readiness for change or a lack of capability for change. This may point to the need for some sort of adaptation first of all, with the use of more participative change approaches to build a

Change in action

Illustration 3.4

Change at ASDA

In 1991, ASDA the supermarket chain was close to bankruptcy. When Archie Norman took over as chief executive at the end of 1991, he wanted to change everything about the organization, other than its location in Yorkshire. Financial stability was restored within Norman's first year by restructuring, which involved selling off non-related parts of the business, property and some stores, and revaluation of the remaining stores. A rights issue was used to raise funds for the transformation, to reposition ASDA as a leader in fresh food and clothing.

Many levers and mechanisms were used. Head office was reduced from 2,000 plus staff to about 1,350 to make ASDA a store-based company. To support this trend, monthly board meetings were moved into the stores, with lunch in the store canteen. During the visit, Board members had to talk to customers and 'colleagues' (there were no managers and staff in the new ASDA). Layers of management were taken out of the structure, and within the stores, each product group, such as the bakery or the fishmongers, was set up to be run by a team with their own profit and loss account. Recruitment policies were changed to find people who wanted to serve the customer and who liked selling. Share options were also made available to staff on the same terms as executives.

To create an involvement culture rather than a control culture, some of the many initiatives put in place included surveys of staff opinions, 'listening groups', and a 'Tell Archie' suggestion scheme with rewards for good suggestions. Such initiatives were symbolic of the new desired working environment, as were other initiatives. The only reserved parking space at head office is for the company Jaguar, which is awarded each month to whoever brought about a large increase in sales.

The head office was designed to fit with the new emphasis on open communication. In the open plan office, even Norman only had a desk, with many meeting rooms for discussion and an absence of status symbols. ASDA baseball hats indicated that the wearer needed space for thinking time. Many charts, news items and customer comments were displayed.

By 1995, although the culture change was not complete, ASDA was in a healthy financial position, there had been a 30 per cent increase in customers, and sales growth was better than that of the competitors.

(Edited from an original article, 'ASDA's Open Plan', in the 4 December 1995 issue of *Management Today*, with permission of the copyright owner, Haymarket Business Publications Limited.)

readiness for change, and/or more personal development interventions to build a capability for change. Alternatively, the power of the change agent to deliver transformation may be limited, in which case early interventions may be to do with the use of political levers aimed at building support and a stronger power base for the change agent.

Yet there are implications of the scope of change which have to be taken into account when making the design choices. Ultimately, if an organization is to deliver transformation it needs to drive in change to the central assumptions and beliefs in the paradigm, which means that at some stage it may need to target values, or at least behaviours with the intention of driving in value change. If the target is values, then change is likely to take some time. This also has implications for the range of levers and mechanisms, as explained in Chapter 2, as at some point it will be necessary to invest in education, training and personal development interventions. If the organization is not cash rich, this may limit its ability to invest in such change levers. In such circumstances it may be necessary to first target behaviours through a full range of levers and mechanisms, such as structures, systems, routines and symbols, and then support these changes through time with appropriate education and training.

However, the issue of physical spread throughout an organization also brings other dimensions into consideration. If, for instance, the change is limited to one functional division which is located within one nation-state and employing similar types of staff, then the change process is less complex than trying to lead a change over a multidivisional global corporation.

3.6   *Preservation*

Preservation is the extent to which it is essential to maintain continuity in certain practices or preserve specific assets, either because they constitute invaluable resources, or they contribute towards a valued stability or identity within an organization. Assets include tangibles such as money, buildings and technology but also intangibles such as know-how, and staff loyalty or pride in the employer or product (see Figure 3.4).

3.6.1   *Assessing preservation*

A key criteria for the change agent to consider is the extent to which there is a need to preserve the status quo within an organization. There are two aspects to preservation. The first is being clear about what the organization's assets are, both tangible and intangible. The second is deciding upon what should or should not be preserved in a change process.

Organizational assets include both tangibles and intangibles. In the same way that a small business valuation will include both a costing for property or technology plus intangibles such as 'goodwill', so too

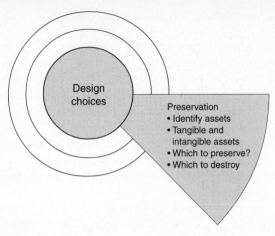

Figure 3.4   Contextual features for preservation

larger organizations need to consider sources of both tangible and intangible competitive advantage. A resource audit can help identify what these assets might be. The concept of a resource audit is introduced in *Exploring Corporate Strategy*, Chapter 4. Resources are identified within four categories – *physical, human, financial* and *intangibles*. These categories of resources also need to be analyzed to assess whether they are still relevant for the organization, and if they are, whether they are easy to imitate by competitors, or whether they are unique and difficult for competitors to imitate.

It is important that all resources that contribute to an organization's competitive advantage are retained during the change process, but it is particularly important that the change process does not lead to the loss of the resources that are unique and difficult to imitate. These resources are often the more intangible assets such as the know-how, or 'tacit knowledge' of particular staff. Tacit knowledge can be described as an informal and almost instinctive understanding of, for example, organizations, customers or products, probably acquired through experience. The important aspect of tacit knowledge is that it is not formally held within an organization in the form of written policies or procedures, instead it is retained in people's heads. Since it is not written down or systematized in any way, it is hard to imitate and pass on to others. Yet this informal knowledge, precisely because it is not formally produced, is often a source of competitive advantage because it is not easily replicated by other companies (2).

Some of the downsizing that went on in the early 1990s resulted in the precipitous removal of more experienced managers from corporations. They were often perceived as an easy target for redundancy because of their age and pension holdings. However, their hasty removal from the organization often resulted in a loss of tacit knowledge. Illustration 3.5 contrasts the experiences at British Telecom with that of Glaxo Pharmaceuticals. The voluntary redundancy programme at BT led to the loss of many of the people whose knowledge the company needed. Glaxo Pharmaceuticals identified the need to retain certain staff and initiated change in a way designed to keep these staff. Chapter 4 explains how this was done in more detail. The issue is that if a change agent does not understand what aspects of the existing organization need to be preserved, or how such assets can be replaced if lost, the change process may have unanticipated and damaging outcomes.

The extent of preservation is in part dependent on the scope of change. Arguably the more that has to be retained, the less the scope of change. Yet it is necessary to address preservation as a separate question. If an organization needs to undergo transformation, it is possible to overlook the existing sources of competitive advantage that

Change in action

Illustration 3.5
Two different approaches to change

British Telecom

BT were forced to implement a large and radical downsizing programme in order to remain competitive in the 1980s – this involved shedding some 120,000 staff out of 240,000. They opted to run a voluntary redundancy programme. Unfortunately in so doing they found that they were often obliged to hire back into the organization, at consultancy rates, many of their former employees who had recently taken a redundancy package. This was because many of the staff they had made redundant had essential knowledge of how to make the organization work. The knowledge they held was customized to BT and therefore difficult to obtain in the external job market.

Glaxo Pharmaceuticals UK

In the late 1980s Glaxo Pharmaceuticals UK (now Glaxo Wellcome following a spate of mergers and acquisitions) knew that its customer base was changing. Also its most successful product was due to come off patent in the mid-1990s. Glaxo realized that change was necessary. It also recognized that as it employed some of the best qualified staff in the labour market it could not afford to alienate them by implementing changes that might cause them to exit from the company. It designed its consequent change programmes with this in mind.

reside within the organization. This is particularly the case if the 'assets' are to do with people who can find good employment elsewhere.

Finally, it must be recognized that there may be intangible, cultural aspects of the organization that need to be retained, such as staff loyalty, a team spirit, or extensive staff collaboration which in turn leads to sources of advantage such as creativity or better customer service. If an organization's competitive position is based on its staffs' creativity or customer service, then any change process that unwittingly destroys these features of the culture will damage the organization. Aspects such as staff loyalty or team spirit can also be used to help facilitate the painful process of change. Similarly, when professional service firms, such as the large accountancy and consultancy organization KPMG, undertake change, they have many young, motivated and talented staff. This has to be an asset in any change circumstances, as again such staff members can be used to facilitate change.

A cultural web analysis can help to identify some of these features. Therefore, a cultural web analysis needs to be used in two ways – first to consider what aspects of the organization need to be changed, and second to consider what aspects of the organization need to be specifically retained, either because they will contribute to future competitiveness, or because they can be used to facilitate the change process.

3.6.2   *Preservation and design choices*

If preservation of hard to replace assets is important, particularly intangible assets embedded in the existing culture, then a number of design choices become clear. For instance, revolution in which many aspects of the organization are changed simultaneously would be a risky change path. Similarly, a target of outputs could be dangerous as this could lead to many unintended behavioural side effects.

If preservation is more to do with the retention of particular staff groups, particularly if these staff are seen as highly desirable assets in the external labour market, this has implications for the style of change. To avoid alienating them a collaborative or educative style of change may be a safer route than a directive approach. If the staff group concerned is a group that values their autonomy and independence, such as university lecturers, then direction and prescription of behaviours or values is likely to be inappropriate, and it might be that a change target of outputs would then be appropriate.

On the other hand, organizations seeking true transformational change will have to give up, or even destroy, features of organizational life that in the past might have been assets but now represent barriers to change. The emotional attachment to such features may make this hard to do. Managerial and staff mindsets about what leads to success, and about what is the right way of doing things, may need to be abandoned.

This is about 'unlearning'. Unlearning implies that people have to throw out unhelpful behaviours or ways of thinking to make room for new ways of thinking. If these old ways of thinking have become taken-for-granted assumptions for individuals, then challenging them and giving them up can be a painful process for staff. This may mean that change needs to follow a more top-down, directive change approach.

The need for unlearning also has implications for the range of levers to be used. If there is sufficient time and money, unlearning can be achieved by investment in levers to do with training and development. However, if inapplicable practices are deeply embedded within an organization, particularly if there is little time for change, the imposition of changes to working practices through structures and systems may be necessary, accompanied by visible destruction of aspects of the organization that symbolized the past. This is the approach taken by Ralph Halpern at Burtons, described in Illustration 3.3 above. A forceful and directive approach may mean that staff who cannot adjust to the changes asked of them given the rapid change timescale leave. On the other hand, if staff are unable to adapt to the new ways of working required of them, they can become a liability to the organization rather than an asset.

3.7   *Diversity*

Diversity is to do with the degree of diversity that exists among the staff group(s) affected by change. Change may affect groups or divisions with different subcultures, or different national cultures. Staff may also differ in the way they identify with the organization – through their team, job, department, division or the whole organization. Professional groups may identify more with their profession than their employing organization (see Figure 3.5).

3.7.1   *Assessing diversity*

Many change texts assume that organizations are homogeneous. This is usually far from the truth. There are three aspects to diversity that can impact on the appropriateness of any change approach:

- The extent to which there is uniformity or diversity within an organization. Diversity can occur within an organization because of the existence of different *national cultures,* different *subcultures,* or different professional or *occupational groups* between divisions and departments.

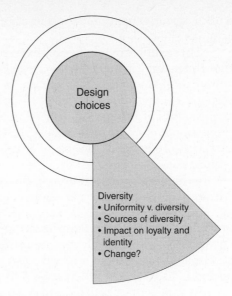

Figure 3.5   Contextual features for diversity

- The impact of these sources of diversity on staff loyalty and commitment to the overall organization.
- The extent to which the change agent wishes to reduce or increase levels of diversity as part of the intended outcomes of the change process.

If a corporation is spread over several different countries then issues of diverse national cultures must be taken into account (3). A change initiative designed in California may be quite unacceptable to a south-east Asian national culture. The issue of cross-cultural management becomes less of an issue in truly global corporations where the culture of the staff is so international that common approaches are possible despite different geographic locations. However, truly global or transnational corporations remain rare. The more diverse the operations and national units the more difficult it is to introduce common change processes at anything more than a visionary level. The implementation of that changed vision may have to be left to the discretion of the geographic unit concerned.

Another source of diversity is that of professional groups. At Glaxo-Wellcome within the UK division there are differences between the culture of the sales units and the culture of the Research and Development scientists. This means that any change process at a national level would have to be able to appeal to both of these different groups. There can also be departmental or divisional subcultures within an organization. The more subcultures that exist, the more complex the design process.

These different sources of diversity in turn affect employee loyalties and commitment. If the source of diversity is national culture, to what extent would a local employee in a developing country agree to a corporate change if she or he felt that it threatened the national security or safety of her/his country? Similarly, staff who are members of professional or vocational bodies, such as lawyers, may feel allegiance to those professional norms of autonomy before allegiance to any organizational norms. Alternatively, employees may show more loyalty to their trade or staff union. The tradition of collective bargaining within an organization may alert change agents or managers to the existence of diversity within the workforce. At a more basic level, staff may identify more with their immediate work or peer group than they do with the whole employing organization (4). Similarly, head office staff may identify more with an organization than geographically dispersed field staff (see Illustration 3.6).

In some organizations it may be clear that employees do identify and should identify with their employing organization. For instance, it would be strange for a priest not to identify strongly with the Roman Catholic church. Yet employees can derive a sense of identity from many different sources. Senior managers can erroneously assume that their strong allegiance to the employing organization is shared by the rest of the staff. Change agents should not assume that the staff feel that the 'organization' is worth the pain of individual change.

Having identified the levels of diversity or uniformity within an organization, the change agent may consider addressing these as part of the change process. An organization may be too diverse with insufficient unifying elements for commercial effectiveness or the mainten-

Change in action

Illustration 3.6

Diversity and identity in retail banking

The retail banking sector in the UK was obliged to undergo a major transformation because of industry level changes such as new entrants to the sector, new technology, etc. The need for change was obvious at Board level but the banks also had to convince their geographically dispersed bank staff. When designing their change process they found that the field staff identified strongly with their immediate work group and local branch but felt the organization, as represented by their head office, was remote and not a source of identity. This meant that the change agents had to work with the branch staff's sense of reality, not their own.

ance of management control. This can happen as a result of rapid growth or increasing internationalization where units start to grasp too much autonomy from the centre. Alternatively it may result from many mergers and acquisitions as at EDS Europe (see Chapter 1). In these situations the change interventions may need to include actions to promote more unity of purpose.

Conversely, the organization may have become too uniform, with conflict or dissent eradicated from everyday working behaviours. Alternative ideas are not considered and different personality types are either not allowed to enter the organization or are ejected once inside. The result can be a company of clones who all think and behave alike and have fixed views on how business should be conducted. Whilst their views fit the marketplace the business may succeed; but if the market changes they may struggle to change in order to meet new forms of customer or competitor demand. Here the change issue becomes one of promoting diversity within the organization. However, this is more to do with the *scope* of change.

3.7.2   Diversity and design choices

If there are high levels of diversity based around different national cultures, then a target of value led change, if time allows, can cross these boundaries. Likewise, common output targets can be prescribed across the globe. Hewlett-Packard is a multinational corporation which has existed with the same statement of organizational values for over sixty years – the HP Way. Furthermore, that values statement is used throughout its operations across the globe. The values statement has a universal message about respect for other people that is meaningful for people wherever they live and whatever their religion. They also have a business planning system and performance management system which are common to all national and business divisions within the corporation. Thus staff objectives are derived from a common set of measurements and changes in these outputs can be targeted as change mechanisms. What Hewlett-Packard does not do is to prescribe common behaviours across its multinational corporations. A programme that emphasizes tightly prescribed behaviours cannot be introduced across diverse national groups within the same organization because it would clash with behavioural norms within national societies.

High levels of diversity also has implications for change roles. In a large corporation, either national or international, local staff may identify more with the head of their business division rather than the overall chief executive of the whole corporation. Therefore, in identifying change leaders it may be wise to devolve responsibility down to business unit heads.

The change start point may also be affected by high levels of diversity. It may be unwise to unfurl a change process across a whole corporation if diversity exists across divisions or departments. In the aftermath of its major downsizing programme, BT has purposefully tried to promote new forms of working practices (such as new contractual arrangements, management styles and forms of assessment) within its newly established divisions. These working practices differ from those found within its established business divisions. The new divisions are not therefore socialized into the old BT culture. Depending on the success of the changes in culture, working practices and management styles in the new divisions, BT may choose to then apply these across the whole of its 120,000 staff.

Diversity can also affect the change path. When undertaking a merger or acquisition, the initial change phase may concentrate on unifying the cultures of the two organizations involved. Similarly, if an organization already has subcultures within it as a result of, for example, previous acquisitions or mergers, and this diversity needs to be reduced for the planned changes to work, then again the initial change phase may involve interventions aimed at unifying the different cultures.

The presence of diverse professional or vocational identities needs to be taken into account by any change process, particularly if the groups concerned are powerful. A role could be created for a professional representative within the change design team, in the same way that union involvement would be sought, to increase the acceptability of any proposed changes to that representative's peers. If this is not possible, then a change style that incorporates education and collaboration may be necessary in recognition of the freedom and autonomy professionals normally have within their work. Behavioural prescription is also less likely to be received well by professionals because of the need they often have for high levels of autonomy. For example, teachers are likely to react negatively to the imposition of directives that limit their discretion in the classroom.

If the change is directed at a homogeneous group of employees, it may be possible to dictate behavioural changes as targets for change, or use organizational values as the change target. For example, the counter staff at McDonalds fast food outlets respond to the exact definition of their behaviours. Indeed this is part of the product that McDonalds is selling. Similarly, if an organization has a relatively homogeneous group of employees who identify strongly with the organization as a whole, top-down change programmes are more likely to succeed. Likewise, a strong organizational identity may mean that the Chief Executive is seen as a leader for all staff, and therefore is the natural choice for the role of leading change.

3.8   *Capability*

Capability assesses how good the organization is at managing change. *from* Aspects that require consideration include the location of change *where* expertise within the organization, how much change the organization and its staff have experienced in the past, and the degree of expertise for handling change at an individual, managerial or departmental level (see Figure 3.6).

3.8.1   *Assessing capability*

It is important to question whether an organization possesses the necessary skills and abilities to manage change before embarking on change design and implementation. A change agent should not design an implementation process that the organization is not capable of delivering. The research on change is littered with examples of organizations which either implemented inappropriate change designs, or attempted change designs that were too sophisticated for their levels of change competence. This is also why many of the change initiatives that are heralded as transformation actually result in reconstruction.

Capabilities need to exist at three levels – the individual level, the managerial level and the organizational level. Individual capability is about the ability of individuals within an organization to manage change within themselves. Anyone who has lived through a personal

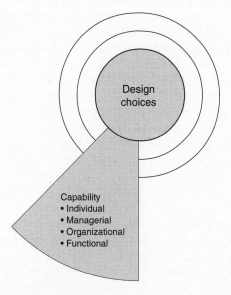

Figure 3.6   Contextual features for capability

crisis such as a bereavement or divorce will understand that personal change can be an overwhelming experience. However, the more reflective the individual, the more they can expect to learn from the experience, and hopefully then be able to manage the process more effectively if it reoccurs.

Learning about individual change is part of a process called personal development. This involves individual staff members developing a competence for handling change at a very personal and sometimes emotional level. Many mainstream MBA and Senior Executive Development programmes contain courses focused exclusively on this topic. They usually incorporate some form of experiential learning.

The organizations which sponsor employees on these courses are not simply concerned with the gains made at an individual level by the staff who attend these courses. The sponsors are also aware that it is the organization which gains if its staff are capable of managing the personal impact of organizational change for themselves. It can save the organization considerable amounts of time and money if this capability is embedded within people. Staff may show less resistance to change, or may need less persuasion from their peers or managers to change. Resistance at an individual level is often not directed at the change but towards the change process itself. Various models for understanding the process of personal transition are described in Chapter 5.

A second level of capability is at the managerial level of change. How able are line and general managers to counsel and help their staff through the process of change? For instance, does the organization's management possess the appropriate communication skills to convey a clarity about the change and a commitment to their staff? Do they possess the change counselling skills needed to help their staff through change? Are any managers experienced in dealing with a number of different change initiatives at one time? Does the organization know which managers within their staff have a high degree of competence at managing change?

Research that examined organizational transformation in eight different organizations over a nine-year period concluded that line manager capability was a key differentiator in accounting for the differences between success and failure in the different change histories of the companies (5). In companies that successfully transformed or changed the researchers found:

- Line managers followed through consistently on change initiatives, whereas, in companies that struggled with change, the line manager response was inconsistent.
- There was a focus on a few clustered and coherent interventions. Thus, the line managers were not faced with a bewildering array of change initiatives.

- Managers were assessed and held accountable for managing change and were also rewarded for their efforts in this area.

A third level of capability for managing change is vested at the organizational level. Change units can be established anywhere within an organization. Some change experts may be located within strategic planning units, Chief Executive Offices, Human Resource functions, or specialist change units called Organizational Development departments. As well as displaying expertise within the broad subject of change, they may be specialists in their own right in the areas such as management development, top team development, management of high potential staff, or internal communications. All of these functions and skills can contribute to an organization's overall capability in handling change. The example of the RMI initiative in the National Health Service (NHS) (discussed later in this chapter, section 3.9.1, Illustration 3.7), discusses a series of problems with the change approach. Many of these appeared to be due to not only a lack of funds but also a limited change capability.

Finally, there is also a difference between an organization's ability to manage change incrementally and an ability to manage big-bang change (see Figure 2.2). By their very nature big-bang change programmes attract greater attention. Research has shown that companies who possessed a competence at this level also display certain skills (5):

- They know which levers to pull in order to achieve rapid change. Senior managers know which change initiatives could instantly tap into sources of staff motivation. Traders in the City of London are motivated by rewards and bonus systems. These are potentially key levers in achieving change within investment banks. In other organizations different levers are key .
- They possess an ability to design big-bang programmes. They know how to run pilot events, how to roll out cascades of workshops and run multimedia communication events. They often maintained specialist change units within the organization.

Other organizations have a capability to manage incremental change. Enduring multinational and global companies such as Hewlett-Packard or Citibank have developed a special ability to ride the waves of change over decades rather than years (6). Such organizations achieve this through a number of means:

- They constantly scan the external and internal environment.
- They use this information continuously to fine-tune their internal control mechanisms such as business planning systems or performance management systems. These systems act as railtracks between the strategic apex of the company and the non-managerial operating core.

The systems are used continually to send new objectives down through the company and to send information on business performance back up to the top. In the same way that a baby develops motor skills gradually using messages from the brain sent down through its nervous system to its limbs, so these management systems act as an organization's nerves.

- They promote the use of loose organizational structures that can be continually reshaped in response to changes in the marketplace or labour markets.
- They often possess a relatively stable yet implicit set of cultural values that endure over time. No matter what changes occur these values give the companies a cultural stability such that the informal identity of the organization is never overstretched in the minds of the employees.

This suggests that a capability in incremental change is based upon four skills: constantly scanning the external environment, using management systems as information and communication systems, promoting flexible organizational structures and maintaining elements of cultural identity for the purpose of consistency.

The People Process Model can be used to assess levels of change capability within an organization. Specifically it checks out transformational competence in three areas – organizational transformation, transformation of future leaders, and the ability to transform the workforce. This model assesses the strength of linkage between individual behaviour and corporate strategy through the sophisticated use of people management processes and systems. For more detail of this framework and how to use it see Appendix 2.

Capability is a difficult feature to assess in the short term. At an individual level there exists a plethora of psychometric tests that can indicate change capabilities, particularly among managerial staff. At the level of the organization it may simply require a resource audit of which staff have had experience of managing large-scale change programmes either in their current company or with previous employers. Surprisingly enough, depending on the size of the organization, a simple questionnaire or focus group sessions with staff may uncover valuable experience in this area.

3.8.2   *Capability and design choices*

Capability influences the choice of change path. Transformational change, whether evolution or revolution, is harder to achieve than realignment. This may mean that whilst transformation is the preferred change path for an organization, it is not an option because the organization lacks the capabilities listed in the previous section. The organization needs to start with adaptation or reconstruction first. For instance, earlier change may entail developing managerial capability. Managers may need to be taken through development initiatives to enhance their understanding of change and their ability to manage it. If the ultimate aim is evolution, business planning systems, including performance management systems, may also need to be established to aid an incrementalist approach.

When considering change targets, value led change is probably the hardest form of change to achieve as it requires skill to purposefully and successfully penetrate the values and attitudes of staff and to change them. At the very least the organization would need to be able to demonstrate an Organizational Development capability, with perhaps a team of development specialists who either have a knowledge of personal change, of have access to consultants who have this knowledge. Some organizations have change consultancy teams with such capabilities who act as internal contractors within the organizations. A change style of collaboration, for example, may also require particular skills such as facilitation. Capability, therefore, also affects the choice of change roles. Consultants may need to be involved in a change process to compensate for a lack of change capability within an organization.

The choice of change levers is also affected by capability. For example, symbolism can be used as a powerful change lever but in inexperienced hands symbolic change can be counterproductive (see Chapter 6). Similarly, using Human Resource Management systems, such as recruitment and selection or reward systems, or change levers requires the staff in the Human Resources function to possess both an operational excellence in these areas and a strategic understanding of the power of these systems as change mechanisms (see Chapter 6).

3.9 Capacity

Capacity considers how much resource the organization can invest in the proposed change both in terms of cash and staff, and how much time managers have to devote to change (see Figure 3.7).

3.9.1 Assessing capacity

Many of the change programmes written up as showcase pieces feature large corporations undertaking change. The danger is that small to medium-sized enterprises try to mimic these larger programmes but without the same capacity available for investment in initiatives. The result can be overambitious changes announced at senior management level which fizzle out at lower levels because there is no means to manage a big-bang change. It is therefore necessary to consider

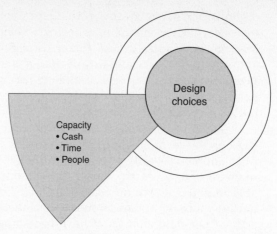

Figure 3.7 Contextual features for capacity

what key resources are limited in any specific change scenario. These can, in part, be assessed through the use of a resource audit, already discussed in section 3.6.1 above.

Capacity can be divided into three main areas – cash, time and people:

- *Cash*: Any change interventions that involve management development programmes, particularly off-site, are likely to be expensive and require considerable investment. Physical change assets, such as new technology, can also be expensive. Symbolic change, such as the relocation of offices or redesigning existing office layouts, can also require cash investment.
- *Time*: Difficult questions need to be addressed about how much time is available for senior managers to devote to leading the change. Middle managers often feel squeezed by the pressures of change. They are expected to implement several different change initiatives whilst at the same time continuing to deliver on all their normal performance targets. If a change agent wants line or general managers to give attention to change initiatives then he or she needs to consider creating time for them. Some organizations remove managers' responsibility for certain routine tasks for a limited period of time in order to create time for the implementation of change. These issues are discussed in Chapter 7.
- *People*: The issue of capability has already been considered, but quantity is also relevant. Are there sufficient people or managers who are competent in the management of change and committed to the change itself? Are these people sufficient to create the momentum needed for the change to be carried out?

The case study on the NHS initiative RMI (see Illustration 3.7) demonstrates the impact of limited investment. The limited resources given to the change project in terms of investment in systems, time and communication significantly contributed to its less than successful implementation. The failure to invest sufficiently in the management of the initiative resulted in even more money being wasted as a result of a failed change process.

3.9.2 Capacity and design choices

Cash capacity affects the choice of change path. Big-bang programmes may be costly. Incremental change is less expensive, but only if the required infrastructure of management systems and line manager capability is already in place. If not, then substantial investment will be needed to build up that systems and managerial capability.

Likewise, value led change, if it is to be successful, involves a heavy investment in the communication, education, training and personal development change levers that will need to be used to achieve the target of value driven change. Investment is needed in the form of both managerial time and money. A change target of outputs or behaviours is much cheaper in terms of time and money, but may not deliver the change that is needed.

Higher levels of capacity, in terms of time, cash and people, are needed for collaborative, educative or participative styles of change (see Chapter 2, section 2.4). Less time and money is needed in the short term for directive styles of change – although there is always the risk that managing the resistance caused by a directive style of change if used inappropriately (again see Chapter 2) may be more costly in the longer term.

Choosing the right people for the key roles in change management also raises questions of capacity. The chief executive may be the company's most charismatic leader but if she or he simply does not have time to devote to the leadership of the change process then alternative candidates need to be considered. If the company has little time but does have cash then there is the option of bringing in an external change consultancy to help manage the change, or assembling an internal change action team to lead it through the organization.

3.10 Readiness

Readiness for change is to do with how aware staff are of the need for change and how willing and motivated they are towards the change. Readiness is also to do with how much support there is generally for the change, and how much understanding there is of the scope of change needed (see Figure 3.8).

Change in action

Illustration 3.7

The Resource Management Initiative

In 1986 the Resource Management Initiative (RMI) was introduced to the NHS and piloted in six hospitals and six community health service sites. This initiative was part of wider reforms which were aiming to allow hospitals to opt out of district control and become self-governing trusts, and at the same time make GPs budget holders allowing them to refer their patients wherever they thought they would receive the best treatment.

The RMI aimed to provide clinicians and other hospital managers with the accurate and immediate information in order to help them manage the broad range of resources for which they were responsible. In so doing, it was hoped that RMI would also encourage them to take an interest in the management of the hospital in which they worked. Part of the response to this initiative was to develop a package of information systems called Case mix systems. Documents about the RMI stressed that it would be a bottom-up initiative that would involve the service providers in the design and management of the change. Equally, recognizing the specific needs of each hospital unit, RMI was to be planned on a local basis rather than imposed in a uniform manner across the whole of the NHS.

The stakeholders in the case

RMI project team

These teams had access to considerable funds for implementing the structural and cultural change required, and the backing of government and NHS officials. However, to the vast majority of hospital employees they were simply outsiders with no power. They were not respected as they had limited clinical or managerial experience.

The clinicians

RMI was not seen as primarily concerned with the quality of patient care and therefore not of central importance to the clinical staff. Furthermore, it was seen as threatening the professionalism and therefore the autonomy of the clinicians as it introduced budgetary controls and planning systems. RMI also brought in the idea that management as a discipline could contribute to the provision of quality patient care. The structural reorganization around hospital management boards also continued.

Illustration 3.7 continued

The change processes

Information technology and systems

There was great divergence in the way that IT issues were handled between hospitals with the consequence that hardware and software were purchased with little thought about congruence with other systems. There was a lack of training generally in IT and IS and a perception that the information that would be gathered using these systems would benefit accountants more than doctors.

Communication

There was inadequate use of different communication initiatives throughout the RMI with many junior level staff only learning about the change through rumour and gossip. This was partly due to the fact that staff had no time to read the scarce written literature that did get through about RMI. The communication budget for the initiative was too low for its purpose, particularly given the level of resistance felt towards RMI by many medical groups.

Training

Training was also scarce. Few hospitals had a planned approach to training staff in RMI, and even where it was provided the staffing levels on the wards prohibited nurses from attending the courses! The lack of facilities within hospitals which could be used for computer training were extremely limited. In a climate of technophobia this only helped to harden attitudes against the RMI.

Change styles

Whilst the rhetoric used by both the project teams and the sponsors of the initiative emphasized the consultative and participative nature of the process there was little evidence of this taking place. Instead people perceived it as being imposed on them from the top. This is unsurprising given the lack of investment in training and the inadequate formal communication channels in existence.

Whilst some of the resistance to RMI was based on principle, much of it was the result of the way in which it was being implemented within the hospitals. Staff were offered no incentives for making the initiative work and RMI soon began to be seen as 'yet another under-resourced, ill-conceived and poorly implemented programme of change that would have little effect'.

(Adapted from A. Brown, *Organizational Culture*, 1995, London: Pitman.)

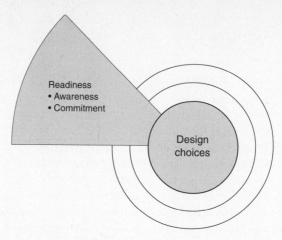

Figure 3.8   *Contextual features for readiness*

3.10.1   Assessing readiness

This feature helps change agents to assess how prepared staff are for change. There are two aspects to readiness – the degree to which staff are aware that change is necessary, and the degree of motivation staff feel towards change.

Staff can be aware at a rational level of the need for change but be unprepared at an emotional level to embrace change at a personal level. Alternatively, even an awareness of the need to change may be missing.

A senior team of an organization may be expert at anticipating future market trends over the next five to ten years. The team may recognize that the organization needs to start to change now in order to be able to respond competitively to the changing environment. However, if the organization is in good health, with excellent profits and high staff satisfaction, the problem the senior managers face is how to demonstrate the need for change to lower levels of staff.

It can also be that people within an organization understand the necessity for change but are not committed or motivated to change themselves. There can be a number of reasons for this. First, staff can perceive that the organization's need for change and their need to change are two entirely different issues. It is possible to interview staff about the changes in their external business context and the changes that their organization is undergoing internally in response to these changes. The language that staff will use to explain these changes may be the rhetoric that their senior managers have used to explain the changes. However, the same staff often display little understanding of how they might have to change themselves at a very personal level if the organizational changes are to occur.

Second, it can be that the staff do understand the meaning of the change but that there is little they can gain from the change. The personal cost of change, in emotional pain and time invested, may be so high that the gains that the change process promises certain individual members of staff are insufficient for them to embark on change themselves. This is sometimes the reason for staff taking early retirement from career posts. In education in the United Kingdom, the changes brought about by governments in the 1980s and 1990s had a radical impact on school teachers' everyday working lives. They were required to engage with much more assessment of their own work, and national assessment of pupils' work. This required more paperwork at a task level, and an openness towards appraisal of themselves at a personal level. For some the changes were too much in content, with little apparent gain for teachers at an individual level. They therefore opted to leave the teaching profession.

Third, some organizations have developed their bureaucratic cultures to such an extent that staff are divorced from the roles they have to play. In these cases it is quite possible for staff to anticipate that their job will change, and that the organization will change, for these are the structures of working life. However, they would see the idea of personal change as unnecessary as all that is required of them at work is to fulfil a particular role.

An example of this from a retail bank concerns the emergence of a 'new careers' model in the 1990s. Many mature corporations at that time faced the problem of corporate renewal. They needed to change from being top heavy, slow and bureaucratic into customer-focused, entrepreneurial organizations. One of the change mechanisms used was the removal of job security and the creation of a new psychological contract with employees. The rhetoric that accompanied this new contract told employees that they could no longer expect a job for life with the corporation, nor a career based on numerous small promotions as they worked their way up the rungs of the corporate ladder. Instead they should expect to work for a number of different employers during their working lives and should ensure for themselves that they were equipped for this new life of job mobility. Interviewed about these changes, staff in a retail bank could explain at a rational level that change had occurred, what that meant for them in terms of future careers and security and what they were going to do about it. However, the same staff simultaneously completed an in-depth questionnaire which measured their attitudes and orientation to many aspects of working life. One question asked them about future employment prospects: 90 per cent of the staff at the bank responded that they expected to stay working at the same bank for the rest of their working lives. Therefore, however much they could rationally talk about the idea of 'new careers' they had not accepted its implications for themselves at a very personal level.

Assessment of an organization's readiness for change can be made formally through mechanisms such as staff attitude surveys, or more informally through mechanisms such as focus groups. Some organizations who have the appropriate skills to do so run the attitude surveys or focus groups themselves. Others (see Natural History Museum example, Chapter 1) employ consultants to help. Consultants may also be employed to encourage greater staff honesty and openness since the use of consultants can give the staff the sense of greater anonymity.

3.10.2   *Readiness and design choices*

A low readiness for change has implications for the change path selected. If an organization has a complacent workforce, the change may need to take a change path that is big-bang in nature but only achieves (deliberately) realignment rather than transformation for the organization. This high impact change design may be necessary in order to shake staff out of their complacency in readiness for a subsequent more fundamental change initiative. The example of Glaxo Pharmaceuticals UK Ltd given in the next chapter illustrates this tactic.

If personal change is not perceived as necessary by staff when it is, this also impacts the change style. The change agent may need to lead a participative or collaborative campaign which engages the personalities of the staff involved. Merely directing staff to change may be insufficient. Change levers to be considered when there is low readiness for change, or a low recognition of the need for personal change, include personal development courses for senior managers and other levels of staff which encourage them to recognize the need for change. Where staff understand the meaning of the change but perceive little gain from it, the change agent may need to accept that some staff will not change and therefore contemplate voluntary or compulsory exits from the organization.

Likewise if there is low readiness for change it may be impossible to take a bottom-up approach to change since this requires extensive staff involvement. Instead, top-down change may be necessary to kick start the process. Alternatively, change agents could consider using pockets of good practice or pilot sites to start change initiatives in parts of the organization where there is a readiness for change. These pilot sites could symbolically act as role models for the rest of the organization.

A low readiness for change is likely to necessitate a change role of leadership. Anyone who is to lead the change must demonstrate two things to the rest of the organization: an absolute belief or passion in the need for change and a commitment to change themselves. The change leader must also demonstrate a visible manifestation of that change to all staff in the organization in terms of behaviour as well as words. Therefore, senior managers who are potential change champions need to be assessed against these criteria. Otherwise, they may espouse the need to change to the rest of the organization whilst contradicting what they espouse with no change in their own working practices

When the organization displays a high readiness for change then change champions may find themselves pushing on an open door. The menu of design choices is increased.

3.11 *Power*

Power examines where power is vested within an organization. It is to do with the identification of the major stakeholders (within and out-side the organization) and individuals or departments which hold power in the organization. Other issues include whose support must be canvassed and how much self-discretion is possessed by the change unit (see Figure 3.9).

3.11.1 *Assessing power*

Power can be understood on many levels. Here it is considered from two perspectives – the personal power exercised within organizations by individuals or groups of people and the power of the organization to determine its own future.

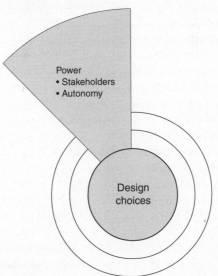

Figure 3.9   Contextual features for power

Understanding the personal power and politics within an organization, and identifying the major power brokers, is critical before any design choices can be made. The best choice in design terms may not be achievable because of powerful coalitions who may block the change because of their own agendas. To give a practical illustration, in the health service the medical consultants are powerful figures (see Illustration 3.7). Any change agent within a hospital needs to be able to convince a critical mass of consultants that the change is necessary in order to get processes implemented. Similarly, at KPMG, Colin Sharman still had to convince a critical mass of other partners of the need for change (see Chapter 2, Illustration 2.6).

In organizational terms, many change texts assume that an organization's management team have a full latitude of discretion in terms of the choices they can make about change. In reality, many organizations are constrained in what they can undertake by their relationship with other institutions. Illustration 3.8 describes how Jürgen Dormann, the Chairman of the German pharmaceuticals conglomerate, Hoechst, was constrained in his restructuring by the reaction of the stockmarket to an earlier strategic decision he had taken which investors had not liked.

As another example, public sector organizations contemplating change may not be allowed to choose the obvious or best course of action because of the constraints that are placed on them by their political masters. The privatized utilities in the UK were given trade boundaries beyond which their commercial endeavours were not allowed to go. The NHS in the UK arguably has not been able to undergo the changes its professional and managerial staff might have wanted because it has been subject to varying strategies from a succession of both different ministers and different governments.

However, this lack of room for manoeuvre is not restricted to those sectors where there is a governmental connection. In private sector organizations change agents face other constraints on their decision making because of forces beyond the organization. For instance, membership of a group of companies can be a constraint. The WH Smith example in the next chapter illustrates a change situation in which the division concerned cannot release itself from its role as a cash cow within the broader group which impacts upon its choice of change approach. There is also the presence of shareholders or institutions like the stockmarket. Whether the stockmarket will endorse a change may be a major influence on any decisions (see Illustration 3.8).

A useful way of assessing who has power and their position on the proposed change is to use stakeholder analysis. This has already been discussed in *Exploring Corporate Strategy*, and is discussed further in Appendix 3. A stakeholder analysis enables a change agent to

Change in action

Illustration 3.8

Hoechst Marion Roubles

Jürgen Dormann, the 58-year-old chairman of Hoechst, the German chemical and pharmaceuticals group, learnt about the power of stakeholders in 1998. Having once been the darling of the stockmarkets by declaring that he would allow his own performance to be judged by the financial markets, he now admits he has made errors in managing investors' expectations.

Things started to go wrong when, as part of his strategy for restructuring the conglomerate, he promised to float Hoechst Marion Roubles (HMR), the pharmaceuticals business. Hoechst Marion Roubles had been built by bringing together Hoechst's drug operations with Marion Merrell Dow of the United States and Roubles Uclaf of France. The plan was to float HMR in order to provide funds to buy the remaining stake that Hoechst did not own in Roubles Uclaf. The Roubles minority shareholders could then swap their stake for shares in the newly floated HMR.

In the event, an opportunity arose to sell another division within Hoechst and that raised sufficient funds for Dormann to buy out the remaining Roubles Uclaf shares without handing out HMR shares. The wisdom of the strategy in business terms has been proven but the investors have not forgiven Dormann.

Other events in the conglomerate have combined with the HMR episode to cause a depression in Hoechst shares. By May 1998 they had underperformed the shares of Germany's top 30 companies by 30 per cent in the previous 12 months. Dormann admitted that in handling investors' expectations 'we have done a poor job. We are on the learning side. It will improve ...'. Yet until Hoechst was more valued by the stockmarket Dormann accepted that it would stay aloof from the pressures towards consolidation felt elsewhere in the industry.

(Adapted from *Financial Times*, Profile, 8 June 1998.)

consider what they can do to gain support for their proposed changes from those who have power and are either against the proposed changes or are ambivalent to them. It also enables a change agent to consider how weaker stakeholders who are for the proposed changes can be used to help endorse change.

3.11.2 *Power and design choices*

Power, or lack of it, can influence the choice of change path taken. Where a business division may badly need transformational change, they can be prevented from embarking upon such a route because other more powerful divisions, or the group's centre, block their actions. Equally a powerful parent can be a strong facilitator of change.

Powerful individuals may block the change path in the same way. A powerful chief executive who feels a potential threat from the proposed change can squash a plan for transformation in favour of more modest realignment routes. Equally, an over powerful change agent or executive can insist on a change process which is disproportionately large in comparison with the problem it is trying to address. However, the agent or executive concerned may see this as a way of raising their profile and visibility within the organization.

In circumstances where a change agent does not have the power to carry out the type of change they want to implement, they may choose to first go for a realignment change phase. The levers and mechanisms deployed would then be about winning the change agent the power she or he needs. The WH Smith example in Chapter 4 illustrates this.

Powerful individuals, such as managing directors or chief executives, can push through top-down and directive change. However, where the agent has identified powerful groups within the organization whose support and commitment is needed then a more collaborative style may be appropriate. This is one of the learning points from the NHS case study described in more depth in Chapter 4, and from the RMI case study in this chapter (see Illustration 3.7). Had the project groups worked harder to convince the medical staff of the merits of the initiative, it may have been given a better reception.

Paradoxically, highly powerful individuals such as chief executive officers who take a leadership role can be counterproductive when the target for change is values and the culture they are trying to remove is one based on blame and fear. If the CEO is seen as a bully but leads the change, staff will merely start to mimic the desired values because they feel threatened. This will not lead to significant change and the issue will never be addressed due to the atmosphere of fear.

Power is critical when assigning roles within a change process. If a change champion or leader is to be appointed then the change agent needs to pick a powerful individual or provide the individual with powerful backing. Then they also need to consider other powerful stakeholder groups and consider incorporating them in some way into the change process, particularly if these groups could be obstructive.

Specific change levers to deal with power include techniques such as breaking and re-forming both formal and informal power structures within organizations, using the existence of cliques, networks and those with influence to gain buy-in for change, and resistance management. Chapter 6 discusses the management of politics in more detail.

3.12 Summary

This chapter has discussed the need to analyze the change context in order to avoid using inappropriate change formulae. This contextual analysis is the key to successful change for it is the context that should drive the design choices that are made rather than personal bias on the part of the change agent. In particular the chapter has:

- Explained the use of the change kaleidoscope as a diagnostic framework for mapping the change context.
- Described each of the eight contextual features of time, scope, preservation, diversity, capability, capacity, readiness for change and power.
- Discussed the design implications of each of the contextual features from the kaleidoscope.

This chapter has also outlined the various diagnostic frameworks that can be used to understand these contextual features. The next chapter explores the interaction between these change context features and the design choices through a series of in-depth case studies.

Notes and references

(1) For full story of SAS turnaround see J. Carlzon, *Moments of Truth*, 1987, New York: Harper and Row.

(2) See J.B. Barney, 'Looking Inside for Competitive Advantage', *Academy of Management*, IX, 4, November 1995, pp. 49–61.

(3) See G. Hofstede, *Cultures and Organizations: Software of the Mind*, 1980, Maidenhead: McGraw-Hill.

(4) See K. Legge, 'Human Resource Management – A Critical Analysis', in J. Storey (ed.), *New Perspectives on Human Resource Management*, 1989, London: Routledge, pp. 19–40.

(5) See L. Gratton, V. Hope Hailey *et al.*, *Strategic Human Resource Management*, 1999, Oxford: Oxford University Press.

(6) See V. Hope Hailey, 'Transforming Organizations through People Management', *Management Focus*, 10, Summer, 1998, pp. 4–7.

4 Analyzing the change context: making change judgements

4.1 Introduction

The previous chapter explained how to analyze the change context using the change kaleidoscope. Eight change context features were outlined: time, scope, preservation, diversity, capability, capacity, readiness for change and power. This chapter uses five extended case studies to expand the reader's understanding of how to use the change kaleidoscope. Its aim is to help the reader identify the critical contextual features in each case and understand their implications for the design choices.

This chapter is deliberately different in style from the other chapters due to the nature of the material used. The descriptions of the case studies are as rich in contextual features as space will permit, but in a real situation much more detail would be seen by the change agent. Each change feature within the kaleidoscope is analyzed in every case. Through this case study analysis the chapter examines:

- how to understand change context using the change kaleidoscope;
- how to identify which contextual features are critical;
- how the analysis of context is linked to the decisions made about change.

Some examples of the diagnostic tools that were suggested as useful analytical aids in the previous chapter are used to examine the organizational contexts. These include the cultural web, the People Process Model and stakeholder analysis, all of which are described in detail in the appendices at the end of the book.

4.2 Case Study: WH Smith News

This case study looks at the change experienced by one division within the WH Smith Group in the UK. At the time it was written the WH Smith Group was predominantly a retail group, with a large chain of newsagents/booksellers, specialist bookshops, music/media shops and a distribution business. The distribution business is the subject of the case study. The case study describes the change process put in place by the division at the end of the 1980s and the beginning of the 1990s. The case demonstrates the problems faced by mature corporations that are seeking corporate renewal.

This case study (see Illustration 4.1) shows the constraints on change design that can flow from having a low capacity and capability for change, and how powerful stakeholders can constrict the choices available to the change agent. It also illustrates how the concept of change path allows for change as a multi-staged process. Capacity and capability may need to be developed within an organization before the desired scope of change can be implemented.

4.2.1   Analysis of WH Smith News

A cultural web and a stakeholder analysis are helpful frameworks to use in order to understand the scope of change required and the power blocks within WH Smith News (see Figures 4.1 and 4.2).

4.2.2   The kaleidoscope of WH Smith News

If we move around the kaleidoscope we can see clearly how the organization measures up against the various features. Due to the increased competitive pressures within their industry, the organization needed to instigate some form of change fairly quickly as *time* was not on their side: they had lost a large amount of business to TNT. However, their position within the WH Smith Group meant that they provided an important cash cow function to their partner divisions. As the stakeholder analysis shows, this meant that the organization's *power* was constrained because of its membership of the larger group, even though the larger group was supportive towards the changes. The house managers were also tremendously powerful and the change agent needed to work with them rather than against them. Part of the reason for this was that the house managers had valuable tacit knowledge about how the business worked which needed to be *preserved*. This was necessary because, until that knowledge was formalized and therefore shared, it was crucial for keeping business going as usual through the change process. Thus the house managers were both the means through which to achieve change and yet also the blocks that were preventing change from taking place.

There were some positive aspects to the change context. All employees, managerial and non-managerial, felt a strong *identity* with the organization. This translated itself into loyalty and staff commitment which the senior management wished to preserve. If they lost the staff's loyalty they were not in a position to buy it back using financial inducements. The strong identification with the paternalistic company also allowed it to extract long working hours from the staff.

Change in action

Illustration 4.1

WH Smith News

WH Smith News was the largest distributor of newspapers and magazines in the UK, by both market share and turnover, and was part of the WH Smith Group. This Division had 4,300 employees in 72 wholesale houses and over 22,000 retail customers. The group set broad financial and growth targets for the News Division, which had a large degree of autonomy on how to achieve them. Since the News Division was the cash rich division within the group, effectiveness in achieving financial targets was vital. In 1989 the WH Smith Group instigated a process of corporate renewal. The need for change in the News Division was particularly strong as in 1988 the division had lost £40 million of business overnight to the non-unionized rival TNT.

The prevailing style of management was characterized by the group CEO as 'autocratic, tempered by paternalism. The values of the business were loyalty, security and obedience to orders.' The nature of work within the News Division also generated strong traditions. The business is '24 hours a day, 7 days a week, 364 days a year' (only Christmas Day is not worked). The hours are long, deadlines are tight and much of the work, particularly in the warehouse, is physically demanding, all of which has engendered a 'macho' culture. However, the pace and deadline-driven nature of the business together with clear success criteria generated a high level of excitement and motivation among staff, despite the low wages. As one manager said: 'Once you are in it becomes a way of life and there is a very strong sense of identity among employees.' The company has always prided itself on being a caring company, an expression of the paternalism which runs throughout the division. There are two clear messages for staff: do not challenge the house manager's status or authority and do not challenge decisions.

It was decided to instigate a process of cultural change in order to implement a new managerial style of 'directness, openness to ideas, commitment to the success of others, a willingness to accept personal accountability and the strong development of teamwork and trust'. This was seen to be crucial in order to deliver the strategic intent of enhanced customer focus and increased productivity. In part the responsibility for this lay with the HR function.

The house managers were key to the change process but they could not be overtly attacked at first as they were also key to maintaining the cash cow relationship that the division provided for the rest of the group. They also held

The organization was relatively homogeneous, with few subcultures existing within the division. There was therefore a low degree of *diversity*.

As the cultural web (Figure 4.1) shows, the pre-change paradigm of the organization was one of success with a paternalistic control cul-

tacit knowledge in the form of 'the way things are done around here'. The absence of any kind of systematic recruitment, selection, appraisal or communication system meant that a textbook transformational change would be difficult without any systems to support it. Equally if the HR function had demanded a strategic role and dictated the changes, it might have alienated the managers. The division also needed to maintain the cohesion and strong staff commitment that had been elicited through the paternalistic culture. Their position within the group as a cash cow, the low profit margins and the resultant inability to invest in staff, created constraints on their capacity to implement change.

A female personnel manager was appointed from within the group. She was one of very few women managers within the division and certainly the most senior. She did not initially demand a place on the executive council, but instead set about formalizing personnel systems and offering to take some of the administrative burden from house managers. In this way she started to handle recruitment and selection, delivering many of the house managers' training needs and handling the collective bargaining. She gradually established a personnel function which dealt with all the human resource issues.

She also introduced a survey of management style with the aim of countering what was seen as the strongly deferential culture within the division. The document was sent to all News Division staff by post and allowed them to comment on the performance of their manager on 30 different characteristics. The aggregated data was published and shared among all employees. The fact that this information was generated bottom-up gave the personnel department permission and legitimacy to act on the insight that they already possessed before the survey was completed.

In adopting a more bureaucratic service to the line managers, and by seeking to assist rather than confront or overwhelm through more value-led cultural change, the personnel manager won many friends and made few enemies. Shortly after her arrival she was invited to join the executive board for the division. As a result of her work, which slowly formalized and systemized the personnel systems and restructured the division, the business may now be capable of the more radical transformational change that is desirable but was not originally achievable.

(Adapted from L. Gratton, V. Hope Hailey *et al.*, *Strategic Human Resource Management*, 1999, Oxford: Oxford University Press.)

ture and employees who were unquestioningly loyal yet expecting jobs for life. As such, a cultural change to 'directness, openness to ideas, commitment to the success of others, a willingness to accept personal accountability and the strong development of teamwork and trust' challenged some of the most deeply ingrained historical ways of behav-

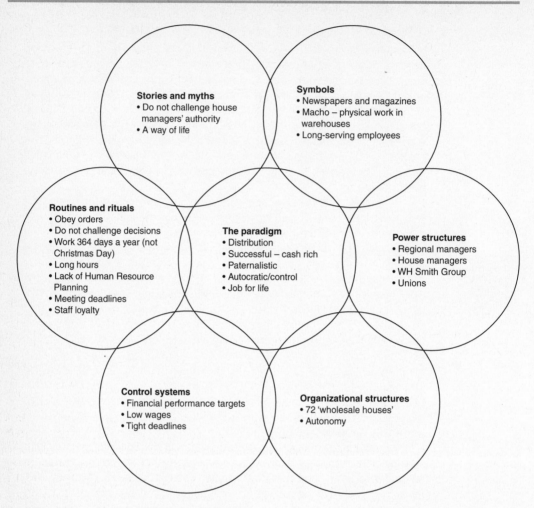

Figure 4.1   WH Smith News cultural web

ing. Therefore, in terms of *scope* the organization needed to undertake fundamental transformational change .

The major gaps were in the two aspects of *capacity* and *capability*. In terms of capacity, the division's relationship within the group meant that the division had to meet its financial obligations first. Furthermore, the industry sector itself was a low-profit-margin business, which meant that compared with businesses such as pharmaceuticals or financial services the business had little surplus cash for investment in a change process. In addition, the change capability was very low: staff had never had the chance to develop an expertise in this area. There was a strong internal labour market, so their exposure to

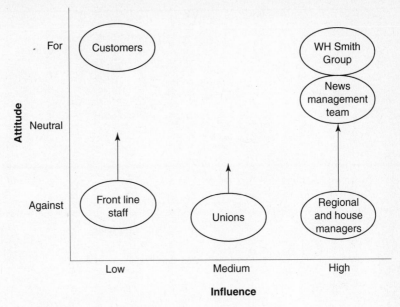

Figure 4.2 *WH Smith News stakeholder analysis*

change in other contexts was extremely limited. Their managers had extremely limited experience of managing staff through change processes, and little understanding of the nature of personal transition. At an organizational level within the division there was no specific change unit or department with an expertise in change. Indeed, the training and development department was very underdeveloped. Having said that, they did have the expertise of the WH Smith Group HR department at their disposal.

Last, but not least, the organization's *readiness for change* was very low. The house managers were reluctant to break from tradition, and given the poor history of communication throughout the division, had little understanding of their role and contribution within the group as a whole. They needed strong persuasion that change was in their best interests. Rather than confronting them head on with the barrage of changes necessary, an alternative route was adopted whereby their support was sought in return for services given to them by the HR manager. By offering to provide basic personnel administrative services to them, the manager started to centralize, standardize and formalize those services. All of this was achieved without appearing to threaten their power base.

4.2.3   Key contextual features of WH Smith News

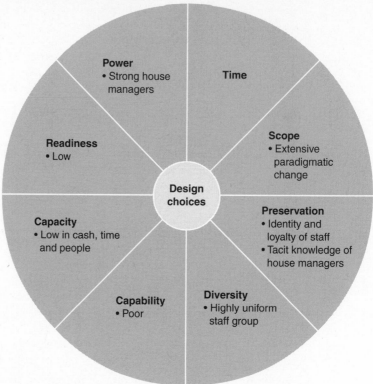

Figure 4.3   Key contextual features of WH Smith News

4.2.4   Design implications for WH Smith News

Change path

When considering the nature of change, because time was of the essence, a big-bang approach appeared to be necessary but there were constraints on this. Big-bang change might have alienated the house managers. They possessed a great deal of the tacit knowledge that keeps the business going. Until that could be formalized and centralized within the division's office, any sudden change might have jeopardized the smooth running of the business. Furthermore, the division's cash cow position within the group was another constraint on rapid change as it might have threatened the cashflow through to the other businesses. There were also relations with the union to consider. Therefore the division lacked the capacity and capability to effect big-bang change.

The organization's change in business strategy meant that the workforce needed to become more customer focused. The desired results of the changes (increasing personal accountability, directness, openness, teamwork and trust) required a paradigmatic change in the basic assumptions and beliefs of the workforce, both managerial and non-managerial. The appropriate change path might therefore have appeared to be evolution. Yet, this was not possible because the division lacked the formal infrastructure of performance management systems[1] and the informal management know-how that was needed. They needed to put these in place before they could manage to let change evolve. In short, they lacked the capacity and capability to implement transformational incremental change.

The only option left open to them was to follow a change path of adaptation in the first stage, which allowed the personnel manager to build up the infrastructure necessary for incremental change of a paradigmatic kind. The design choices are therefore discussed with three different phases of change in mind: the short term as illustrated in the case history, and implications for change in the medium and long term.

Change target

Although the desired change in the longer term involved changing staff's values, neither behaviours nor values were tackled in the short term as the priority was to design a process which built up the organization's capability at a systems and infrastructure level, and tackled the politics of the situation. In the medium term targeting behaviours would be possible. This was because of the high uniformity and compliance of the non-managerial staff, who were not likely to resist the tight prescription of behavioural change. Further change initiatives geared towards values could then be implemented in the longer term.

Change roles

At this stage in the organization's development, the change could not have been led by a complete outsider to the business or group. Outsiders would have lacked the legitimacy needed to work with the house managers. In contrast, it could not be designed from within as there did not appear to be any change competence within the division. Therefore, the choice was made to appoint the current senior management team to lead the change process but aided by an insider/outsider, the HR manager from within the larger group.

---

[1]   Performance management systems are systems which specify for staff their personal objectives and the measures against which their performance is assessed. These systems are also used to identify individual's training and development needs and to determine rewards.

Change style

The process needed to be delivered using different styles for different levels. Given the power position of the house managers the process needed to either let them collaborate in its design, or be implemented in a participative fashion. With the non-managerial staff, directive styles of change would be acceptable. However, the risk with that choice was that the directive nature of the process itself would serve to reinforce the old command and control type culture that the change was meant to erode. In the medium term the change process could experiment with more participative forms of change for the warehouse staff.

Change start point

Change was unlikely to take off through bottom-up initiatives. Staff at the lower levels of the organization might have had potential for initiative but only had experience of top-down management-driven ideas. In the medium term relying totally on top-down change might also have been risky as senior managers themselves might have been ambivalent about the need for fundamental change. Having established the infrastructure needed in the initial change phase, there would be strong arguments for starting pockets of good practice in the medium term throughout the division. If the personnel manager targeted change initiatives at particular managers whose current managerial style was closest to the new espoused values, then those managers could start to act as role models for the rest of the organization. This would allow the personnel manager to test out the effectiveness of the transformation change strategy using pilot sites before implementing it throughout the organization.

Change levers

In the first phase of adaptation two forms of change levers are employed. First, the personnel manager established new control systems in the form of human resource management policies and procedures into the division. This allowed her to centralize some procedures and to take control away from the house managers. It also allowed her to gain information on staff performance. The management style survey and the customer satisfaction survey also added information to the central database, but they were also political in nature. Had the personnel manager started to impose changes in management style on to the house managers based on her own judgements, she could have been accused of not understanding the business. By using the views of both the workforce and customers she was armed with powerful reasons for persuading the senior and house managers that change was necessary.

4.3 Case Study: an NHS Trust

This case study (see Illustration 4.2) demonstrates that high diversity and power within an organization can have consequences for the design of change. The National Health Service (NHS) within the UK is a complex organization. The case examines one hospital within the service that has gained Trust status – this means that it has gained a degree of autonomy over its destiny, even though it is still working within the broader service. Its complexity exists on many different levels. First, there are many different types of staff working within the NHS: doctors, nurses, therapists, support staff, administrators and managerial staff. Second, there are many powerful stakeholders in this hospital context: the government, the regional health authority, the consultants and then the organization's management.

4.3.1 The kaleidoscope of the NHS Trust

Given that this was a newly created trust, *time* was not so much of a pressure as it is in other change situations. Nevertheless, for such a new organization there was much that they wanted to *preserve*. The idea of public service through the NHS was a strong motivator for staff. Commitment to high medical standards and patient care was also strong. Like the WH Smith case earlier, this commitment to health care resulted in the staff being highly dedicated even though the pay of junior doctors and nurses was comparatively low. In addition to wishing to preserve this staff commitment, the hospital was also anxious to retain its top consultants. Therefore, any change design had to avoid alienating or annoying them. The *scope* of the process was realignment as the change to being an NHS Trust did not involve fundamentally transforming the way work is conducted in the hospital. Staff's taken-for-granted assumptions about healthcare, the NHS, or being a doctor or a nurse were not affected by the change.

In terms of *readiness for change*, the situation at the trust was complex. The NHS was subjected to continual change because of the variations in public spending and the political changes of governments. This had resulted in NHS staff experiencing change fatigue and a feeling of both powerlessness and hopelessness in the face of continual change. Therefore, there was an expectancy of continual change but it was not experienced as a positive phenomenon. Instead, it was seen as something that is imposed upon the service by people or institutions from outside which required them to respond. In contrast, the newly acquired trust status of the hospital demanded that the hospital takes a more proactive stance to determine its future, one that the staff were less accustomed to.

Capacity for change is a complicated issue. There are always low

Change in action

Illustration 4.2

An NHS Trust

A London NHS hospital with close to 2,000 staff and a strong commitment to teaching and research gained trust status in 1994. Trusts were formerly hospital or community services which, under the terms of the UK conservative government's reforms of the NHS (1991) have severed links with district health authorities to become independent bodies. The establishment of trusts as providers of health care was intended by the UK government to bring greater accountability for taxpayers' funds and enhance efficiency within the NHS by encouraging trusts to act like private sector organizations. Trusts are self-governing and have their own board of directors. Each trust is required to present a business plan.

This particular Trust was organized into four clinical directorates each of which was based on the specialist medical units within the hospital. These included renal units, cardiac units, spinal injuries units, paediatric units and others. Each of these health specialisms, when demarcated into a clinical directorate, bears a strong resemblance to the concept of business units in the private sector. At the head of each of these units was a clinical director who fulfilled a management role. In addition there were four corporate directorates which supported the four clinical directorates. The corporate directorates included finance, human resources and information systems. However, this restructuring around trust status had unintended consequences in terms of the cohesion between directorates. Staff felt that 'there is an almost exclusive

financial resources within the NHS, although since the hospital was a new foundation it had less financial demands placed on it for rebuilding infrastructures. The Trust did have the resources of the health service at a regional and national level which it could choose to contract in. It traditionally invested in medical training and education for clinical staff and organizational/management training for administrative staff.

In terms of their *capability* for change, staff were used to learning and education. The medical staff were also used to the continual improvement of medical techniques and therefore accepted change in that area. There was low investment in aspects of personal development for medical staff. There were, however, specialist change units within the NHS which had knowledge of organizational change, if the trust was able to use them. In some parts of the trust the staff were highly educated and intelligent people who, if approached in an appropriate manner were probably capable of learning very fast indeed. In some ways, therefore, this organization must have contained some capability for change.

Illustration 4..2 continued

focus on the department at the expense of the trust in general'. Employees identified more with their professional group or with their speciality than with the interests of the Trust.

There has been increasing involvement of medical staff in management. However, one problem associated with doctors becoming more involved in management is that many do not wish to move away from their prime motivator, patient care: 'What I enjoy is treating patients. I don't want to fight for resources …'. The credibility of individual staff and their individual power comes from working with patients rather than from any managerial position.

The ability to change policies and practices to reflect new structures and working conditions was limited by the influence of the professional groups within the Trust. For example, the different professional groups had their own training, development, appraisal and career management processes. The medical consultants were very influential and it was said that for any change to succeed it was essential to 'get the consultants on board: they are still powerful figures'. The organization's central HR department could not, therefore, take a lead role in these areas. Similarly, the lack of a common performance management and monitoring framework had hindered the implementation of the Trust's corporate strategy. Different systems and management styles persisted.

Paradoxically, this public sector organization had one common unifying issue: commitment to their customers (the patients). However, commitment to their employer, the hospital, was less of a cohesive bond.

(© Veronica Hope Hailey, 1998.)

When examining *diversity* within this trust we can see a very complex picture starting to emerge. Although there was high identification with the health service as a whole for the medical staff, the next source of identity was the professional or vocational group. For junior doctors this is because it is the clinical group within this and other hospitals that determines their career progression. Anxious about their job prospects, young paediatricians, for example, will be more concerned with impressing other practitioners within paediatrics within and beyond the Trust than in impressing the organization's senior management. The medical staff did not identify with the trust primarily; their main loyalty was to the NHS. Nurse turnover ran at about 35 per cent but the majority of nurses from this trust leave the hospital to work in other parts of the NHS.

In contrast, the administrative and managerial staff probably felt more identification with the organization as this was the primary focus for their work. The danger lay in the managerial staff assuming that their medical colleagues shared the same interest and commitment to the trust. These aspects also contributed to the degree of diversity within the organization. There were numerous subcultures within the trust. The trust straddled a variety of occupational labour markets because of the wide range of jobs within one hospital. There is a split in the objectives and norms of those working in management and those in the medical or nursing professions.

Power, therefore, was vested in the consultants and, in particular, the clinical directors. In order to achieve changes in organizational or managerial practices within the trust these people had to be persuaded on two fronts. First, they had to be convinced of the need to change and be prepared to put on a public show of commitment to the proposed changes. Second, they had to be convinced of the need to apply some of the changes consistently across all directorates for the good of the whole trust, perhaps in some cases, at the expense of their own professional clinical directorate.

4.3.2   Key contextual features of the NHS Trust

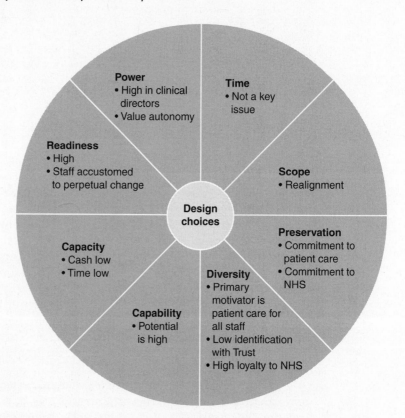

Figure 4.4   *Key contextual features of the NHS Trust*

4.3.3   *Design implications for the NHS Trust*

Change path

The scope of the change meant that realignment rather than transformation was necessary. When considering the nature of the change
required, there might have been an argument for some short-term
burst of change activity in order to establish the notion of the Trust as
an important entity within the minds of all staff. Other change could
only be achieved incrementally over time through influencing the consultants. As the consultant group was so powerful it is difficult to contemplate change without addressing the contextual issue of their
power. It may be necessary to start a change path of reconstruction,
moving on to adaptation.

time!
(which they
don't have
due
to
change
gov's)

Change target

Among the medical staff there was a strong meshing of personal
values with the values of the NHS: they identified with the purpose of
the NHS. However, there was less evidence of staff identifying with
the trust. The change agent could choose to frame the change with
their strong sense of values towards the NHS and their patients, without focusing much on the Trust. Behaviours as change targets would
be inappropriate for some groups within the hospital, such as clinicians, who would perceive prescription of behaviours as interfering
with both their professional training and their needs for high latitudes
of discretion. Clinicians could be targeted using output measures such
as budgetary targets, and performance targets to effect behavioural
change in the longer term.

Change style

Given the diversity of the workforce, the change agent needs to consider different styles of change for each group. For the consultants a
collaborative or educative style is most appropriate because of the
powerful position they hold within the workplace, and their need for
autonomy. In contrast, with low level support staff it may be possible
to use a more participative style. The managerial and support staff are
key to the success of the change as they can be expected to identify
more with the hospital than their colleagues within the professional
and vocational groupings. Therefore, a style that elicits their commitment is essential for the change to be successful. The energy and
enthusiasm of the management and support staff is essential for there
to be a sufficient critical mass to drive the change through.

Change roles

The contextual issues of capacity and capability throw light on the issue of roles. Clinical directors must symbolically champion the change as they are such powerful figures, but do they have the time and knowledge to manage such a process? Therefore, managers must design the change but be prepared to let it be implemented through the medical directors for it to have legitimacy and credibility, and a reasonable chance of success.

Change start point

Bottom-up change is unlikely to be successful as the NHS is such a hierarchical organization and staff would be unaccustomed to taking risks or decisions without referring them up to the senior team. Also staff in this Trust appeared to lack the readiness for change to participate in and drive such a change process. An alternative approach is to encourage pockets of good practice within some of the more progressive clinical directorates, thereby providing positive role models for their peers to observe. Top-down initiatives would be dependent on the support of the consultants.

Change levers

The Trust's management can use a combination of budgetary controls and human resource management systems to support the target of change outputs for clinicians. Whichever are used, the change agent should consider using levers that address the key unifying motivator of patient care for all medical staff. Extra training and development courses in specific aspects of medical care could be offered as an inducement to accept the changes. Staff may be motivated to accept the change by having the opportunity to extend their range of medical knowledge in return for changes in working practices.

Symbolic levers could also be used to increase a sense of identity with the hospital. Examples of symbolic levers include social events that emphasize the importance of the hospital as a unit, such as: fundraising for specific units within the hospital; senior management team events which bring together managerial and clinical staff; and visits by patrons of the hospital. To explain the purpose of the changes the change agent could implement communications initiatives through a variety of media such as newsletters, team briefings and open meetings between senior management and staff.

4.4 *Case Study: Hewlett-Packard*

Hewlett-Packard is a famous multinational corporation which employs over 90,000 staff throughout the globe. It started life manufacturing scientific test instruments but over the following sixty years went through several mutations until now a major source of its turnover is derived from the laser jet printer market. It has a good reputation as an inventive hi-tech company, and an outstanding reputation for the practice of good people management. This case study (see Illustration 4.3) examines how these practices contribute to its ability to change or 'mutate' incrementally over time.

Change in action

Illustration 4.3

Hewlett-Packard

The Hewlett-Packard approach to change is both simple and complex at the same time. Established for over sixty years and operating throughout the globe this mature multinational has to battle with what practices can be kept universal and which have to be localized. This localized customization of practices is necessary to recognize the diversity that exists within the corporation both within different business divisions, different functions, different professional groupings and different national cultures.

They therefore practice two forms of change simultaneously: both gradual realignment and short-term big-bang breakthrough change initiatives. The latter are most easily identifiable. These breakthrough initiatives are called Hoishins and rapid change on these particular issues is expected within 12 months of the Hoishin being put on-line. A change initiative on diversity is an example of a Hoishin – business or geographic units will be expected to meet certain targets on diversity within an agreed time frame. Diversity in this sense means encouraging a range of working patterns, family-friendly policies and less discrimination towards minority groups. How this specific breakthrough is to be achieved is determined by the particular national unit or product group.

The more interesting aspect of change is the way in which the corporation changes incrementally over time, but also over national boundaries and other divisions that characterize its heterogeneous corporate nature. Essentially three main frameworks are used which are common across the whole corporation. These frameworks exist to give stability within the organization despite the continuous change that the corporation is required to instigate in order to remain competitively responsive.

The first framework is a strong values statement called the 'HP Way'. Although these values have been present since its founders launched the company in 1937, the HP Way was first formalized and institutionalized in 1947. It attempts to foster individual freedom within a strong belief and value system. So the HP Way focused on a 'Belief in our People' which incorporated:

> Confidence in and respect for our people as opposed to depending upon extensive rules, procedures and so on; which depends upon people to do their job right (individual freedom) without constant directives.

Illustration 4.3 continued

Hewlett-Packard is viewed by its staff as having an outstanding organizational culture and over the years the HP Way has taken on the image of the Apostles' Creed: a shared statement of beliefs but one that can be interpreted in many different ways by different churches within the Christian religion. In the same way the HP Way is used in all the different countries in which Hewlett-Packard has offices, but those offices make sense of it in terms of their own national culture. It is almost as though its shared symbolic image is more important than living it as a shared reality. As one senior manager said: 'it's an assumed culture'. This perhaps is its strength: as a corporate ideology it allows for different interpretations of its words. Thus in HP there is a common language but the meaning of the words are different across divisions.

> 'There is a huge amount of "white space", "the bit in the middle", that is not quite clear how it actually works.' (Senior Manager)

> 'It's remarkably confused as to what it is but it's very strong.' (Middle Manager)

> 'If you ask anyone about the HP Way they will give you a different answer about what they believe it to be. People find it difficult to put their finger on what it is.' (Non-managerial staff)

This allows Hewlett-Packard to achieve an assumed cultural consistency and at the same time a cultural flexibility. Within each microculture a fit is sought but, importantly, always through informal rather than formal methods of selection or appraisal, and covertly but strongly reinforced through peer pressure. Furthermore, many staff found it difficult to articulate how it was achieved. There was little talk of strong induction training in the values statement.

There also appear to be very different cultures between the divisions. Thus the differences between a division of support engineers (with needs for reliability and security) and a division of sales staff (with needs for instant hits, fast pace) are acknowledged and worked with:

> 'there are variations in style across business units ...'

> 'sales are quite different in Hewlett-Packard as in many organizations ...'

In the research and development department it may be acceptable to wear jeans and to work whatever hours of the day you wish; whereas in sales and distribution, it is essential to wear suits. This is in contrast to many corporations who insist on adherence to an all-embracing corporate image.

The flexibility and intangible nature of the culture does not only operate at the level of the individual, but also allows for reinterpretation of the HP Way at a corporate level, at a global level and at a divisional level. For instance, at the corporate level, many people assumed that the HP Way had formally stated a commitment to lifetime employment. This has never actually been explicitly stated in the original HP Way. Therefore, when faced with difficult decisions about downsizing in 1992 in the wake of the economic downturn, it was possible for senior management to successfully remind staff of the historical emphasis on business performance and Management by Objectives:

Illustration 4.3 continued

> The HP Way is respect for the individual, but they have to deliver results. This is not a holiday camp. We do a lot of things to create a positive environment for our people to succeed. People forget the 'having to succeed' part and can confuse some of the down-side of not succeeding with an abandonment of the HP Way ... You can't grow and make a profit by just being nice to people. (Senior Manager)

The critical issues that the managers identified in helping the HP Way to work across national boundaries were: (1) that the national unit manager had to have the capacity to 'meld' the national culture with the HP corporate culture but in a sensi-tive and covert way; and (2) that the use of a corporate building design was extremely important in covertly and symbolically reinforcing some consistency in approach. Very few managers within the UK unit had expatriate experience . Thus we were witnessing a very nationalistic unit within a Californian company.

The second and third frameworks that give both stability and flexibility sim-ultaneously are the business planning process and the performance management systems. These act like the nervous system linking the corporate brain to the limbs on the periphery of the organization. The same systems are common across divisions and professional groupings, although the objectives they send down and performance results they send up are obviously individualized. Yet behaviour is still not prescribed. Targets or outputs are laid down in the form of personal objectives, but not behaviours. The company states that the reason for this close attention to outputs and objectives is paradoxically the promotion of individual freedom, innovation and entrepreneurial spirit. As one of the original senior man-agers explained:

> Early in the history of the company, whilst thinking about how a company like this should be managed, I kept getting back to one concept: if we could simply get every-body to agree on what our objectives were and to understand what we were trying to do, then we could turn everybody loose and they would move along in a common direction.

So, individuals have their personal objectives defined for them but how they achieve those objectives in terms of innovative activity or specific behaviour is for-mally left undefined.

In summary, the establishment of clear targets and objectives (the what) does not necessitate the means of achieving those objectives (the how) also being prescribed. This can be contrasted with many bureaucracies where the functions and actions (the how) are prescribed. However, neither is Hewlett-Packard an 'adhocracy' and the pervasiveness of the planning systems prevents it from becoming a free for all. Instead, we see in the planning systems a Taylorist, engin-eering approach applied to management. Targets and objectives are coordinated globally in such a way that, in the division where this matters, entrepreneurial spirit or innovative thought can be allowed to flourish within defined business par-ameters. The HP Way supplements this by giving the organization shared cultural stability through prescribing a loose set of values with which the diverse group-ings that make up HP can identify.

(Adapted from P. McGovern and V. Hope Hailey, 'Inside Hewlett Packard: Corporate Culture and Bureaucratic Control', in S. Sackmann (ed.), *Cultural Complexity in Organizations*, 1997, Thousand Oaks, California: Sage.)

Achieving short-term business objectives

1. Are individual and team objectives linked to business goals?
There is strong linkage as the business objectives of the overall strategic plan are clearly articulated to the individual and are transformed into clear objectives which are discussed and agreed on an annual or biannual basis. At HP the ten-step plan and business fundamentals are designed to cascade annual objectives from the corporate plan to the business unit and hence to the individual. Also a device called 'Framework' relates annual business objectives to job characteristics, individual skills and short-term training needs and development. From attitude surveys it was clear that individuals perceive a linkage between their job behaviour and performance and business strategy.

2. Do performance metrics and appraisal reflect business goals?
There is medium linkage as the metrics are reliable and valid but still reflect short-term business targets.

3. Are individuals and teams rewarded for business-focused performance?
There is strong linkage as team and performance outcomes are accurately measured and directly related to the achievement of business goals; a proportion of the remuneration package reflects business-goal-oriented outputs. The relationship between the achievement of business goals and pay is clear to the individual.

4. Does training reinforce and support business goals?
The key technical and managerial competencies, skills and techniques required to deliver the business objectives have been systematically analyzed and shared with managers. In HP there is a range of on-line and off-line training and development opportunities; most felt the organization encouraged the development of new skills.

Preparing for long-term business success

1. Does the organization do long-term scanning of HR issues?

4.4.1   *Analysis of Hewlett-Packard*

The change capabilities at Hewlett-Packard (HP) can be assessed using the People Process Model (see Figure 4.5).

4.4.2   *The kaleidoscope of Hewlett-Packard*

Hewlett-Packard is a difficult organization to understand. Much of its change expertise is embedded within the organizational processes and management practices that have evolved over its sixty-year history. This expertise is therefore difficult both to reveal and to imitate. The corporation's managers can achieve breakthrough change and change

This refers to the idea of scanning labour markets in the long term in order to understand the implications in terms of training and development, recruitment and selection and succession planning. For instance, does the scanning suggest that there will be sufficient people in the external labour market to meet the needs of the long-term business strategy? If not, should the organization grow its own through training and development? Are there people already internally who with development will be able to bridge these gaps or does the organization need to start recruiting them in from outside the organization now to develop them over the longer term? In HP this activity is carried out at various levels within the company on a national, regional and international basis.

2. Is there a long-term HR Strategy?
Yes.

Transforming

1. Does the company have established processes for transforming leaders?
A high potential track for very successful staff has been established in the mid-1990s.

2. Does the company have established processes for transforming the workforce?
Strong line managerial skills ensure continual counselling of staff as change goes on. People felt confident about their own skills and ability to compete in the longer term.

3. Does the company have established processes for transforming the organization?
There is good evidence of continuous incremental change through the ten-step process, business fundamentals and big-bang reconstructive change through the 'hoishin' process.

Note: This extract only gives the results of the analysis from the People Process Model.

Figure 4.5   *The People Process Model of Hewlett-Packard*
(Source: *Adapted from L. Gratton, V. Hope Hailey* et al., Strategic Human Resource Management, *1999, Oxford: Oxford University Press*)

slowly over *time*. They have learnt the skill of implementing change across their global corporation. Since they have learnt how to change continuously the *scope* of the change is realignment. They have also learnt the skill of running both reconstructive and adaptive forms of realignment simultaneously.

The paradox is that as an organization HP is highly *diverse*. It practices across different national cultures. However, it operates as a multinational, seeking a blend between the national culture and the corporate culture within each country that they work in. It employs few expatriates, within the UK national unit, and its staff are essentially national rather than international in culture when compared with other global companies. Their functional or product divisions also have their own subcultures.

Yet, within this diversity HP also achieves high organizational identity. Successive attitude surveys conducted by external researchers demonstrate a strong commitment and loyalty to the organization and a belief in its ability to succeed. Staff talk about really caring about the fate of the organization and of being proud to say that they work for HP.

Senior management are very clear about what it is they want to *preserve*: the broad values statement, the HP Way and the tradition of Management by Objectives (MBO). This gives them a cultural stability such that the organizational identity is never so stretched that the staff lose sight of what the organization stands for. They also maintain the business planning system and the performance management system within the broad label of Management by Objectives. These act like the nervous system of a body, transmitting and receiving information, communication and knowledge throughout the company. They too give a constant framework with which the staff identify. HP is clear about the practices it wants to preserve, and all else can be continuously changed, renegotiated and flexed. They therefore achieve change incrementally.

Other companies have values statements, business planning systems and performance management systems yet they do not perform in the same way as HP. This is because a further *capability* lies in its staff and particularly its line managers. If you asked managers within HP what was essential for getting on in HP they would give the standard reply of meeting business targets, but in addition they would add that it would be impossible to get promoted unless the person had recognizable and proven people management skills.

These informal skills include developing staff, communicating with staff and counselling staff on careers and performance. People's contribution to performance is constantly appraised on an informal basis by managers and peers. Appraisal becomes merely annual confirmation of what has been said throughout the year in normal conversations between managers and staff. These highly honed people management skills give HP a terrific capability in managing change because its managers constantly realign their staff performance, behaviour and expectations.

The analysis using the People Process Model shows the capability captured in change management systems that HP have developed over the years. They demonstrate excellent management practice in the activities concerned with delivering short-term business results.

However, more significantly they are able to align these short-term activities with the issues identified by their long-term business forecasting. The planning and monitoring systems constantly send information up and down the corporation, so the managerial interface constantly communicates what is changing and how employees can respond and be supported in this change. In addition to the informal change expertise vested within individual line managers, HP also has a high *capacity* for change as it has comparatively good access to financial resources.

As there is an expectation of continuous transition, the staff are aware of the need to constantly adapt working practices and committed to the need to change in order to improve. There is high *readiness for change*. There appears to be a balance of *power* between the corporate centre, the business divisions and the national divisions.

4.4.3 Key contextual features of Hewlett-Packard

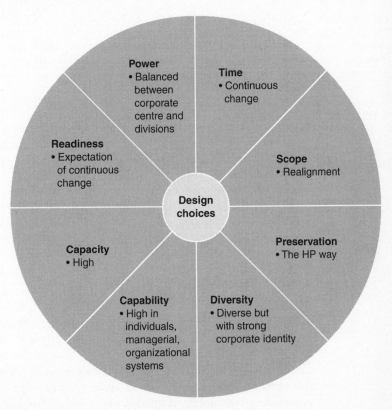

Figure 4.6 Key contextual features of Hewlett-Packard

4.4.4   Design implications for Hewlett-Packard

Change path

Hewlett-Packard appear to operate simultaneously with two different types of change: reconstruction and adaptation. It may appear that HP has never undergone transformational change but unless we track their detailed history over time it may be difficult to distinguish between moments when adaptation became evolution.

Change style

Hewlett-Packard achieves change through matching the style to the type of change required. The business targets or change initiatives are decided at the corporate centre and then given to the individual business or geographic unit. The staff participate in deciding how to achieve these targets, but they do not collaborate in the setting of the overall change targets. Other areas that need changing are addressed using different styles. For instance, when the company experienced high levels of stress the senior management implemented an educative programme for staff on sources of stress, using the talents of athletes and brain specialists to emphasize their message.

Change roles

Hewlett-Packard appears to assign different roles to different individuals according to the type of change required. Project groups may be set up for Hoishin initiatives, although the CEO will give backing to these short-term initiatives. Line managers take responsibility for both short-term and long-term change initiatives and are measured on their competence and achievements in this area. However, this is a feasible design choice because of the line's capability in people management.

Change targets

Given its background in research and development the corporation believes in promoting individual autonomy. Therefore, it seeks to maintain values and continually targets outputs rather than behaviours. The individual is left to decide how to achieve something, in discussion with the line manager if necessary. This also means that the corporation can deal with its diversity – the values statement appears, symbolically at least, to operate across borders in a way that prescribed behaviours could never do. Likewise, the business planning system and the performance management system operate across national and functional divisions. They prescribe the outputs for the corporation.

Change start point

Change appears to start top-down. However, ideas about change are received from all levels and areas of the organization. Change may be formalized through top-down initiatives but informal change ideas do come bottom-up through the organization.

Change levers

For incremental change HP uses the business planning and performance management systems as levers, which is consistent with a target of change outputs. As was described earlier, these systems act as a nervous system within the whole corporation. Just as the body shares the same nervous system but gives the limbs of the body different instructions in order to achieve different movements, so HP employs the same systems but the messages they carry will be specific to different units within HP. This is what enables them to respond to both local and global needs at the same time. By meshing the business planning systems with the performance management systems it is possible for the corporation to align employees behind the business strategy. The objectives that an individual is given, the rewards they do/do not receive and the training and development that they undergo all send powerful messages about how employees are to change – yet exact behaviours are never prescribed. As the business objectives, rewards and training and development change over time, so employees change incrementally.

For the short term, big-bang initiatives called 'hoishins' specific levers will be chosen that are capable of delivering rapid change. These levers will include both systems and symbols as a means of changing outputs. For instance, when the UK division started to record unacceptable levels of employee stress (in the eyes of the senior management) various short-term change initiatives were put in place. Symbolic interventions included using a famous British athlete to lead fitness routines around the office; bringing in medical experts to explain the impact of stress on both the brain and the heart; and reorganizing the physical layout of the offices so that those who spent most time at their desks were positioned nearest to the windows to ensure maximum exposure to daylight as a way of reducing stress. All of these interventions were both practical and symbolic in nature.

Change in action

Illustration 4.4

Lendco – a retail bank

The financial services revolution in the UK, starting in the 1980s with the deregulation led by the Conservative government, broke down the traditional lines of demarcation between different types of providers. Consequently, there was intense competition fuelled by new entrants and new forms of delivery into the marketplace. This coupled with the impact of new technology has led to a drive to cut down costs. In the 1990s the market matured and the banks were left struggling to find new ways to compete.

Lendco's major businesses were segmented into separate business units. In addition it embarked upon a cultural change programme with the intention of moving the bank away from what senior management described as an authoritarian culture which had bred a child-like dependence within the staff and a general climate of fear and blame. Lendco directors sought to gain a culture that fostered individual responsibility and excellent people management as they believed that this was the means of achieving improved customer service. However, the major problem for the bank in this respect was that the potency of the old culture was tied into the type of staff who chose banking as an attractive career because of its stability, predictability and strong internal career paths. These sort of people often did not naturally possess high levels of individual autonomy and were likely to find the transition to the new culture extremely problematic. The problem was exacerbated in Lendco by the fact that there was a perception within the bank that the old culture was being dismantled without a clear alternative. Every change that was implemented seemed to

4.5   Case Study: Lendco – a retail bank

This case study (Illustration 4.4) looks at a high street retail bank which needed to undergo transformational change. The case brings out the problems of achieving such change when there is low capability and an equally low awareness of the need for change. It also brings out the complexities of employee loyalty.

4.5.1   The kaleidoscope of Lendco

In terms of *power* the structure of the retail banks in the UK was such that there was a significant divide between the branches scattered all

Illustration 4.4 continued

the staff like another blow to the old accepted way of doing things, rather than something that was new or better being introduced.

At the same time a major part of the same change programme was the strategy to 'empower' line managers in particular, so that they took complete responsibility for the management of people away from the personnel department. This was a point identified by the senior management as a key source of competitive advantage. In practice, however, bankers still stuck to banking and persisted in giving lower priority to people issues. It appeared that deep in the mindset of the average bank manager was the idea that you were only a good manager if you were a good lender.

Contrary messages about the importance of business targets versus people targets meant that the former in practice gained priority in a branch manager's mind. Despite providing people management courses and personal development plans, the people management skills of Lendco's line managers remained a constraint. Many branch managers still felt that managing people was what personnel did.

Furthermore, the downsizing and segmentation of the business had a marked effect on the status and activities of the line and branch managers. The branch had moved from being a complete point of delivery for products and services to merely a retailer of those services and products which are now designed centrally. Branch managers lost status and morale was lowered.

The branch managers were key in delivering the new culture that the bank was trying to achieve, but for many reasons they did not have the capability to deliver this change.

(© Veronica Hope Hailey, 1998.)

over the country and the head office. The head office staff assumed themselves to be quite powerful because that was where the senior managers were located. The business divisions, such as investment banking or the international division, were often located in the City and perceived themselves to be a sophisticated and separate group of people compared with the branch network staff.

Yet, the branch managers were in a very powerful position. As they were scattered all over the country, they could not be directly supervised through a person-to-person managerial system. Admittedly, developments in new technology have meant that their work flow and targets can be closely monitored, yet their influence remained. They were the main source of both communication and interpretation of head office edicts; they could therefore put whatever spin they wished on information as it cascaded down through the organization.

The standardization of approach that the bank's retailing strategy demanded required more centralized forms of control. Much of the bank's activity over time could be interpreted as gradually trying to extract the power from the branch networks.

The bank's senior managers were very powerful and as such, control was put on the strategic agenda for discussion and consideration. Traditionally, directors within the banking sector are bankers by experience and qualification. There may have been a problem in getting them to consider softer issues such as change management and people management capability. Their position as major stakeholders may have blocked this. Equally the stock market's drive for short-term business results may cause blocks to be put on substantial investment in longer-term change initiatives.

Time does not appear to be a major issue – there was no immediate crisis on the visible horizon. Yet, time will become an issue if the bank does nothing, due to the new entrants into the banking world, and the new forms of delivery that are being embraced by both old and new members within the marketplace.

However, the lack of financial crisis contributed to the low *readiness* for change within the branch network. Whilst senior managers and some head office staff understood the need for change, this was not shared by staff in the field offices. The lack of awareness of the need for change, meant that the commitment to change was a theoretical issue. One can only speculate that the long lengths of service to the bank may have acted as a twin edged sword in this respect. On the one hand, staff may have felt such loyalty to their employer that they were willing to try to change for them. On the other hand, their lack of exposure to other forms of working, and their attachment to the traditional working practices of old-style retail banking, might have made them very uncommitted to any form of change.

The issue of *preservation* is also interesting. The bank would like to preserve the levels of loyalty it has enjoyed in the past. However, it only wants to preserve them at its price. What this means is that it does not want to preserve a commitment to long-term contracts of employment and job security. What it should also consider is the tacit knowledge that is held within the branch offices: perhaps an understanding of local or regional businesses, and the profile of customers within the area and their specific needs. The more the bank centralized, the greater the chance that these assets would be lost. Other more tangible assets which it needs to question the value of preserving include the capital investment in the branch infrastructure. New entrants are finding cheaper ways of delivering a banking service or selling financial services products, telephone banking and super-market banking.

In terms of *capacity* for change, the bank had some financial capacity to invest in change management but only if the senior management deemed it necessary.

The bank does not appear to have had an enormous *capability* in change management terms. There was little evidence of a body of expertise existing at an organizational level in the form of an experienced and sophisticated Organizational Development department. At managerial level, the most important players are the branch managers. Yet few of them have experienced change outside Lendco, and there appears to be little investment in embedding an understanding of change management within these people.

In some ways the situation is even worse for two reasons. First, the branch managers probably assume that they are expert in change management because of the technical banking changes they regularly incorporate within their work. Yet, they have little or no experience in managing the softer aspects of change, themes which are picked up in Chapter 6. Second, because of trends in human resource management, the corporation has actually given back responsibility for people management to the branch managers but without necessarily establishing whether they have a competence or capability in this area.

At an individual level, the staff who worked in the bank often chose such a career for its security and stability. They may not enjoy change at a personal or emotional level. They were certainly unaccustomed to it, and may resist change due to their feelings of confusion.

The bank enjoyed quite low *diversity*. Despite the differences between the branch network and the international or investment divisions mentioned earlier, the branches of the banks are very homogeneous in culture, staff groups, roles and customers. However, in terms of identity, the picture was more interesting. The staff did identify with the bank, but their primary source of identity was their local branch, or at most, their region. They had little identification with head office, and a tangible 'them and us' attitude had grown up within the network.

In terms of *scope* the bank needed to achieve transformational change in the longer term. It needed to transform itself from being a banking business to being a retailer of financial services. This would require the bank fundamentally to change the way it does business in terms of beliefs, assumptions and behaviours.

4.5.2   *Key contextual features of Lendco*

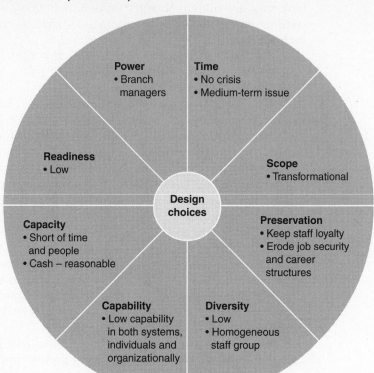

Figure 4.7   Key contextual features of Lendco

4.5.3   *Design implications*

Change path

Ideally, the bank would want to carry on changing incrementally, but because of the lack of readiness for change the change agent would have to consider some more visible and symbolic changes instead. Initially, the bank would be wise to start with some short-term adjustments to existing working practices in order to prime the organization for the transformational change it requires. In addition, it had a low capability in change management. This would have to be developed before the organization is ready to tackle transformation.

Change target

Changing the organization's paradigm or values is the long-term target as values will have to be changed in order to achieve transformational change. However, the bank needs to build up its capability first, and address the staff's low awareness of the need for change. Behaviours would be a good initial starting point, perhaps in tandem with changing outputs. By directly focusing on behaviours the line managers are given a change target that is tangible to assess. To the staff it symbolically indicates that change is necessary.

Change roles

As it is still a dependency culture in the early change stage much of the initiative would have to be backed by senior management. The HR function would hold little credibility in the branches and therefore these initial change forays must be driven by a business manager. At the same time as starting these adjustments, the organization could consider forming some change action teams, in preparation for the bigger transformational change ahead. These change action teams need to be carefully selected. Existing powerful stakeholders need to be included, but only those with a reasonably positive attitude to the transformation needed. In addition, the change agent needs to identify some new young blood, preferably from the branch network who could join these teams. To enhance the change capability within these teams the bank could consider bringing in external consultants.

Change start point

Initially the change would need to start top-down, certainly in the reconstruction stage as there would be no impetus for change from the bottom of the organization. Before going for the large-scale transformation, the bank could additionally experiment with proposed new working practices in pilot sites.

Change style

A mix of directive and participative styles is appropriate. The reconstruction change initiatives need to be introduced in a directive way to demonstrate that change is not a debatable question. In the long and medium term the larger transformational change could be participative in the way that it is rolled out. The bank needs to shift the culture from dependency/paternalism and to get staff to take responsibility for their own destiny. If senior management persist in directing all change they will merely perpetuate the existing values and attitudes.

Change levers

Initially, the organization needs to enhance some of its basic management control systems, such as performance management and communication. The reason for this is that without these centralized control systems the bank's senior management remain dependent on the branch managers for communicating and implementing the change. Also if the bank wants to move away from a paternalistic command and control type culture to one where employees and line managers are more empowered, then the form of control operating within the bank needs to move from the personal control of individuals to control through management systems.

To consolidate the initial change target of behaviours, a competency framework could be introduced. Those competencies could be used across all performance management systems and selection criteria and form the basis for training and development activities. Outputs can be targeted through the performance management system. Whatever change path the bank takes, given that it needs to transform the skills base of the organization, the introduction of change-oriented management development and general training is likely to be necessary. This will also provide senior management with information about the change capability within the organization. It

Change in action

Illustration 4.5

Glaxo Pharmaceuticals

Glaxo is an international pharmaceuticals company, although this case study is based on its UK division and particularly focuses on the sales divisions prior to the merger with Wellcome. Glaxo was, and is currently, hugely successful, but at the time of the case study, the late 1980s, was under threat from expiring patents on its products and from massive changes in the UK marketplace.

The need for a planned cultural change programme within Glaxo was identified within the business strategic planning process in 1988. The aim was to become more customer oriented in terms of, for example, quicker response times. Recognizing the important contribution that the excellent management of staff could potentially make to the bottom line, the Managing Director gave significant support to the Human Resources Director's initiative to design a set of behaviours that would be critical to business success in the future.

An attitude survey run throughout the company revealed some disturbing attitudes and organizational characteristics. First, there was an attitude of complacency among the staff. Staff recognized the changing nature of the marketplace within which Glaxo was operating, but there was insufficient awareness of the responsibility and contribution that was necessary on the part of each member of staff in order to sustain the success of the company. Second, there was an organizational characteristic of slow decision making, threatening Glaxo's ability to respond quickly to the needs of the marketplace. Third, there were strong functional divides within the organization contributing to the slow pace of decision making. This hindered the development of any sense of shared responsibility for business success.

Both the Managing Director and the HR Director recognized that if these were not tackled they would severely hamper the organization's ability to respond to the

will give them the opportunity to identify possible change agents and those who do not have the competence to act in this capacity.

The longer-term transformation would need to focus on communication mechanisms, participative workshops and personal development as means of tackling values, beliefs and mindsets at a deeper level. It is only through addressing this deeper level of value that the bank can achieve the paradigmatic change it requires in order to respond to changes in the marketplace. However, these value-led initiatives will need to be accompanied by changes to all structures, systems, symbols and organizational routines if individuals are to change their behaviours in a way that is consistent with the new values.

4.6 Case Study: Glaxo Pharmaceuticals

This case study (Illustration 4.5) considers the problems of managing

Illustration 4.5 continued

changing nature of the customer – the National Health Service in the UK – and the increased competition within the marketplace.

Focusing initially on behaviours rather than values, a description of the behaviours necessary for the Glaxo of the future was drawn up. In conjunction with consultants from a management college, the senior management team were put through an outdoor development course that enabled them to understand and experiment with these new behaviours. It also enabled them to understand at a personal level the depth of change that was necessary on the part of individuals if the desired change was to be achieved. The course proved so successful that the experience was repeated for a further 700 staff members within the organization. Staff were invited to revise the behaviours spelt out in the programme called RATIO, in terms of their own jobs and roles so that each characteristic could be fleshed out.

A series of complementary change initiatives was implemented. First a values statement was issued stating the values that should underpin the behaviours that Glaxo was trying to achieve in RATIO. A second initiative was the institution of project groups. These were encouraged in order to break down the functional divides and promote amoebic like structures to emerge within the organization. A third initiative was the relocation of Glaxo. Members of the senior management team battled to ensure that maximum symbolic use was made of open plan working in order to chip away the functional divides through open and easy communication. A later initiative has been to incorporate RATIO within a set of managerial competencies.

All these initiatives were designed to unfreeze the complacency within the organization and to enhance staff's readiness for change. Two years later a much larger change programme was instituted focusing on radical business process re-engineering.

(Adapted from L. Gratton, V. Hope-Hailey *et al.*, *Strategic Human Resource Management,* 1999, Oxford: Oxford University Press.)

change at a time of success. The organization does not appear to be under any kind of threat externally; the staff are happy, satisfied and trust their senior management. Yet the directors can see that in the longer term the company will need to transform itself. They choose to start this process of change sooner rather than later, in order to manage the process carefully.

4.6.1   The kaleidoscope of Glaxo Pharmaceuticals

The key contextual feature here is *readiness for change*. As the corporation was very successful the staff saw little need to change. They also had complete faith in their senior management's ability to respond to change, and generally showed, through the attitude survey, a confidence in their employers that most companies would envy. However, as the senior management knew that this complacency was the very thing that could threaten their dominance in the marketplace they had to work hard to erase it.

The organization appeared to have plenty of *time* – their main product was not due to come off patent until the mid-1990s and this was the late 1980s. However, in order to make the workforce aware of the need to change, the management needed to create a climate of urgency. Therefore, although they could have handled this change gradually over time, they did the change in a big-bang way over short periods of time. The *scope* was in fact realignment rather than radical transformation. However, the nature of the change appeared more radical because of the need to wipe away the complacency of the staff.

The *capability* for change within the organization was mixed. On the one hand, there was not a great deal of expertise in handling the change programmes they used, hence the buying-in of consultants. However, the workforce in any pharmaceuticals company is extremely well educated and perfectly capable of absorbing new concepts and behaviours quite fast. In that sense they had a higher capability than other organizations.

Likewise, whilst they had to buy in resources in the form of consultants to help them run the change programme, they equally had a financial *capacity* to invest money in a programme of this size. They were also able to invest a considerable sum of money in making sure that the architecture and design of their new buildings mirrored the organizational changes they were trying to embed.

They were also fortunate in the sense that since they were only dealing with one division, the sales divisions, they were attempting to change a relatively uniform group of people. Had the change been intended to go wider within the corporation, then it would have run up against problems of *diversity* in the form of different occupational groups and different sites. People identified with the organization –

they liked working there. However, they were still highly educated people who could not be treated as though they had no need for autonomy or minds of their own.

There were the usual power blocs within the organization – the heads of the trading companies, and the sales managers in the field. However, *power* does not come over as an unusually salient feature in this case study.

Finally, there was much that Glaxo wanted to *preserve*. It did not want to alienate the mass of the workforce as the company already employed some of the best people in the labour market. The vast amount of knowledge, intellect and potential possessed by the workforce would not be easy to replace. Glaxo wanted to remove the complacency but not the positive aspects of its staff. At this stage of the change it did not know which staff would be suitable for the new ways of working. The work on RATIO and management competencies would enable Glaxo to analyze its skills base against projected future demands.

4.6.2   Key contextual features of Glaxo Pharmaceuticals

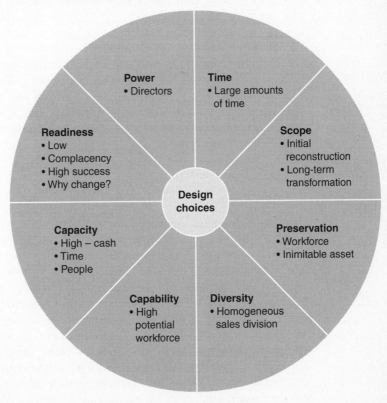

Figure 4.8   Key contextual features of Glaxo Pharmaceuticals

4.6.3   Design implications for Glaxo Pharmaceuticals

Change paths

The outcome Glaxo wanted from this first phase of change was a form of realignment. However, because of the complacency within the division, the change itself had to be done in a big-bang way which implied it was more radical than it was in reality. In effect the management were destabilizing the status quo as a precursor to more fundamental change. So, the change was a form of reconstruction.

Change start point

Due to the staff complacency, the senior management was forced to drive this change top-down. As the staff were content with the status quo, there was no incentive for them to start change in a bottom-up fashion. One of the objectives of the change process was to make it clear that continuation with the status quo was untenable. Therefore, pockets of good practice, as a design option, would not have delivered the high visibility that the change process needed.

Change roles

For the same reasons of needing high visibility and symbolic impact, the senior management had to lead the change. The HR department did substantial work designing and planning the various change initiatives, but it was the Managing Director who was seen as the main change champion. The project groups acted as a form of change action teams – their importance was far more symbolic than performance driven.

Change target

Prescribed behaviours seemed to work well with the workforce because of their tangibility and their link with jobs (through job profiles) and perceived business relevance. The change agents were also able to focus on using values because of the relative uniformity of the division. Although there were subgroups within the sales division, there was a greater homogeneity than there would have been had the change needed to be implemented across the whole corporation. For example, had they included research and development scientists in the change process they might have found it more difficult to target behaviours. This is because the scientists as a professional group might have objected to the threat to their autonomy that the prescription of behaviours represented.

The second wave of the change process, which focused on values,

seemed to be less successful than the behaviour-led change. One explanation for this may be that they tried to introduce the values using the
same implementation techniques that they had used for the behaviours, RATIO. As value-based change is aimed at achieving fundamental transformational change, more probing methods may have
been necessary. As it was, it appeared easy to ignore the values initiative.

Change style

In order to increase staff's awareness of the need for change the division chose a participative style of change process. However, it was not
collaborative. The senior management had decided that the organization should change – it merely wanted the staff to participate in the
events building up to that change, and give them some ownership over
the change process.

Change levers

A key lever was the use of management development, in particular the
senior management's outdoor development weekend, and the subsequent change workshops that were held for all levels of staff. This is
unusual given the emphasis on behaviours. Management development
is more commonly associated with a targeting of values, but was
needed here to get senior managers to realize that behavioural change
meant they had to change. The behaviours encapsulated within
RATIO were linked into a management competency framework that
could be extended across the whole human resource management
system of recruitment and selection, performance management,
including both rewards and development.

Other significant levers were the symbolic office relocation and
their symbolic use of interior design in the new offices. Emphasis by
the senior managers on mirroring the organizational changes with the
new open plan offices allowed them to send powerful messages about
the change to the staff. There was also the symbolic use of project
groups to promote the idea of cross-functional working.

4.7   Summary

This chapter has explored the use of the change kaleidoscope through
the examination of five extended case studies of companies undergoing
change. These case studies have illustrated both the complexity of
change and interrelated nature of all the kaleidoscope features. None
of the individual features can be considered in isolation from the other
seven characteristics. Furthermore, the contextual features shift

through time as illustrated by the WH Smith News case. The pattern of features at one time will be altered by the changes put in place. The features, therefore, have to be reassessed before choices are made about future changes.

In particular the chapter has considered three main areas

- How to use the change kaleidoscope to understand the change context in depth.
- How to identify the key contextual features in any change situation that influence the design choices and therefore the change approach. As the case studies illustrate, certain contextual features may be critical in one organization and of minor significance in another.
- The implications of each assessment of these features for the design of change.

Having established the link between change context and change design choices, the next three chapters explore the design and management of the transition process.

5

Designing the transition: the implementation path

5.1 Introduction

So far, this book has discussed the initial planning and design for change implementation. Chapter 2 introduced the design choices that need to be made. Chapters 3 and 4 discussed how to assess the key contextual features of the change situation, and how to use these factors to judge what change approach to take. As yet, little has been said about the design of the more detailed steps to achieve the implementation of the desired change approach, or for that matter, once change gets underway, how to manage the implementation. This is the focus of the next three chapters – the design and management of the actual transition:

- The notion of three change states, the *current* (where the organization is now), the *future* (where the organization wants to be), and the *transition* (how to get to the future state), is introduced. All three of these states need to be understood before embarking on implementation, although the focus of this chapter is the transition state.
- The concept of a change *vision* is introduced, and it is explained how this aspect of the future state needs to be considered before moving on to design the transition.
- The need to diagnose barriers to change that may be encountered during the transition is discussed. Barriers arise primarily from organizational culture and stakeholders.
- The notion of the transition state is expanded to explain how it encompasses three change phases – unfreeze, move and sustain.
- The concept of the transition curve is explained to illustrate how the organizational transition process of unfreeze, move and sustain is underpinned by the personal transitions of individuals within an organization.
- Consideration is given to how to design a series of levers and mechanisms, and how to sequence their deployment, to achieve the chosen change approach, and move the organization through the transition from unfreezing to ultimately sustaining the changes.

Chapters 6 and 7 look in more detail at some of the levers and mechanisms involved in managing the transition to make change actually happen.

5.2   *The three change states: the current, the future and the transition*

There are many different ways of conceiving the overall change process, some use more colourful language than others, such as 'awakening', 'mobilizing' and 'instishionalizing' (1). However, it is commonly accepted that during change it is necessary to consider three states – the current, the future and the transition (see Figure 5.1) (2).

Essential inputs to the diagnosis of the current organizational state are an understanding of the organization's competitive position and the need for change, but this must be accompanied by an understanding of the internal organizational context. It is also necessary to develop some sort of vision or strategic intent of the desired future organizational state. The transition state, the process of changing the organization from what it is now into the desired future organization, can only be designed once it is understood what the current organizational state is, and what the desired future organizational state looks like.

As stated in Chapter 1, we are assuming that readers of this text already have an understanding of how to diagnose the current organizational state, and how to develop an outline of the desired future state, from either *Exploring Corporate Strategy* or some other text. This chapter will therefore say little else about the current state, but will give some further consideration to the future state, particularly in terms of developing a *vision* for the future. Without an understanding of what the future organization will look like, it is difficult to diagnose barriers to change, design appropriate levers and mechanisms, or measure whether the desired changes are taking place.

To achieve change it is necessary to:
1. Assess the current organizational situation.
2. Define the desired future organizational state.
3. Determine how to get there.

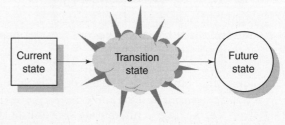

Figure 5.1   *Three change states*

The transition state, the process of actually making the desired changes happen, often receives less attention than it merits. Implementation is conceived in terms of the up-front planning for change, with scant attention to managing the transition process itself. Yet the transition state is not like either the current or future states. It is not possible to move from the current to the future state overnight. It might be possible to redeploy and relocate people in terms of named job roles and locations over a weekend, but to change the behaviour of those people, and particularly to change the organiz-ation's shared values and beliefs, will take much longer. This is why this chapter and Chapter 6 are devoted to a discussion of the range of *change levers and mechanisms* that can be deployed during the tran-sition state to achieve the desired end result. The special *management* and *resource requirements* of the transition state are discussed in Chapter 7.

5.3   The future state: developing a vision

Frameworks such as the cultural web (already discussed in Chapters 2, 3 and 4), can help with the development of a vision for the future by providing a picture of what the desired organization looks like. However, it must also be possible to explain the future state to an organization's employees, so a vision is about more than drawing up a new cultural web. It is also a mechanism for communication. This text will therefore treat the vision as having two parts to it – a vision state-ment, and an image of the future organization encapsulated in the new cultural web for the organization. The web itself is unlikely to be a good communication vehicle since it is a framework that has to be explained before people can make sense of it.

5.3.1   What is a vision?

Since the 1980s, there has been an increasing emphasis on the need for a powerful change 'vision', or picture of the future, if change is to be successful. Transformational change in particular usually consists of a number of projects and initiatives. Without a unifying vision, these initiatives can appear to be unrelated, confusing and piecemeal. A vision gives change recipients a target to aim for, and the incentive and energy for change. It should also generate commitment to change.

A vision is usually a qualitative expression of the desired future state. There are various descriptions of what constitutes a good vision, but generally three aspects are mentioned. A vision encapsulates what the organization is trying to achieve; a rationale for the changes to be undertaken; and a picture of what the future organization will 'look like', which incorporates something about the values of the new organization and what is expected of employees. In addition, visions need to appeal to the majority of an organization's stakeholders, and comprise realistic and attainable goals (3).

5.3.2   Vision statements

A vision should be expressed in such a way that it can be communicated effectively to employees in a way that is memorable. Employees will find it difficult to remember overly long and complex messages. Few individuals are able to remember even a page of detail, so a memorable vision statement is likely to be short and to the point. If a vision cannot stimulate interest and some degree of understanding in a short space of time, there is still more work to be done. A good vision statement should also be exciting and challenging. Furthermore, employees need to understand how they can help make the vision happen – they need to be able to link what they do on an everyday basis to the achievement of the vision (3).

Some of the most famous vision statements include that of Komatsu, the Japanese earth moving equipment manufacturers, who wanted to 'Encircle Caterpillar'. Caterpillar were the industry leader in Komatsu's sector at the time. Similarly, Honda wanted to become a second Ford, a pioneer in the automotive industry. These statements show that using examples, metaphors or analogies can help to express succinctly what is required to employees without using jargon.

Other vision statements may be addressed more specifically to a particular change initiative, rather than longer-term evolution. SKF, the international bearings manufacturer, implemented transformational change in the way it dealt with customers seeking replacement bearings for those in a piece of machinery or a car that had worn out. In this market, known as the aftermarket, traditionally bearings were sold through dealers and distributors with little concern for helping customers identify and fit the appropriate bearings. The vision developed for the aftermarket division was simply 'Trouble Free Operations'. This phrase captured the need to start providing not just bearings, but services to the aftermarket customers, and to become market focused rather than a production-led organization (4). However, visions do not have to be a succinct two or three words. Chapter 6, Illustration 6.1, describes the changes undertaken by the Birmingham Midshires Building Society in the early 1990s as they attempted to reorient the society to deliver better customer service. Their vision was: 'By being the FIRST CHOICE for our customers, our people and our business partners, we will grow, profitably.' FIRST also doubled up as a mnemonic for the new organizational values of Friendly, Informed, Responsive, Service oriented and Trustworthy (5).

A vision statement can also be communicated through behaviours as well as words, particularly the behaviours of the senior managers in an organization. The role of symbolism during transitions is discussed in more detail in Chapter 6.

5.3.3   Using the web to help formulate a vision

A picture of what the future organization looks like can be developed by drawing a new cultural web. This exercise is called 'rewebbing' in *Exploring Corporate Strategy* (Chapter 11), and is a useful way of building a picture of the future organization since the web incorporates not just new structures, but also what sort of symbols, routines and control systems are needed (6). Illustration 5.1 shows the current and future webs developed by an organization referred to here as Metto, the European division of a chemicals business. This illustration shows how the web can capture the key elements of change required. Metto wishes to undertake a fundamental change from an internally-focused, manufacturing and product-oriented organization, to one which puts customer needs first, and offers excellent service on a pan-European basis. Power structures, routines and rituals, structures, symbols and so on all need to change to support this.

Developing an outline of a new cultural web is an important exercise early on in the design of the change process, even if there is as yet no vision statement. Questions considered in Chapters 3 and 4, such as the scope of the changes to be undertaken by an organization, cannot be answered unless there is at least an outline of the desired future state.

5.3.4   Identifying levers and mechanisms

The process of drawing up a new cultural web also leads to the identification of levers and mechanisms for change, in terms of structures, systems, routines and symbols (6). This can be seen from Illustration 5.1 of the Metto web. However, the cultural web cannot be used to capture all levers and mechanisms by any means. In particular, interventions to do with communication and personal development, in order to achieve an awareness of the need for change, or an ability to manage and undertake change among employees, have to be considered separately, and are given due consideration in Chapter 6.

5.3.5   Linking vision development to design choices

The change approach selected affects the way a vision for the change process should be developed. For example:

- If the change approach selected is *top-down* and *directive*, as may be the case for a reconstruction or a revolution such as that undertaken

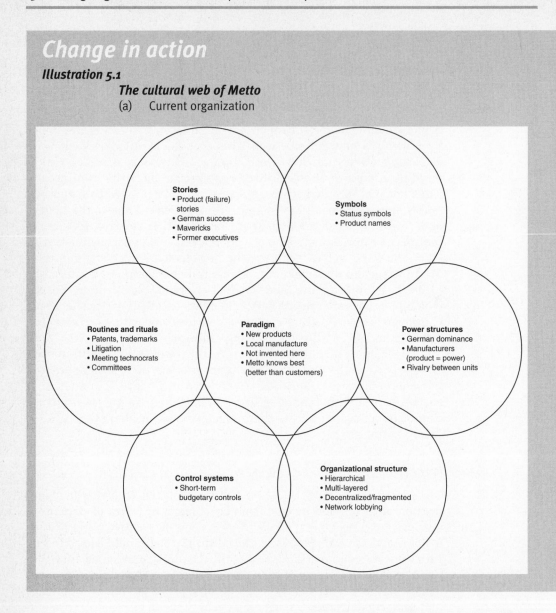

Change in action

Illustration 5.1

The cultural web of Metto

(a)   Current organization

by Ralph Halpern at Burtons (Chapter 3, Illustration 3.3), or Richard Surface at Pearl Assurance (Chapter 3, Illustration 3.2), then a vision statement and a future cultural web can be developed by one person, such as the chief executive or the managing director, particularly if this individual is in the change role of leadership. Alternatively, the web and vision statement can be developed by the senior management team. When drawing up the future web and identifying levers and mechanisms for change, the choices made should be based on the

Illustration 5.1 continued

(b)   Future organization

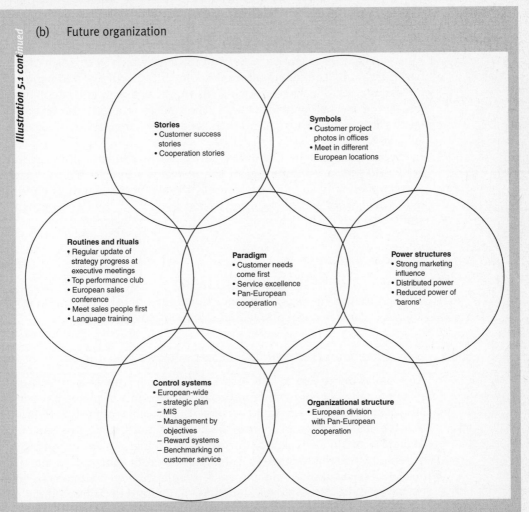

(*Source*: G. Johnson, 'Mapping and re-mapping organisational culture', in V. Ambrosini, G. Johnson and K. Scholes, *Exploring Techniques of Analysis and Evaluation in Strategic Management*, 1998, Hemel Hempstead: Prentice Hall.)

intervention target selected (outputs, behaviours or values), and the change levers chosen to achieve this (see Chapter 2, section 2.7).

- If the change approach and style is to be more *bottom-up* and *collaborative* as at the Open University (Chapter 2, Illustration 2.3), then a wider range of employees can be involved in the process of vision and cultural web development. Vision statements do not necessarily 'appear' from an individual's sudden burst of inspiration; they may have to evolve gradually through a lot of hard work. Organizations may choose to use external facilitators to help achieve widespread employee participation, or use senior managers to lead the process (3). This is likely to depend on decisions already made about the change roles (leadership, team, external facilitation), which in turn should be based on contextual circumstances to do with capability and capacity for change. Again, when drawing up the future web and identifying levers and mechanisms for change, the choices made should be based on the intervention target selected, and the change levers chosen to achieve this.

- In circumstances where a more *participative* change approach has been selected, a combination of the above two approaches to vision development may be selected, whereby the senior managers, or change team, design an initial web and vision statement, and then consult staff.

5.4   Barriers to change

Once the future state for the organization is understood it is possible to diagnose the barriers to change. Most barriers to change arise from the old organizational culture and organizational stakeholders

5.4.1   Identifying barriers to change and levers to overcome them

Any vision developed of the future will encapsulate new structures, systems and ways of behaving that have to be put in place, but without consideration of existing barriers, it is possible, almost by default, to leave old systems and ways of behaving in place, and these can subsequently prove obstructive. For example, one organization undergoing change wanted to move to a structure of profit centres in a move to devolve responsibility and increase middle manager empowerment. However, old control systems, such as centralized decision making on levels of resourcing and recruitment, and authorization of certain types of expense claims and expenditure were initially left in place. As a result the middle managers perceived little increase in their scope for discretion or autonomy. Interventions needed to be put in place to address these barriers if change was to progress.

This example illustrates that existing *organization cultures* provide some of the strongest barriers to the implementation of change. If the existing organization culture and the potential barriers to change it creates are not understood from a technique such as cultural web analysis, the way the organization and its members operate may continue to be driven by the existing culture, rather than by the desired new ways of behaving. For example, a web analysis would have revealed the barriers provided by existing control systems to successful implementation of profit centres in the example given above. In the

Metto example in Illustration 5.1, the existing culture presents several barriers to the desired integrated European organization, and the aim to offer high quality customer service. These include the historical emphasis on new product development from a technical point of view, and rivalry between business units to develop different products. The symbols were all to do with technical excellence, such as the CEO talking to the 'technocrats' rather than salespeople, and the technical literature and photographs on the office walls. For change to be successful, the range of levers and mechanisms deployed needed to address these issues.

However, as emphasized in Chapter 3 when discussing the need for preservation, change does need to avoid throwing out positive aspects of an organization alongside the negative aspects. Therefore, when examining the cultural web, attention should be paid to not just the barriers to change, but also those aspects of the organization that are either an asset or a facilitator of change and need to be retained.

Powerful stakeholders can also provide significant barriers to change. The way such stakeholders are likely to react to the proposed changes should have already been built into the design choices made from the consideration of power as one of the contextual features. However, it is also important to understand the way different stakeholders will respond to change as implementation progresses, and then consider how this is to be tackled. This is to do with issues of resistance management, which is discussed in more detail in the next chapter.

5.4.2   *Summarizing barriers and facilitators of change: force-field analysis*

It is helpful to summarize the analysis of barriers to change, along with identified facilitators of change, in a force-field analysis (see Figure 5.2) (7). Force-field analysis provides a pictorial overview of the main problems that need to be tackled, and helps to focus the debate about which levers and mechanisms need to be developed to overcome identified barriers. It may be that barriers created by, for example, old control systems can be overcome by simply removing these systems. If, on the other hand, the barriers are to do with the risk averse nature of employees, or a focus on production rather than customer service, a wide variety of structural, symbolic, communication and training interventions may be needed to get the employees to change.

The guiding principle of force-field analysis is that the *current* organizational state is maintained by a series of forces for and against change. Although there may be driving forces for change present, such as a declining competitive situation, these forces are as yet not strong enough to overcome the restraining forces against change resulting from the existing way of doing things, possibly because their existence

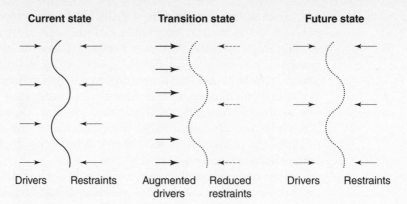

Figure 5.2   *Force-field analysis*

is not recognized throughout the organization as yet. Therefore, over-coming barriers to change is not just about identifying levers and mechanisms that can be put in place during the *transition* to decrease and/or remove the restraining forces. Another approach is to also con-sider levers and mechanisms that can be used during the transition to strengthen and/or augment the driving forces, thereby using an increased pressure for change to overcome the restraining forces.

Illustration 5.2 shows a force-field analysis for the situation at WH Smith News prior to the changes discussed in Chapter 4. The per-sonnel manager's early change initiatives were about gaining the sup-port of the house managers to reduce the likelihood that they would use their power to obstruct her initiatives. The deferential nature of the old culture was also eroded by the management style survey con-ducted by the personnel manager. Yet if the organization was to become customer-focused, with teamworking and greater personal accountability, at some point the personnel manager also had to put in place levers and mechanisms to deal with other barriers, such as the control culture in which non-managerial staff did not question decisions – or make decisions, the low change capability, and the lack of HR systems. Overcoming these barriers could also be assisted by the deployment of other levers and mechanisms to augment the driving forces for change. This could include interventions to increase the awareness of the need for change and the implications of this through-out the organization, which in turn might require improvements to communication mechanisms.

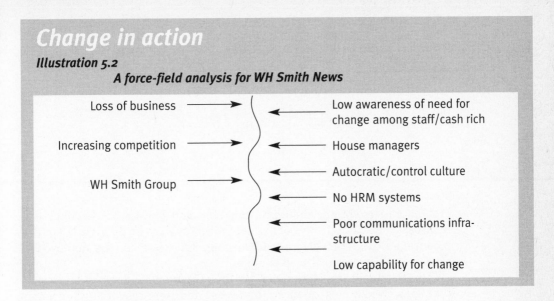

Change in action

Illustration 5.2
A force-field analysis for WH Smith News

Loss of business ⟶ ⟵ Low awareness of need for change among staff/cash rich

Increasing competition ⟶ ⟵ House managers

WH Smith Group ⟶ ⟵ Autocratic/control culture

⟵ No HRM systems

⟵ Poor communications infra-structure

⟵ Low capability for change

5.4.3   Linking barriers to identification to design choices

Linking the identification of barriers to change to design choices is more to do with identifying levers and mechanisms to overcome the barriers compatible with the change levers selected as part of the design choices. If the aim is to target behaviours ultimately to achieve value change by the use of a range of levers and mechanisms from the structural to the symbolic, the sort of approach taken by Archie Norman at ASDA (see Chapter 3, Illustration 3.4), then the levers and mechanisms considered should include such interventions to both tackle the barriers and increase the drivers. As discussed under unfreezing tactics below, use can be made of symbolism to challenge existing ways of doing things and promote awareness of the need for change. If the aim is to target values, and the chosen change levers include communication and education interventions, then these sorts of interventions should also be considered to overcome restraining forces and strengthen the drivers of change.

5.5   Designing the transition state: the organization level

Once the design of the future state has been completed, and it is known what barriers to change have to be overcome, it is then necessary to design an implementation path to deliver the future state. This involves thinking about which levers and mechanisms to deploy and in what order. Of course, many levers and mechanisms will already have been identified. The future culture web will contain details of any new structures, systems, routines and symbols needed. The consideration

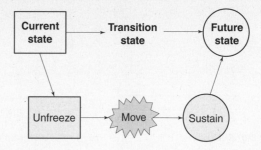

Figure 5.3   Three phases of transition

of barriers to change should have led to some decisions about old structures, systems and ways of behaving that need to be dismantled or discouraged, and the levers and mechanisms that can be deployed to achieve this and facilitate change.

To provide more shape to the way the identified levers and mechanisms should be sequenced, and what additional levers and mechanisms may be needed, it is helpful to subdivide the transition state itself into three other phases – unfreeze, move and sustain (see Figure 5.3).

This model is based on the one devised by Lewin (8). The original model referred to unfreezing, moving and refreezing:

- *Unfreezing* is about making people within an organization ready for change by making them aware of the need for change and dissatisfied with the existing ways of working. It is about creating the readiness for change among the workforce, at all levels from senior managers downwards, discussed as part of the change kaleidoscope in Chapters 3 and 4. Change is a painful, difficult experience for both organizations and the individuals within them. To undertake change people need to feel that the problems and the pain change will cause are outweighed by the need to change.
- *Moving* is the implementation of the needed changes through the selected range of levers and mechanisms.
- *Refreezing* involves embedding the changes throughout the organization to ensure members do not relapse into old patterns of behaviour.

The principle of unfreezing is still widely acknowledged as an important part of any change. Managers introduced to this model will often comment that on reflection they can see that the change process within their organization stumbled along rather than acquired momentum, because the staff within the organization were never 'unfrozen' and made ready for change. Similarly, the concept of refreezing is still recognized as having some merit, as it seems that without efforts to indicate that change is over, change drift can set in. A common comment from managers is that the change processes within their organizations have been left unfinished, since no real attempt has been made to institutionalize the required behavioural and attitudinal changes throughout the organization. The result is a continual backsliding of staff into old ways of behaving and a confusion over where the change process has got to.

On the other hand, it is also often commented that refreezing is an inappropriate term to use in modern organizations. Many organizations move from a radical change into an ongoing incremental change process of continuous improvement. This is why it is more common for the refreeze phase to be referred to as sustain or institutionalize. These terms embody the need to instil the new behaviours and attitudes throughout the organization and signal the end to major change, whilst avoiding the implication that there will be no more change and that the organization will become static.

5.5.1   Unfreezing

Unfreezing an organization sounds simple enough in theory, but is far more difficult in practice because it is about making individuals ready for change. The use of logic and rational argument will not necessarily be enough to convince individuals who may stand to lose a lot by change, or who may have to undertake personal change themselves, or have to invest considerable effort into the change process, that there is a strong need to change.

Unfreezing may occur because a significant change in the environment has led to a decline in the organizational performance that is tangible to all employees, such as the arrival of new competitors leading to a sharp decline in market share, or a take-over or sell-off. This may lead to a felt need for change that can be capitalized on, or possibly even a crisis. But this is not always, and is in fact rarely, the case. If no crisis or felt need for change is evident, then unfreezing has to be managed in some way. There is a variety of different means that can be used and the following section lists only some of them.

5.5.2   Questioning and challenging the status quo

A variety of techniques can be used to encourage staff to question the appropriateness of the existing way of doing things for the organization's longer-term survival:

- Encourage debate about the appropriateness of the current way of operating. This was the technique used to unfreeze the partners and senior managers in KPMG. Illustration 2.6, in Chapter 2 reveals that workshops were run to encourage the KPMG partners to debate the need for change. The senior management conference was used to encourage debate among senior managers about the need for change and what type of change. However, as Chapter 2 also points out, not all levels of staff were involved in these sorts of initiatives, and therefore it could be argued that an awareness and acceptance of the need for change was not generated throughout the organization.

- Disseminate information showing how the organization compares poorly with the organizations with which it competes. This could be done through the use of internal communication media, or it could involve the chief executive of an organization using the business press to tell staff that the organization is performing poorly (9). The fact that the chief executive is talking openly about the organization's performance legitimizes debate.

- Introducing techniques such as 360-degree appraisal, whereby subordinates are given the opportunity to appraise their managers, as well as being appraised themselves by those managers. This can legitimize debate about existing management styles and barriers to change within the organization.

- Questioning and challenging may also be achieved by the symbolic means discussed next.

5.5.3   Symbolic breaks with the past

Making symbolic breaks with the past is about doing things differently to indicate that things are changing. This may then also legitimize questioning and challenging the status quo. There are many different ways of achieving this:

- Senior managers can indicate by their behaviour, or the way they dress, that things are different. John Browne, Chief Executive of British Petroleum, wanted to foster a culture of teamwork and accessibility at BP, so he positioned his office on a middle floor of the company's head office in London, rather than on the top floor. The office has no door, and is next to an open plan area occupied by Browne's fellow executives. Instead of a door, the office has a sliding panel which Browne can close if he requires privacy (10). If managers wish to foster a culture of more open communication, they can run question and answer sessions and workshops on the change process, at which they answer all questions honestly. They can also make a point of being visible in the offices, initiating both social and work-oriented conversations with all levels of staff.

- Changes can be made to the way things are done. Older staff due for promotion may be passed over in favour of outsiders with a different skill-set, and other types of staff may even be made redundant. This is a particularly powerful unfreezing mechanism in any organizations where jobs were always for life and promotion was often linked to length of service rather than performance, although there are not many such organizations left these days. An example would be the move by many of the large UK accounting firms in the early to mid-1990s to make non-performing partners redundant for the first time ever.

- Changes may be subtle. If there is to be more of an emphasis on customer service and less on technical product aspects, then this can be supported by indications of a power shift from production to marketing. Examples of this include giving marketing a larger budget, or moving senior marketing people to more prestigious offices closer to the MD and therefore the central seat of power. Illustration 5.3 reveals that Ericsson Australia tried to use these kinds of symbolic breaks with the past in the early 1990s. To indicate that the organization was to become more focused on customer services, a new structure was

Change in action

Illustration 5.3

Change at Ericsson Australia

In the early 1990s, the MD of Ericsson Australia, Kjell Sorme, attempted to change the organization from a bureaucratic, technology-focused company, to one with a focus on customer service as well as engineering. Specialist customer divisions became the drivers of the business, with the more technical divisions, such as design and engineering, supporting them. The workforce was reduced from 2,500 to 1,800, with the largest cuts in manufacturing. New recruits have been taken on since, but into service and marketing roles.

By 1993, despite additional initiatives, such as a mission statement, a strategic plan and many change projects, it was realized that these initiatives alone were insufficient. They did not enable individuals to understand in what way they had to change. Therefore, a new mission statement was developed for Ericsson, and a programme called Leading Change put in place for all senior and middle managers, which ran from October 1993 to March 1994.

The main focus of Leading Change was to challenge the existing way of thinking within the organization, and to better equip managers with the necessary change skills. Each programme started with an address on the need for change from Sorme, followed by video interviews with Ericsson customers. These interviews contained the customer's assessment of their relationship with Ericsson and their future expectations. The rest of the course introduced the managers to a number of change tools tailored to suit Ericsson's needs. The aim of these tools was not only to challenge existing mindsets, but also to encourage the programme participants to have a commitment to the changes needed at Ericsson and a sense of urgency.

(Adapted from: Fiona Graetz, 'Leading Strategic Change at Ericsson', *Long Range Planning*, 29, 1996, pp. 304–11.)

developed in which specialist customer services divisions became drivers of the business, which the technical functional divisions had to
support. Manufacturing staff numbers were also cut, whilst staff numbers in marketing and service departments were increased with new
hires. However, in Ericsson's case, these initiatives proved insufficient
to unfreeze the organization.

● Symbolic breaks with the past may be more direct and challenging.
Illustration 5.4 describes the change process undertaken by William
Grant and Sons. The symbolic breaks here included the relocation
from West to East Glasgow, the loss of some old employees and the
taking on of new employees, the dismantling of the old organizational
hierarchy, and the setting up of the employee forum. This example
also illustrates that unfreezing is not enough on its own to enable
employees to undertake change. At William Grant, the employees may

Change in action

Illustration 5.4

Implementing change at William Grant and Sons

In the mid-1990s, William Grant and Sons, a Scottish distiller, underwent a
major change. The aim was to move to a team-based organization and leave
behind the old autocratic, paternalistic culture. The bottling plant and administration was moved from West Glasgow to Motherwell in East Glasgow. Some of
the employees from the old plant did not relocate, so new employees from
Motherwell were taken on. The entire workforce was split into teams varying in
size from 3 to 30, who were to run themselves like mini businesses with control
over their own budgets and resources. An employee forum was also established to discuss pay and conditions. As part of the move to teamworking, each
team was supposed to spend an hour each week looking at ideas for improving
their part of the business. But these meetings did not work. The HR Director
compared it to 'drawing teeth'.

A consultant was employed to run a programme of workshops, a series
of two-day events, for all employees, at all levels. The first event took place in
1995 in Motherwell and was for 280 people. For each event, employees gave up
their Sunday, and the event then ran on into the Monday, for which production
was stopped at whichever plant the event was being held. The point of the programme was to help individuals come to an understanding about the way they
and others work, so that they could then see a possible way forward that would
enable self-improvement. The workshops focused on individuals even though
the aim of the programme was to do with better teamworking. Using the programme 'Mindstore' as the starting point, each team has subsequently set
itself goals to improve the way it operates that part of the business.

(Adapted from: Eileen Fursland, 'Breaking Tradition Takes Great Bottle', *People
Management*, 12 September 1996, pp. 34–7.)

have recognized that change was inevitable, but further personal development was required by staff to enable them to work in their teams in the way the vision for the organization required them to do.

5.5.4   *Drastic measures and shock tactics*

Some symbolic changes may be quite ruthless, verging on shock tactics. Such shock symbolic moves could involve wholesale closures or sell-offs of parts of the business that used to be core to the identity of the organization but are no longer. This is common in take-over and turnaround situations. These moves can challenge the very essence of an organization's beliefs about its identity as the following examples demonstrate:

- ICI, previously one of the world's biggest industrial chemicals producers, made a shift into sensory perception products such as fragrances and toothpaste flavourings, in the late 1990s. This was to be achieved by the rapid and wholesale sell-offs of the old core ICI businesses, such as the industrial chemicals division, and the purchase of new businesses. Acquisitions and sales totalled in excess of £9 billion between 1997 and 1998 (11).

- Apple Computer, the manufacturer and vendor of Apple PCs, needed to undertake change in the early 1990s when its products became overpriced and underpowered in comparison with competitor offerings. Apple expanded its product range to move out of its niche market position, and brought out many new products. Apple also reduced costs by consolidating buildings, cutting cafeteria subsidies, and cutting some projects and marketing activities. There were many layoffs. Jobs were moved out of California: 'The Campus' ceased to be the centre of the universe for Apple. One of the holy grails of Apple, that virtually everything was done in-house, was also challenged. The manufacture of components that could be bought elsewhere was subcontracted (12).

- When Ralph Halpern effected change at Burtons to refocus the business on retailing (Chapter 3, Illustration 3.3), he closed down the 'feudal castle', Hudson Road factory in Leeds. Richard Surface at Pearl Assurance (Chapter 3, Illustration 3.2) halved the organization's product range and reformed the salesforce. One thousand jobs were lost.

5.5.5   *Communication, education and training*

This approach could be described as the softly, softly approach to unfreezing. It links into the change management style of communication and education discussed in Chapter 2, although it is also compatible with more participative change approaches. The idea is that if staff are exposed to a different way of thinking and operating they will then use the new set of behaviours required in their working environment. This is often used in combination with one of the other approaches. To return to the example of Ericsson Australia in Illustration 5.3, the use of structural changes to unfreeze the organization were supported by the use of education and communication interventions in the shape of a new mission and vision statement, and the Leading Change programme. This programme is a classic attempt to unfreeze individuals since it embodies three components – making people aware of the need for change, making them aware of the types of changes needed, and equipping them with some of the capabilities needed to then carry out the changes. It is an example of an intervention targeted at changing attitudes and values, rather than just behaviours or outputs.

5.5.6   *Earlier reconstruction or adaptation*

The notion of unfreezing also connects back to the discussion in Chapter 2 on change paths. Sometimes, the unfreezing for an evolutionary or revolutionary change is an earlier change. The examples of this given in Chapter 2 include General Electric and British Airways. In both instances, the initial turnarounds were effected through much 'slashing and burning', which acted in part to unfreeze the organizations for the more fundamental and transformational culture changes which had to follow. However, it must be realized that earlier change may not on its own be sufficient as an unfreezing mechanism. At British Airways, staff had to be made aware of the need for additional cultural change. This was achieved through personal development, in the form of a programme called 'Putting People First' (13). Illustration 5.5 describes how Oticon, the Danish manufacturer of hearing aids, carried out a restructuring followed by more radical transformational change. Again, the start of the second phase of change required more unfreezing interventions, which at Oticon was attempted by a large number of symbolic initiatives.

5.5.7   *Linking unfreezing to design choices*

As with all change interventions, the unfreezing tactics need to be context-specific. What works in one context will not work in another. A key aspect of any successful unfreezing tactic is likely to be novelty, which means doing things differently from the way they have been done in the past. An understanding of an organization's *administrative heritage* may, therefore, be helpful here, especially if an organization wants to communicate a real commitment to change.

Administrative heritage is to do with the organization's history and particularly its change history. It is about the types of events and

Change in action

Illustration 5.5

Unfreezing at Oticon A/S

At Oticon A/S, the Danish manufacturer of hearing aids, subsequent change also required additional unfreezing. The new CEO, Lars Kolind, carried out radical surgery on the organization in the late 1980s, to reverse financial losses and stem the decline in the organization's competitive position brought about partly by competitors' use of new technology. Overhead costs were cut, unprofitable product lines were cut, and 10–15 per cent of the employees at headquarters were made redundant.

However, Kolind wanted Oticon to become a leader in creativity, innovation and flexibility. He wanted to establish an organization consisting of just one team of 150 employees at head office focused on development. To achieve this he wanted all employees to adopt a greater variety of job roles and flexibility, and to eliminate unnecessary work, replace paper with an information system and eliminate office walls. This involved combining the development staff from one office with the management staff at head office, and required additional tactics to make staff ready for such an extensive change. Despite some fierce opposition, in August 1991 Oticon moved to a new office. There were no walls, offices or partitions. Employees had a desk, and sat with the project team on which they were working at any particular time. The central lifts were replaced with a spiral staircase. Traditional job descriptions were scrapped and all employees had to forge their own job roles. Kolind arranged press coverage of the move, and even auctioned off the furniture from the two old offices at an auction to which all staff were invited, to indicate that there was no return.

(Adapted from: R.M. Gould, 'Revolution at Oticon A/S', A and B cases, case numbers OB229 and OB230, 1994, IMD, Lausanne, Switzerland.)

traditions that are remembered by the members of the organization. For instance, previous change attempts may have been always initiated in the same way, perhaps by the appointment of new managers, and the announcement in memos and meetings that changes and some restructuring are to take place. If following these past change initiatives, staff have then seen little change, this would not be a good way to launch a new attempt at change. The approach taken needs to be visibly different. Otherwise, staff will assume that the message of change equals no change, as it has done in the past. Alternatively, it may be that previous change attempts have been very successful, but the changes have been incremental in nature, whereas now the organization needs to undertake radical and more fundamental change. Again, it would be unwise to initiate the latest changes in the same way as previous changes.

The key contextual features will also affect the decision on which sort of unfreezing interventions to use. For example:

- An organization with *little time* to deliver change, and a *low readiness* for change, in which the change agent has the *power* and needs to impose change through a type of *reconstruction* or *revolution*, will need to achieve unfreezing quickly. More dramatic and directive means of unfreezing, such as symbolic breaks with the past and shock tactics, may be necessary. See the example of Apple given above. This would also be consistent with a change approach in which the intent is to *target behavioural* change.

- An organization with *more time* to deliver change, whether through *adaptation* or *evolution*, can utilize techniques such as encouraging a questioning and challenging of the status quo, or communication, education and training. This was the approach taken by Glaxo (Chapter 4, Illustration 4.5). Use could also be made of symbolic breaks with the past, particularly if there is a low readiness for change and time could become a factor if change is not initiated, such as at the retail bank, Lendco (Chapter 4, Illustration 4.4).

- When there is more time, the choice of unfreezing tactic(s) may also depend on whether the change agent has selected a *participative* or *directive* change approach, and the degree of power of the change agent. A change agent with little power can possibly do little other than to encourage questioning and debate to build support. Change agents with more power can utilize a broader range of tactics. The *change target* should also be considered. For example, if the aim is to achieve *value change*, then communication and education, or even personal development interventions, are more likely to be needed as at Lloyd's of London (Chapter 2, Illustration 2.7), if staff are to understand the new values the organization is trying to develop.

- *Diversity* can require the use of different unfreezing tactics for different groups of staff. Chapter 4, Illustration 4.2 describes the situation at an NHS Trust. It is pointed out that different styles of change may be needed for different groups of staff such as consultants and managers. Therefore, different unfreezing tactics would also be needed. For example, tactics such as education and communication are more likely to be appropriate for consultants since this is consistent with the suggested collaborative change style and acknowledges the power they wield – they cannot be compelled to change. For managers, it may be possible to use participative techniques which encourage challenging and questioning.

- If the aim is to deliver change in a bottom-up fashion, then the change agent may need to establish initial communication and workshop seminars to stimulate debate and encourage staff to take ownership for moving the change agenda forwards.

- If an organization ultimately wants to deliver *transformation*, but is either in *crisis*, or for some reason such as a lack of capability or lack of change agent power as at WH Smith (Chapter 4), is unable to embark on a transformation immediately, then the earlier reconstruction or adaptation will contribute to a readiness for future more fundamental change.

5.6 Facilitating personal transitions: the individual level

Organizations only change if the individuals within that organization change. To an external customer, the behaviour of the people that the customer encounters summarizes what the organization stands for. If an organization wants to change the way its customers see it, it has to change the behaviour of its people. Strategic change has to be driven down throughout the organization. Yet, as Chapter 1 explains, all too often, change management is viewed as something that is 'done' to people. Employees of the organization are treated as passive onlookers who will comply with the directives and objectives issued from the top.

Therefore, to achieve change, a change agent needs to understand how individuals change. Change leaders also need to recognize that they have two parallel sets of tasks to manage: first, leading the organization through change, and second, leading the individual organizational members through that change (see Figure 5.4). This is why change capability, as discussed in Chapters 3 and 4, is so important because part of change capability is having the ability to lead staff through change.

Individual transitions can be likened to the bereavement and mourning process. It is a psychological process that research shows all individuals go through. Individuals will experience feelings of loss, and will have to work through those feelings of loss and come to terms with life afterwards (14). This takes time, although varying degrees of time for different individuals. This text uses two concepts to explain

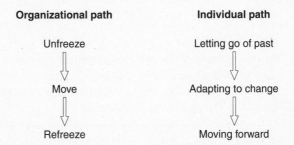

Figure 5.4   *Dual leadership responsibilities – managing the organizational and individual change paths*

how individuals pass through change – the *change equation* and the *transition curve*.

5.6.1   The change equation

The change equation, shown in Figure 5.5, states there are three components that need to be present for individuals to be prepared to undertake change:

1.   The individual needs to feel that the problems and pain that change will cause are outweighed by the need to change.
2.   There needs to be dissatisfaction with the existing status quo.
3.   The proposed changes have to be seen as a viable way of resolving current problems, and the proposed changes have to be seen to be achievable.

Note that the cost of change is not meant to be measurable in financial terms. The 'cost' is more to do with the individual emotional pain and effort associated with change. It acknowledges that change, be it personal or organizational, can be a painful and difficult process for everyone.

This equation is particularly helpful when considering unfreezing. It is also relevant to the discussion in the previous two chapters on readiness for change. Unfreezing individuals is about getting individuals to recognize that change is necessary, and that they have to let go of the past, but also that the proposed changes are desirable in the sense that they will solve the problems the organization is facing, and that they are achievable. An example helps here.

Illustration 2.6, Chapter 2, describes how the changes at KPMG were initiated. One of the steps subsequently taken to make the South-East Region practice, and eventually the whole of KPMG, cus-

$$C = (A + B + D) > X$$

When:

C = Change
A = Level of dissatisfaction with status quo
B = Desirability of proposed change
D = Practicality (risk of disruption) of change
X = Personal cost of changing

Figure 5.5   *The change equation*
(Source: *Adapted from R. Beckhard and R.T. Harris,* Organizational Transitions: Managing Complex Change, *2nd edn, 1987, Addison Wesley)*

tomer-oriented, was to restructure the organization so that audit and consultancy staff were put in common industry-based groups rather than separate discipline-based groups. In one weekend the organization was restructured. Audit and consultancy staff and partners were physically relocated in the KPMG offices to sit within industry groups so as to indicate that from now on they were to work together (15).

This raises the question of whether this relocation was to do with moving or unfreezing. Some managers when asked would argue that it was moving and others unfreezing. Those that argue for the reorganization as a move intervention say it moved the organization towards its future state. Those that argue for the reorganization as an unfreeze intervention say that all it did was to make individuals realize that change was coming. The reorganization on its own did not force individuals to change their behaviours and their attitudes. Sharman agrees with the latter point of view – the reorganization itself had little impact only serving to enable future behavioural change. Indeed, it was commented some time after this initial reorganization that the changes had not been brought down to an individual level. Individuals did not know what they were supposed to do differently (15).

In terms of the change equation, the workshops and conference discussions, and the launch of the '20-20 Vision' followed by the restructuring, were all about creating a dissatisfaction with the status quo and a belief in the suitability of the proposed changes, and then enabling staff to change. This does not mean the restructuring was an insignificant intervention. Unless individuals are made ready for change, they will be less willing and able to undertake change. It takes time for individuals not only to face up to the need for change, but also to then undertake that change. This is illustrated by the concept of the transition curve.

5.6.2   The transition curve

The transition curve (16) describes the process individuals go through during change, and is depicted in Figure 5.6. The transition curve suggests that individuals undergoing change pass through seven stages:

- In *stage 1*, individuals initially experience *shock* when they encounter the need for change, and a dip in their self-confidence due to the need for them to undertake personal change and to do things differently.
- *Stage 2*, *denial*, is a stage when individuals may try to rationalize the changes as not really involving a significant change for themselves. Individuals may try to tell themselves that working in a new role will involve nothing different from their current role. As a result their self-confidence goes back up again, but this denial can also prevent them

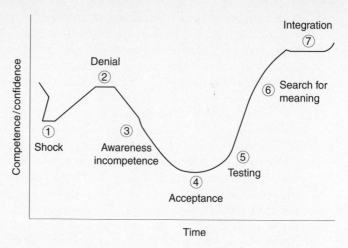

Figure 5.6   *The transition curve*
(Source: *Based on J. Adams, J. Hayes and B. Hopson,* Transition: Understanding and Managing Personal Change, *1976, London: Martin Robertson & Company)*

from moving forwards. Trying to fulfil a new job in the same way as they did their old one may mean they do not perform well.

- To move on to *stage 3, awareness,* individuals need to develop a recognition of the need for personal change. However, acquiring this awareness, which may be prompted by discussion with others, or a recognition that old ways of doing things no longer work, also brings with it a *drop in confidence* as individuals become aware of their inadequacy to fulfil their new role.

- Individuals will be able to move forward to *stage 4, acceptance,* when they can accept the need to let go of the past – to let go of old attitudes and behaviours and adopt new ones.

- *Stage 5, testing,* is to do with identifying and testing out new behaviours, perhaps as a result of training. As new behaviours start to enable individuals to perform more adequately in their new role, confidence starts to build again.

- By *stage 6, search,* the individual is assimilating learning from their successes and failures, and starting to understand why some behaviours work and others do not.

- *Stage 7, integration,* is marked by an integration of new behaviours into the everyday way of working by individuals. There ceases to be a gap between an individual's perceived ability to perform and the expectations placed on that individual.

5.6.3 Experiencing the transition curve

Illustrations 5.6 and 5.7 depict change journeys experienced by individuals. Illustration 5.6 describes the journey undertaken by an individual who quickly adapted to a transition to a new job role, whereas Illustration 5.7 shows an individual who adapted, but found the process far more traumatic than the first. Both examples illustrate well the emotional nature of the individual transitions, and the second powerfully shows how an individual can need a lot of help to get through a personal transition. Some individuals never complete the transition. They get stuck half-way through, and never really recover from the feeling of loss and that things used to be better in the old days.

The headings 'sensing', 'shock' and 'despair' in Illustration 5.7 demonstrate how hard it can be for an individual to let go of the past and come to terms with the need for change. Similarly, the headings 'disorganization', 'realization', 'steadying', 'testing' and 'acceptance' in Illustrations 5.6 and 5.7 reveal the feelings of loss and inadequacy that individuals can experience as they try to understand what is expected of them and what they need to do, but also how there is a gradual

Change in action

Illustration 5.6

A rapid adaptation

Journey	Reaction
Shock	'I was offered the job in the morning and started in the afternoon. I knew what the job was, but there was an awful lot to learn.'
▼	
Acceptance	'It wasn't planned and it meant a significant change to my life, but I welcomed it – I wouldn't have liked to have stayed in my previous job.'
▼	
Testing	'I learnt very quickly, I asked a lot of questions, read a lot and quickly got on top of the job. I gave the appearance of being in control within days – though, of course, there were many months of learning.'
▼	
Moving on	'I'm in control.'

(Adapted from: Roger Stuart, 'Experiencing Organisational Change: Triggers, Processes and Outcomes of Change Journeys', *Personnel Review*, 24, 2, 1995.)

Change in action

Illustration 5.7

A painful adaptation

Journey	Reaction
Sensing ▼	'I'd been getting all sorts of messages.'
Shock ▼	'It was totally contrary to everything that I'd been told.'
Despair ▼	'I felt very criticized, not understood and totally incompetent.'
Disorganization ▼	'I felt totally confused. I thought that I must be going nuts. Had I the right perception? Paranoid? I'd lost all sense of judgement, I felt out of control; Doubt. Am I dreaming this?'
Yearning ▼	'I had vivid dreams, replaying the events leading up to . . . replaying them in different ways. It was like a dreadful nightmare.'
Despair ▼	'I felt isolated but was unable to talk to other people. I had a real feeling of desperation. At one stage, I didn't think I'd survive. It was a desperate time.'
Realization ▼	'I realized that I had no alternative. I had got to get my self-esteem and credibility back into shape sufficiently to carry on. I had to own up and take responsibility for what I'd done; I felt betrayed, cheapened and scapegoated. I was very angry with the organization for blaming me. I am responsible but look what you made me do.'
Steadying ▼	'I moved (within the organization). I spent a long time wilfully forgetting. I started to feel better – a sense of more stability. I was defensive – fearful that things could get out of control again.'
Testing ▼	'I was continuously building anew. I attended courses, some things went well; It took a long time to feel better about myself.'
Meaning ▼	'Getting a clear view of what I'm good and not good at. Developing my understanding of the reality and limits of my relationship with the organization.'
Sharing ▼	'It was important to talk about it.'
Moving on	'I feel powerful. I've put things into perspective and learned from them. It is okay to be me and to trust my perception – and that it's not the only one.'

(Adapted from: Roger Stuart, 'Experiencing Organisational Change: Triggers, Processes and Outcomes of Change Journeys', *Personnel Review*, 24, 2, 1995.)

acceptance that change is necessary. 'Moving on' in Illustrations 5.6 and 5.7 is about the individuals emerging on the other side of change, feeling competent to perform in their new roles.

5.6.4 Linking the management of personal transitions to design choices

Illustrations 5.6 and 5.7 show that individuals pass through the transition curve at a different rate and in a different way. The curve depicts a typical pattern or response rather than a prescriptive route that all individuals adhere to. It also shows that resistance to change is a natural phenomenon associated, like grieving, with a reluctance to give up possessions, people, status and expectations (17).

The concept of the transition curve can be combined with the unfreeze, move and sustain model, as shown in Figure 5.7, to help remind designers of what change interventions in these phases are trying to achieve for the individual recipients:

- The stages of *shock*, *denial* and *awareness*, accompanied by feelings of loss, fits with the change equation and *unfreezing*. Interventions aimed at helping individuals to come to terms with the need for change

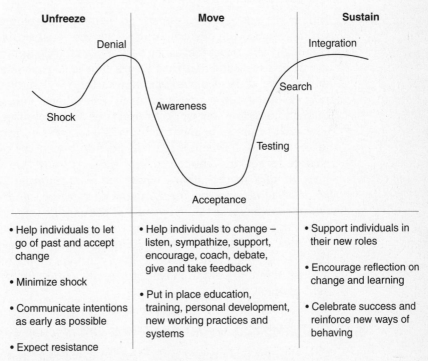

Figure 5.7   Three levels of interaction

and to let go of the past would, therefore, be built into the unfreeze phase through the types of unfreezing tactics discussed above. The unfreezing tactic(s) adopted would still need to match the context and the selected design choices.

- The experience of individuals as they move through *acceptance*, *testing* and *search* will underpin the *move* phase. Thus interventions such as education and training, personal development, new work procedures and systems, and new management styles, which help individuals through these stages should all be included in the move phase. Coaching and counselling, from either internal or external facilitators, for staff who are having problems adapting may also be necessary here.

- The range of *levers and mechanisms* deployed in the *move* phase will need to fit the design choices selected. In circumstances where there is little *time* or *money*, it may prove difficult to provide support through counselling or coaching to staff members who are struggling. There may have to be a trade-off between what is ideal and what is possible. The emphasis may need to be on changes to structures and systems, with imposed changes to roles and responsibilities, and new service and quality targets. If the required change is *transformational* in nature, it will be necessary to drive in value change and not just behavioural change. The levers and mechanisms will need to reflect this with a greater emphasis on personal development, communication, counselling and coaching rather than just skills-based training. Similarly, if a *participative* or *bottom-up* change approach is selected, it will be necessary to utilize levers that encourage staff participation and enable staff to have some say in the way change develops. This may mean greater investment in workshops and cross-functional teams to develop new working practices and procedures.

- The *sustain* phase is about helping the *integration* process. Again the levers and mechanisms used will need to match the design choices of change target and change levers. Interventions that can be particularly helpful in this phase when the *change target* is *behaviours* or *values* include reward mechanisms to reinforce and support behavioural change undertaken by staff. If the change target is *outputs*, such levers may have been used in the move phase. Symbolic interventions can also be helpful here to reinforce change. Since both human resource systems and symbolic interventions as levers of change are discussed in more detail in Chapter 6, this point will be revisited in the next chapter.

5.7   *Designing and sequencing levers and mechanisms*

This chapter has argued so far that to move an organization from the current to the future state, it is necessary to unfreeze the organization and ready the organizational members for change, then to move the organization by putting in place a series of interventions that will lead to the desired changes in values and behaviours, and then finally to sustain the changes to prevent individuals backsliding into old ways of behaving. This chapter has also suggested that many of the levers and mechanisms to use should already have been identified, by developing a new web with new systems, structures, routines and symbols, and by considering the barriers to change and how to overcome them. Unfreezing tactics have also been discussed. Other levers and mechanisms may have been identified when considering the change levers to use as part of the initial design choices. What now needs to be done is to put the unfreeze, move and sustain phases together with the identified levers and mechanisms to determine when to do what. However, it must be recognized that there is still additional work to be done on designing levers and mechanisms, some of which are discussed in more detail in Chapter 6.

5.7.1 Three levels of change

It has already been pointed out above that, particularly if the change is transformational in nature, many communication, education and development interventions may be necessary. These interventions will be in addition to the levers and mechanisms than can be identified from something such as a web analysis, but they are important for facilitating the process of individual transitions. Therefore, the model to be used here in conjunction with the Lewin model is one that reminds us that change involves not just moving and altering the organization, but also the individuals within it. Change can be thought of as occurring within organizations on three levels – individual, climate, and structures and systems (18) as represented in Figure 5.8.

- Changing *individuals* who work in an organization is about changing their skills, values, attitudes and behaviours. The changes have to be supportive of the overall organizational changes desired. For example, if an organization wants to introduce customer–supplier relationships between divisions, but as a result of the change interventions employees start to behave in a way that best protects their own immediate business interests, with little concern for any impact on any other businesses, this is a change, but not one that supports the desired change outcome.
- Changing *structures and systems* is about changing all formal and informal organizational and political structures, all systems, including HR systems, all processes and procedures, and all roles, responsibilities and relationships.
- Changing the *organizational climate* is about changing the way people relate to each other in an organization, and the management style. It

	Unfreeze	Move	Sustain
Individual	Changing skills, values, attitudes and behaviours		
Structures and systems	Changing all formal and informal organizational structures and systems		
Climate	Changing the way people relate to each other		

Figure 5.8   Three levels of interaction
(Source: Adapted from L.D. Goodstein and W.W. Burke, 'Creating Successful Organizational Change', Organizational Dynamics, 19, 4, 1991, pp. 5–17)

may, for example, include changes to how conflict is managed, how decisions are made, how staff are managed and treated, and how open people are with each other. Often what are described as overall features of culture, for example, a blame/control culture, or an open, friendly culture, amount to the organizational climate.

It is possible to start the process of mapping out which levers and mechanisms to use when, by deploying the levers and mechanisms identified in the re-webbing exercise, along with the selected unfreezing tactics, and any levers and mechanisms needed to overcome identified barriers to change, across the unfreeze, move and sustain phases. Symbolic and routine changes are more likely to have an individual impact and affect the organizational climate, whereas changes in structures and control systems are more likely to alter the organizational system in which the individual works. However, faced with the three levels the change agent is forced to consider what additional interventions, such as communication, personal development, reward mechanisms and resistance management, are needed to achieve the individual changes desired.

Exactly how to use the model given in Figure 5.8 is easier to explain with reference to an example. Illustration 5.8 maps out the unfreeze, move and sustain process at Baxi Heating. Chapter 2 has already shown in Illustration 2.9 the degree of change undertaken at Baxi between the late 1980s and 1992/93 in order to become more competitive and profitable. The range of levers and mechanisms used to facilitate this transition was extensive (19).

- *Unfreezing*: Initially, the focus was on improving manufacturing systems. Change was attempted by introducing Just-in-Time techniques and restructuring the organization into teams. However, this proved insufficient to move the organization forward. Much resistance surfaced. It was necessary to create an environment which enabled continuous improvement and greater staff autonomy. The organization

Change in action

Illustration 5.8
Change at Baxi Partnership

	Unfreeze	Move	Sustain
Individual	• Rising costs and declining efficiency • Signs of reduced demand/recession • Communication programme to support Just-in-Time implementation • Redundancies • Consultant-led audit and benchmark of manufacturing capability	• Staff training and development – continuous improvement and re-engineering • Managerial strategic development • Increasing market share for Baxi • Self-management of teams • Company-sponsored night-school education • Clocking on abolished • Appraisal and counselling introduced • New staff restaurant	• Winner of Investor in People • Performance-based appraisal • Continuous learning • 70 per cent increase in profits • Increase in employee share price • Nil grievance and disciplinary issues for next three years
Structures and systems	• Implementation of Just-in-Time in manufacturing plants • Introduction of team-based working • Organization redesign – from functions to product groups • Reduced hierarchy – manufacturing teams	• Continuous improvement teams (CIT) • Business processes re-engineered • New financial systems introduced • Manufacturing sites reduced from 4 to 2 • Reduced finalized goods in stock and work in progress • Manufacturing cycle down from 11 weeks to 24 hours	• European acquisitions and joint ventures • Two business units converted to independent companies • Federal group board structure • Market based IS • CIT presentations – sharing know-how
Climate	• Increasing tensions between shopfloor, management and unions • 1990 Pay negotiations – on pay rates, teamworking and redundancies	• Teamworking • Employee established return to work unit	• Trusting and open dialogue • New product launch – increasing confidence • Dynamic and assertive

(Prepared by Simon Carter, of Transition Strategies Limited, 1992.)

was restructured into product-based groups in January 1990, and there were also some redundancies, a move unprecedented in the organization's history.

- *Movement*: An extensive business process re-engineering initiative was undertaken to drive in the performance improvements needed. To achieve this, staff were trained in continuous improvement techniques and were placed in continuous improvement teams. Teams became self-managing, and many initiatives were put in place to improve the working environment and individual accountability, such as a new restaurant, new HR systems, the abolition of clocking on, and the sponsorship of self-improvement for employees at night-school. The employees supported these changes, even developing themselves a unit to facilitate return to work for employees who had been off work for a long while. As part of the changes manufacturing was also consolidated onto two sites from the previous four.
- *Sustain*: It was Baxi's success following these changes that then acted to reinforce and sustain the changes. Baxi gained the Investor in People award. Profits and the share price increased. There was a new product launch and acquisitions and joint ventures. Other initiatives were also put in place to sustain the changes, such as performance-based appraisal, market-based information systems and sharing of know-how across the business to foster continuous learning.

5.7.2 Linking the sequencing of levers and mechanisms to the design choices

Some managers question whether it is really possible to plan out in advance an entire organizational transition as described in this chapter. The answer is probably not, but this is also affected by the design choices. For example:

- In more *participative* and *bottom-up* change approaches, such as the change process described at the Open University (Chapter 2, Illustration 2.3), later interventions may be dependent on ideas developed from earlier change workshops. Similarly, mechanisms that are to be used to sustain the organizational changes may come about in an evolutionary manner. They may be developed in an opportunistic fashion for the entire organization from initiatives that are being used successfully in just one part of the organization. In such situations less preplanning will be appropriate.
- If the change process is to be more *directive* and imposed, particularly within a *tight timescale*, it may be both possible and desirable to be more precise about what changes are to occur when.
- Even in change processes designed to be more *evolutionary* and *emergent* over time, it is useful to give careful thought to how the status quo

is to be challenged to achieve unfreezing. Further, some of the early choices that need to be made, such as whether reward and selection systems are to be used to sustain the changes or as part of the move phase, do need to be given consideration. One difference between more *collaborative* and more *directive* change processes, may be more to do with who is involved in, or consulted on, the design of the process, rather than the unfreeze, move and sustain path selected.

- *Timescales* have an impact. It is possible that in a *big-bang* change process the different interventions that need to be put in place occur so rapidly that it is hard to distinguish between unfreeze, move and sustain interventions. This appears to have been the case at Pearl Assurance (Chapter 3, Illustration 3.2). When rapid reconstruction is a precursor to more fundamental change, in retrospect all the reconstruction initiatives may become a series of shock interventions which unfreeze the organization for the next step in the overall change path.
- The *change target* can have a major influence. If the target is just *behaviours*, or just *outputs*, as may be the case for *adaptation* as well as *reconstruction*, then the interventions aimed at achieving change in the individual and climate subsystems may be minimal, since more fundamental change to values and management styles are not actually required as part of the change process.

The strength of a model such as the unfreeze, move and sustain model is not to do with the answers it gives, but the questions it forces change agents to ask. Without such a model, it is all too easy to put in place a series of interventions which have little effect because the members of the organization are not ready for change and do not understand what the changes are all about. It is also possible to leave the changes unfinished, because steps are not taken to institutionalize the changes.

Similarly, without the connection of the organizational change process to the individual change process through the transition curve, particularly when attempting to undertake more fundamental change, it is possible to underestimate the range of interventions needed to achieve the required individual changes. It is also necessary to remember that different levels of the organization may be at different stages at different times. Senior managers may have progressed to the move phase whilst interventions aimed at unfreezing lower level staff are still being put in place.

5.8 Key questions to consider when designing unfreeze, move and sustain

Working out exactly what to do to achieve change, even with the outline unfreeze, move and sustain model presented above, is still complex.

---

1. Is there a coherent strategy understood and shared throughout the organization?
2. Are supporting structures and systems under development?
3. Is there a trigger for change or has one been manufactured?
4. Are there visible 'early wins' designed into the change process?
5. Are day-to-day activities aligned to get required outputs?
6. Are the identified barriers to change being removed/dealt with?
7. Are changes supported with symbolic activity?
8. Is communication built into the change process?

Figure 5.9   The eight key questions to consider when planning a

No wonder change agents resort to off-the-shelf recipes or call in consultants. Furthermore, whereas it is assumed that readers will have a knowledge of how to design new structures and systems from *Exploring Corporate Strategy*, there are many other interventions mentioned above that they need to know more about, such as communication, education, management development and symbolic activity, to name just a few. These cannot all be covered in this chapter.

Figure 5.9, therefore, details eight key questions to consider when developing an outline of an unfreeze, move and sustain transition process and the sequence in which the levers and mechanisms should be deployed. It should be noted, as explained extensively above, that the order in which these questions are considered and dealt with may differ from context to context. The eight questions are not meant to be a prescriptive step-by-step list. For example, in a more emergent, and bottom-up change process unfreezing may need to occur before it is possible to get a sufficient mass of people involved to develop a clear strategy. Whereas in a top-down and directive change process it may be appropriate for the change agent to start with the formulation of a clear vision for the organization.

1. Is there a coherent strategy understood and shared throughout the organization?

The overall strategy needs to be translated not just into a clear vision that can be shared and understood throughout the organization, but also broken up into actionable pieces. Any change initiative is likely to consist of a number of major projects, such as redesigning work processes and procedures, office and depot relocations, designing and installing new equipment and technology, job redesign, the introduction of total quality and/or continuous improvement techniques, and possibly business process re-engineering. Furthermore, even a restructuring may involve intermediate steps. It is therefore necessary to create coherence from all these projects, not just in terms of a unifying vision, but also to understand dependencies between projects. The way these projects are to be managed and run will be determined by the change start point and management style selected.

This is a very important step. It is the major projects that will determine most of the resource requirements for the change process in addition to the resources needed to keep the business going during the transition. The projects, their links and interdependencies, and their resource requirements, will form the basis of the change plan. This text does not have space to discuss project management as such, but obviously, in any major change project, project management has a key role to play. At some point a plan, or maybe multiple plans by business division, detailing what is to be done, when and by whom, has to be put together. Progress has to be monitored against this plan.

2. Are supporting structures and systems under development?

Consideration must be given to levers and mechanisms to do with formal and informal organization structures and power structures, information systems, management systems, measurement systems and HR systems. Systems extend from the way budgets are developed to how quickly phones are answered. Most of the needed changes to structures and systems should have been identified by a detailed cultural web analysis, discussed above in section 5.3.3.

At this point it is now necessary to consider when to implement what. Is the new structure to be put in place to enable changes as part of the unfreeze, or are interrelationships and responsibilities within the new structure to be allowed to evolve and then be institutionalized through formal systems and reporting relationships in the sustain phase? Is the new structure to be put in place immediately, or are there to be some sort of interim structure and management mechanisms? Similar questions need to be asked about the new systems. Which are to be used to challenge the status quo, and which to sustain the changes? New measurement systems on, for example, customer service levels, may be used to challenge, and new reward mechanisms may be used to sustain the changes.

It must be stressed, and some people find this extremely frustrating, that there is no prescribed formula for the order in which to do things. The chosen order will depend on the design choices made, but it will also depend on the suitability or feasibility of the proposed levers within the organization's context. Organizations which have recently put in place a new pay structure, or need to engage in lengthy union negotiations to change the reward and promotion mechanisms, for example, may feel that HR systems are an inappropriate place to start. Such an organization may decide that reward and selection systems are to be used to institutionalize the changes, whereas more ad hoc bonuses and non-financial acknowledgement of appropriate new behaviour will be given during the move phase.

3. Is there a trigger for change or has one been manufactured?

This question is about designing the unfreezing process as much as anything else. It has been discussed in some length above, particularly in terms of unfreezing tactics.

4. Are there visible 'early wins' designed into the change process?

Unfreezing can be helped by making demonstrably successful changes early on, which is sometimes referred to as making 'early wins' or 'picking the low hanging fruit'. AID analysis – attractiveness versus implementation difficulty – shown in Illustration 5.9, can be used to help identify which projects should be tackled first to give demonstrable early wins that symbolically indicate that change is first, achievable, and second, going to happen whether individuals like it or not. However, this step may not just be about identifying projects to put in place early on. This step may also include things such as system changes which remove old ways of doing things that staff have consistently identified as a barrier to change. It involves any interventions that the recipients of change can identify as a positive step on the way to change, and that can be used as an example of progress and success.

5. Are day-to-day activities aligned to get required outputs?

This is about understanding which routines to change or remove, and which new routines to put into place, and when. However, it also includes the design of HR systems (rewards, appraisals, selection, training and management development), and giving further consideration to additional control systems that may be needed. As such, it overlaps with step 2. Since HR systems can play a very important role in shaping an individual's behaviour, they are also discussed in more detail in the next chapter.

Routines can be hard to diagnose. Some routines may encapsulate the overall way staff operate. For example, in many service organizations that are not customer focused, and are traditionally risk averse, staff may follow a general routine of 'process before sales', which means that when faced with a form and a customer, a member

Change in action

Illustration 5.9

Attractiveness vs. implementation difficulty

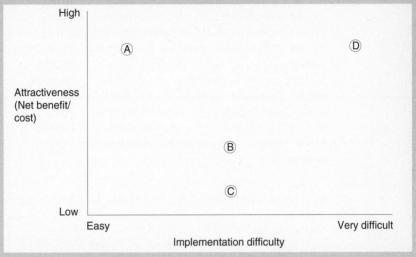

Position projects and change initiatives according to the degree to which they are difficult to implement, and how attractive they are in terms of the benefits they deliver with respect to the costs. When considering difficulty of implementation think about the number of barriers, and likely stakeholder responses to the initiatives. In the above example, project A may be a good project for early wins. The viability of initiative C given its low benefits should be questioned, and project D needs further consideration of what can be done to ease its implementation.

(Adapted from: Tony Grundy, 'Strategy Implementation and Project Management', *Journal of Project Management*, 16, 1, 1998, pp. 34–50.)

of staff will first worry about filling the form in correctly, and the customer and their concerns second. Such routines are likely to be identified as part of the web analysis.

However, managers may not know what all the daily routines followed by their staff are, even though some of these routines may create inefficiencies and blockages to change. Such routines will only be identified when projects examining existing working practices are undertaken, and will have to be tackled at that time. An alternative way of gaining an understanding of routines and ways of working that are blocking change is through much wider participation in the change process by employees. Arguably, the GE Work-Out process (Illustration

2.2, Chapter 2) is a technique for identifying organizational routines which are not consistent with the new desired way of working. Chris Knight, Chairman of Shell Malaysia, used one-day events called 'valentines', a technique borrowed from Ford, to uncover ways of behaving which would inhibit Knight's intent to develop a customer services centre, which was to have the authority to act as necessary to meet customer needs. At each event around a hundred employees from across a range of functions were split into much smaller functional groups. Each group wrote 'valentines' to the other functional groups stating how they felt that group's behaviour could prevent the success of the customer service centre. Each group then selected two of the valentines it had been sent, developed a plan to resolve the selected issues, and appointed a group member to take responsibility for delivery of the plan, along with a member of the group who sent the valentine to help (20).

6. Are the identified barriers to change being removed/dealt with?

If levers and mechanisms have not already been developed to deal with the structures, networks, cliques, stakeholders, routines, control systems and symbols that have been explicitly identified as barriers to change, this must be built into the change process. It also needs to be decided when these barriers should be removed. Some of the old symbols and ways of operating may be removed as part of the unfreezing tactics; other routine ways of behaving may be harder to change and require additional interventions in the move phase.

7. Are changes supported with symbolic activity?

Symbolic activity can be built into all three change phases, with a particular impact on the individual level and the climate, in order to support the changes taking place. This is a very important topic and will be developed further in the next chapter.

8. Is communication built into the change process?

Again, this is an area of critical importance during change, which can be broadened to include education and personal development. It will also be developed further in the next chapter. Broadly, a communications strategy needs to be developed which underpins all three phases of change, to help individuals to both understand and achieve what is expected of them, and to keep them informed of progress and developments.

5.9 Summary

This chapter has explained the concept of the transition state as an intermediate state between where an organization is now and where it wants to be in the future. The transition state requires explicit consideration of how it is to be designed and managed:

- The transition state can be conceived in terms of three change phases – unfreeze, move and sustain. However, it must be recognized that any organizational transition through these three phases is underpinned by the process of individual change and the transition curve. Organizations can only change what they do if the people within them change. A key need is to design a range of levers and mechanisms to facilitate the transition of individuals, and thereby the organization, to the desired future organizational state, and determine how to sequence these levers and mechanisms through the transition.

- To be able to design the levers and mechanisms, it is necessary to ensure that there is a vision of the desired future state. The understanding of the desired future state can also be used to diagnose potential barriers to change.

- Some of the levers and mechanisms to be deployed will be identified when the cultural web is used to formulate the picture of the desired future organization. Others will be identified by a consideration of how to deal with the barriers to change and how to achieve unfreezing. Still others will already have been identified when considering the change levers to use as part of the initial design choices. However, additional interventions, particularly in terms of communication, education, training, personal development, human resource systems and resistance management, also require consideration.

- To help complete the design of the levers and mechanisms, and decide how to sequence the chosen interventions, it is useful to consider the three organizational levels within the unfreeze, move and sustain phases – namely the individual, climate and structures and systems. These levels help to focus attention on the additional levers and mechanisms needed to help individuals through change and facilitate the development of an appropriate organizational climate.

   An additional design complexity is to ensure that there is a match between the selected change approach and the design of the transition state. The next two chapters build on this chapter, by extending consideration of levers and mechanisms such as communication, symbolic activity, human resource systems, and politics, and by considering how change agents should actually manage the transition once it is underway.

Notes and references

(1) Such colourful language is used by N.M. Tichy and M.A. Devanna, *The Transformational Leader,* 1990, Canada: John Wiley.

(2) The concept of change as three states – the present, the future and the transition – is advanced by R. Beckhard and R.T. Harris, *Organizational Transitions: Managing Complex Change,* 2nd edition, 1987, Addison Wesley.

(3) The development of vision statements is discussed by J. Kotter, *Leading Change,* 1996, Boston, MA: Harvard Business School Press. By D.A. Nadler and M.L. Tushman, 'Organizational Frame Bending: Principles for Managing Reorientation', *The Academy of Management Executive*, III, 3, 1990, pp. 194–204. And also by T. Jick, *The Vision Thing (A),* 1989, Harvard Business School Case, N9-490-019.

(4) For full story of change at SKF see S. Vandermerwe and M. Taishoff, *SKF Bearings Series: Market Orientation Through Services*, cases A and B, 1990, IMD, case numbers 591-019-1 and 591-020-1.

(5) See N. Obolensky, 'Birmingham Midshires Building Society', *Practical Business Re-engineering,* 1994, London: Kogan Page.

(6) Re-webbing, along with designing new structures, control systems and routines as change levers, is not discussed in detail in this text, as it is discussed in *Exploring Corporate Strategy*. See also G. Johnson, 'Mapping and Re-mapping Organisational Culture', in V. Ambrosini, G. Johnson, and K. Scholes (eds), *Exploring Techniques of Analysis and Evaluation in Strategic Management*, 1998, Hemel Hempstead: Prentice Hall.

(7) The original development of force-field analysis is in K. Lewin, 'Frontiers in Group Dynamics', *Human Relations*, 1, 1, 1947, pp. 5–41. For some practical advice on developing force-field analyses see T. Grundy, 'Strategy Implementation and Project Management', *International Journal of Project Management,* 16, 1, 1998, pp. 43–50.

(8) The unfreeze, move and refreeze model of change developed by K. Lewin ('Group Decision and Social Change', in E.E. Maccoby, T.M. Newcomb and E.L. Hartley (eds), *Readings in Social Psychology*, pp. 197–211, 1958, New York: Holt, Rienhart and Winston) remains one of the most widely used change models.

(9) B. Spector discusses unfreezing mechanisms in 'From Bogged Down to Fired Up: Inspiring Organizational Change', *Sloan Management Review,* Summer 1989.

(10) See A. Lorenz, 'BP boss drives change through the pipeline', *The Sunday Times*, 26 April 1998, p. 9, for a full account.

(11) See H. Connon, 'Developing a taste for the sweet smell of success', *Observer*, 5 April 1998, Business Section, p. 6, for a report on the repositioning of ICI.

(12) The full story of the changes at Apple is detailed in David B. Yoffie,

Apple Computer 1992, 1992, Harvard Business School Publishing, case number 9-792-081.

(13) This intervention is described in J. Leahey and J.P. Kotter, *Changing the Culture at British Airways*, 1990, Harvard Business School, case number 9-491-009.

(14) For additional information on how individuals experience change, and what helps individuals through the change process, see W. Bridges, *Managing Transitions: Making the Most of Change*, 1991, Addison Wesley.

(15) See the case studies on KPMG within G. Johnson and K. Scholes, *Exploring Corporate Strategy, Text and Cases*, 5th edition, 1999, Hemel Hempstead: Prentice Hall. For additional information on the change process at KPMG see 'KPMG', an interview with Colin Sharman, *Exploring Corporate Strategy: The Video*, by G. Johnson and K. Scholes, 1997.

(16) The transition curve is based on the ideas presented by J. Adams, J. Hayes and B. Hopson, *Transition: Understanding and Managing Personal Change,* 1976, London: Martin Robertson and Company.

(17) This can be seen from texts such as C.M. Parkes, *Bereavement Studies of Grief in Adult Life*, 1986, London: Penguin.

(18) This version of the unfreeze, move and refreeze model is discussed in more detail in L.D. Goodstein and W.W. Burke, 'Creating Successful Organization Change', *Organizational Dynamics*, 19, 4, 1991, pp. 5–17.

(19) More information on the change process at Baxi can be found in C. Bowman and S. Carter, 'Organising for competitive advantage', *European Management Journal*, 13, 4, 1995, pp. 423–33.

(20) This approach to change, along with other approaches, is discussed in R. Pascale, M. Millemann and L. Gioja, 'Changing the Way We Change', *Harvard Business Review*, November–December 1997, pp. 127–39.

6 Designing the transition: levers and mechanisms

6.1 Introduction

The previous chapter explained how to conceive the actual change implementation, the transition state, as having three phases – unfreeze, move and sustain. Chapter 5 also discussed how to diagnose the barriers to change that need to be removed, how to unfreeze an organization, and how to sequence the selected levers and mechanisms throughout the transition. This chapter builds on this, by focusing on the design of some additional levers and mechanisms required to effect change during the transition period. It considers:

- Using communication, both verbal and symbolic, as a lever to facilitate the change process, and help individuals through the transition.
- Resistance management and politics as change levers which can be used to overcome reluctance to change among both change recipients and those who may need to play an active role in change implementation.
- Building new human resource management systems, including the way staff are selected, appraised and rewarded, as levers to support change.
- Using personal development and training to facilitate change.

The chapter also discusses how these interventions can be used to help unfreeze and move an organization, and ultimately sustain the changes put in place.

6.2 Communication during change

One of the key things to remember when communicating with other people is that what the speaker thinks she or he has said, and what the listeners hear, may not be the same thing. Communication is not the transfer of meaning (1), since it is the listener who creates the meaning for themselves. Everyone knows the game of Chinese whispers. Someone whispers a message to their neighbour, who then whispers that message to their neighbour and so on. The message that the last person in the line receives, when recited back, is usually nothing like the message the first person communicated to their neighbour. In reality, even when messages are not communicated by whispers, they still change as they are conveyed from one person to another. This is not just due to an imperfect memory for things that have been heard and read. Individuals communicate in many different ways. They communicate not just by the words and language they use, but also through their body language, the words and phrases they emphasize, and the degree of emotion used.

This is problematic in change situations as the message that counts for change recipients is, of course, the one they have received. The recipients then act on the basis of their interpretation of a message, which may not be the same as the speaker intended. The interpretations recipients arrive at are also affected by a variety of other things, including previous ways of doing things, and personal circumstances and experiences. Communication during change has to be designed to take this into account.

One of the advocated techniques for overcoming misunderstandings is to provide *message repetition*. This is the provision of the same information several times, by repeating the same message in a different way, or by conveying the same message by different means of communication, throughout the change process. Techniques such as verbal and written communication, but also non-verbal and symbolic means of communication, such as changing artefacts or using ritual, behaviour, language and stories, can be used to convey certain messages and implications about change. Effective change agents need to understand the many different means by which they are communicating with their staff, so that they can be conscious of what they may be communicating both intentionally and unintentionally, but also so that they can utilize the *different communication mechanisms* to help get their message across.

6.3 Verbal communication

Verbal communication includes both written and spoken communication. There are four issues to consider – timing, communication channels, message content and message presenter.

6.3.1 Timing of communication

When to communicate what is a serious issue. There is no ideal time. Employees will always want as much information as soon as possible, whereas the designers of the changes may want to give as little information as possible, until they are completely clear about what is to be done. The designers may also be concerned about issues of confidentiality; openness may not be possible. However, change agents need to be aware that:

- Employees resent hearing of change from sources other than management, such as the press (2), and there is a need to control potentially harmful rumours.
- The later the communication, the less the time and opportunity for employees to absorb, understand and adjust to what they are being told. Readiness for change helps to reduce resistance.
- Incomplete announcements and honesty are better than cover-ups (2). If managers are not honest early on, they will lose their credibility. Even if in the early stages of change it is not possible to explain all the details, it may be possible to inform staff of options being considered, and provide timetables of when staff should be informed of decisions.
- Details will always leak out, even if those leading the change have adopted a policy of silence on the changes under consideration (3).

The types of communication needed during a transition can be mapped against the unfreeze, move and sustain model introduced in the previous chapter (see Figure 6.1):

- In the early days of change, communication should be timed to achieve a readiness for change as part of unfreezing.
- As change progresses towards the move phase, the communication should start to focus more on giving individuals the information and support they need to undertake the changes being asked of them, and also on reducing the uncertainty and ambiguity individuals will be experiencing as they attempt to understand 'what does this all mean for me?'.
- Update information on the progress of change and what is to happen next is required throughout the change process, but more so as the momentum of change picks up.

An overall proviso is to remember that the planned communication will never be enough. Communication is the responsibility of not just those appointed to run communication seminars and workshops, but also all managers and supervisors throughout the organization who have teams of people that they need to help through the change process. This also has implications for what should be communicated and to whom.

6.3.2   Communication channels

Figure 6.2 shows the wide variety of communication channels available during change. There are also a variety of informal and ad hoc channels of communication such as conversations over lunch or at the coffee machine. The key to choosing a communication channel is to match it to the audience needs. For example, Ford of Europe uses Business TV to communicate instant information, because there is limited access to PCs in Ford, particularly in the plants. Teletext is

Change phase   Communication purpose

Unfreeze   Creating   Aims: • Unfreeze staff
                readiness   • Challenge the status quo
                                         • Spread understanding of need
                                           for change

Requires rich communication

                Providing   Aims: • Reduce uncertainty/ambiguity
                explanation   • Provide staff with information to
Move   fulfil their role during change
                                         • Enable staff to undertake
                                           needed change

Predominantly requires rich communication

                Providing   Aims: • Keep staff informed of progress
                updates   • Prevent uncertainty/anxiety
Sustain

More likely to be routine communication

Figure 6.1   Communication during change

▶ Videos, videoconferencing and roadshows

▶ Cascaded briefings

▶ Seminars and workshops

▶ Conferences

▶ Briefing notes and/or meetings

▶ Plans and progress reports

▶ Manuals and information packs

▶ Newsletters

▶ Noticeboards and bulletins

▶ Team briefing

▶ Electronic mail

Figure 6.2   Communication channels

updated on an as-needed basis and supplemented with programmes (4). Shell put together a corporate satellite television network in the late 1990s to get across to lower level staff the need for transformation in the company, in case these messages did not get through from their managers (5).

When designing a communication strategy, it is necessary to decide for each piece of communication which channel is most suited to the audience and the message being delivered. As a general rule, in non-routine, complex situations, such as change, richer forms of communication media, such as face-to-face are best. Less rich forms of communication, such as written and electronic means, are more suited to routine, non-change situations (see Figure 6.3)

Since rich communication channels are two-way and face-to-face, they provide an abundance of communication cues. They allow for the expression of concerns, answers to questions, the sharing of interpretations and experiences, and the sharing of problems and solutions. Research consistently suggests that this is the most effective form of communication during change, preferably through small groups, which affords the participants the opportunity to ask questions and air concerns. This approach also enables the message to be targeted to the needs of that particular group of individuals.

However, if individuals involved in change are to achieve an understanding of the behavioural and attitudinal implications of

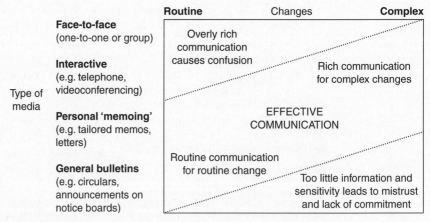

Figure 6.3 *Effective and non-effective communication of change*
(Source: *Reprinted with permission of Academy of Management, P.O. Box 3020, Briar Cliff Manor, NY 10510–8020. R.H. Lengel and R.L. Daft,* The Selection of Communication Media as An Effective Skill, *1988, vol. 2, no. 3. Reproduced by permission of the publisher via Copyright Clearance Center, Inc.)*

change, rich means of communication may need to be more than just face-to-face question and answer sessions. They may include workshops, or even personal development interventions with role play, to achieve *experiential learning*. Developing such management development interventions is discussed later in this chapter.

Illustration 6.1 summarizes the approach to communication at Birmingham Midshires Building Society, during a change process in the early to mid-1990s which aimed to achieve levels of customer service that would make the society the first choice for their customers. This required a cultural shift for the organization. The illustration reveals the value of intensive and rich forms of communication targeted at those who actually need to undertake personal change. It also illustrates how symbolic communication, discussed in the next section of this chapter, in the form of letters of thanks and certificates and awards can be used to powerfully supplement more traditional forms of communication.

Most communications strategies will also utilize many different types of communication, including written communication. To return to Figure 6.1, the richer forms of communication used to achieve unfreezing and explanation may need to be supported by less rich forms of communication. Participants will never remember everything they are told at briefings or workshops. Written documentation can provide useful back-up and reference material. Update information, which is about providing regular information on change progress, can also be provided by less rich channels of communication. Written communication, in the form of newsletters or noticeboard bulletins, for example, can be used to provide updates on progress and plans (see Illustration 6.1). Some organizations use electronic communication for these purposes.

Written communication can be used inappropriately. It may seem sensible to issue manuals when people need information about aspects of their work, such as what to do in particular circumstances, or details of new working practices. If the instructions are for a one-off situation and can be communicated in a one- or two-page memo, this may be true. In situations where the information is more substantial, this is not always so. In times of change, people are busy, stressed and concerned. They are unlikely to sit down and read a manual. The main content of any substantial booklets or manuals may be better covered in some form of seminar, workshop or training, with the manuals issued as reference material.

6.3.3 Message content

Again, the key issue with the message content is to match the detail to the audience needs:

Change in action

Illustration 6.1

Communicating change at Birmingham Midshires Building Society

Birmingham Midshires Building Society, based in the UK Midlands, faced the need for change to remain competitive and independent in the 1990s, following a period of rapid growth in the 1980s.[1] When Michael Jackson joined as CEO in 1990 he needed to improve the performance of the society.

Steps were taken to divest the building society of unprofitable products and services. Following this a change programme was put in place to make the society the 'first choice' for customers, by being **F**riendly, **I**nformed, **R**esponsive, **S**ervice Oriented and **T**rustworthy. The plans were taken forward from 1991 onwards through a series of cross-functional change teams.

The communications utilized during the change programme included:

- *Vision and values statements*: These were communicated to all staff in January 1991 along with the new organization structure through top management road-shows and a 26-page booklet, the *Rocket Document*.

- *Cascade meetings and booklets*: Three booklets were prepared on the strategy and goals of change, the behaviours required of staff, and the society's structure in terms of roles and responsibilities. These booklets were distributed using a series of cascaded briefing meetings from senior to more junior staff. The briefing was completed by early 1992.

- *'Listening to you first' programme*: A staff attitude survey updated annually. The survey allowed staff to suggest actions for change.

- *FIRST Ascent meetings*: The top executive team reported monthly on progress and business performance. The meeting notes were copied, and cascaded throughout the organization.

- *First Edition and Newspoints*: The internal monthly magazine, *First Edition*, was launched in early 1992. *Newspoints* was printed each week and provided information on change progress.

- If the message provides information that is personally relevant, and is couched in language the recipients can relate to and understand, the more likely it is that the message will be understood and retained (6).
- Employees do not just need an organizational vision, they also need a personal vision. In a change situation, the question everyone wants an answer to is, what is going to happen to me? Until individuals know if they will have a job, or where they will have to relocate to, or how their terms and conditions will change, they are unlikely to take in much else (7).
- For the change agents and people who have worked with them on designing the change process, it is too easy to announce just the con-

Illustration 6.1 continued

- *Face-to-Face programme*: Members of the executive team visited branches and departments regularly to learn about staff issues. The agenda was set by those being visited, and from these meetings members of the top team could learn, face-to-face, about the key issues and the things that still needed to be changed.

- *Celebrating wins*: Following an award to the society for customer service, staff members were sent individual letters of thanks and a certificate. They also received business cards with the award logo, presented in a personal silver business card holder, with the vision statement engraved on the back.

- *Customer communication*: Customers received a magazine about the society's products, services and activities. The CEO personally visited customers who had not received the service they expected.

- *Brand character video*: A video reflecting the desired vision and values of the Society was played at the start of any large staff conference or meeting.

- *Open Quality Day*: Held every three months, these days were for about 200 staff at a time. Speakers included staff and external speakers from best practice companies.

- *Hot Ideas*: A suggestion scheme was introduced to encourage staff to come up with changes themselves.

- *Symbolism*: There was a First Choice lapel badge awarded to staff members in response to proposals by customers and other staff. At head office there was a display of staff who had won the First Choice staff member of the year, and staff members of the month.

Note

1. By the end of the 1990s, the Society was the subject of a take-over by the Halifax.

(Adapted from: 'Birmingham Midshires Building Society' in Nick Obolensky, *Practical Business Re-Engineering*, 1994, London: Kogan Page.)

clusions and not explain the thinking that has gone into the decision-making process. This can lead to people asking questions about why particular options have not been considered, when they may have been, and questioning the feasibility and suitability of the proposals (see Figure 6.4).

The message content may also need to be adjusted to meet the different needs of different stakeholders. Although the primary target for communication may be the employees, it may also be necessary to communicate with other stakeholders such as the unions, the customers, the suppliers and the shareholders. Illustration 3.8, Chapter

- Reviewing business objectives
- Exploring needs
- Considering options
- Evaluating solutions
- Announcing conclusions

- Have I got a job?
- What is this going to mean for me?
- How is this going to affect my people?
- How much sense does this make for the business?

Figure 6.4   The communication collision
(Source: Bill Quirke, Communicating for Change, *1995, McGraw Hill)*

3, of the change process at Hoechst reveals that the way shareholders react to change needs to be taken into account. Even staff within one organization may have different information requirements, due to the different ways they are affected by the changes. For example, if change is being implemented by the use of prototypes and then extended, even staff as yet not having to undergo change will still need information on progress.

6.3.4   Who should communicate the change?

In situations of dramatic change, the obvious answer to the question of who should communicate the change would appear to be the senior managers, and preferably the MD or CEO. If senior managers do not personally deliver bad news or news of dramatic change, this can be interpreted as a lack of concern for the welfare of staff, or even a reluctance to give bad news personally. The size of the organization, or the geographic spread, can make it impossible for one or two people to lead all presentations, particularly if there is a need for all staff to hear certain information at a similar time to contain unhelpful rumours, or to avoid the symbolic implication that certain groups of staff are more important to the company than others. Many organizations overcome this by using videos, which are then shown by managers to staff and accompanied by a question and answer session. This may work as along as the managers concerned: are briefed and trained sufficiently to be able to discuss the changes knowledgeably; show enthusiasm for the changes themselves; have adequate presentation skills; and are able to demonstrate empathy and sensitivity where necessary.

In some instances the use of the line supervisor may be more appropriate (8) as they are more likely to be able to translate change into language and terminology that is relevant to their staff. It may also be appropriate to involve managers and supervisors in the second wave of communication, when more detail pertinent to particular groups of staff is being communicated. Update and progress information can also be given by line managers and supervisors.

Anyone that has to communicate change to others needs to have as much information as possible. If managers are asked to brief their staff, but cannot answer their questions, and have no means of feeding the questions upwards to obtain answers for their staff, they are unlikely to generate much commitment for change. Furthermore, when change is to be communicated by individuals who have not been involved in the planning, some thought needs to be given to the issues that might arise, and how these issues should be dealt with. This can be enhanced by collating all questions asked and then issuing answers. Glaxo Wellcome used an advisory board composed of employees from all parts of the organization as part of their communication strategy during their 1995 merger. Members of the board reviewed communications for content and delivery. The intent was to ensure that communications were sensitive to all employees (9).

6.4   *Symbolic activity*

6.4.1   *Symbolism and symbolic activity*

Exploring Corporate Strategy (Chapters 2, 5 and 11) discusses symbolism and symbolic activity in some depth. The points made include the following:

- Symbolic activity includes a wide variety of message sending events, activities and behaviours, as well as the manipulation of organizational artefacts such as status symbols, uniforms, language and logos. It can include rituals (see below), physical organizational aspects, behaviours and language, particularly of change agents and of those in positions of authority, stories, and systems such as reward systems.
- Symbolic activity is anything that conveys something about an organization to the individuals within it. For example, organizations that see themselves as being very successful, often have impressive head

offices located in prime commercial locations, with smart reception areas and polite, uniformed receptionists, and panelled opulent board-rooms. This symbolism becomes a short-hand representation of what the organization stands for, and attaches importance to.

- Symbolic activity is powerful because it has an impact on the way individuals interpret things. The prescription commonly encountered in texts on change, to 'walk the talk', is important, because if all the non-verbal cues about what change means do not support the verbal and espoused messages about change, individuals will interpret the espoused messages as meaningless. If senior managers preach empowerment and greater accountability, but continue to issue orders and countermand decisions made by their staff, then the staff will not believe in the espoused messages of change.

The intent here is not to repeat what has been said in *Exploring Corporate Strategy*, but to emphasize how symbolic activity can support verbal messages of change, and help individuals through the unfreeze, move and sustain process. Illustration 6.2 describes the change process undertaken at a National Health Service (NHS) hospital. It describes the range of symbolic interventions used by the CEO to underpin the changes occurring and gain the support needed. The illustration reveals how symbolic interventions can be used alongside the more commonly encountered structural and political interventions, particularly in situations which involve the need for a culture change.

The illustration also reveals how an aspect of symbolic activity – the behaviour and language of the change agents in particular, and of all senior managers in general – has a tremendous impact. Employees will look to these people for indications of how they should behave. Some organizations do explicitly change language to help foster change. The National & Provincial Building Society initiated a move from a hierarchical organization to a process-driven, team-based organization in the early 1990s. Old language included terminology such as staff, job, procedure, departments, manager, meeting and communications. The new language included players, role, process, teams, team leader, event and understanding. Sporting analogies were used to define team roles such as coach and player (10).

There is a warning that needs to be attached to the use of symbolic interventions. Just as verbal messages can be interpreted differently from the way they were intended by the recipients of the messages, symbolic communication can similarly be interpreted differently from the way it was intended. Chapter 7 returns to this point when discussing the need for monitoring mechanisms during change to understand how recipients are responding to the change initiatives put in place. Symbolic levers and mechanisms are less likely to be suc-

Change in action

Illustration 6.2

Change in an NHS Trust

In 1990, a new chief executive was appointed at GH Hospital. He had to lead a change programme aimed at gaining support from the hospital's consultants, for the change in status of the hospital to a self-managing Trust, as part of the wider ranging NHS reforms. The hospital acquired Trust status in April 1994. However, the changes put in place also involved a turnaround of the hospital.

The CEO adopted a range of interventions. Many hard interventions were put in place including restructuring to clinical directorates, and the update of financial, planning and administration systems. The CEO also utilized political interventions. He used a collaborative change style with much discussion early on with key stakeholder groups, including the leading consultants, and used imposed external changes, such as the arrival of the NHS internal market, to legitimize the change process. There were ongoing discussions with senior and middle managers throughout the change process, and senior management/consultant away-days were held to design a mission for the hospital.

However, a key aspect of the change process was the emphasis the CEO placed on symbolic activity:

- *Behaviour*: The CEO wore jeans and T-shirts and played loud pop music at middle manager away-days to emphasize that the process was also about having fun and experimenting.

- *Rewards*: The CEO sent gifts, such as baskets of fruit, to parts of the hospital which had made particular progress.

- *Ritual*: There were many away-days for all levels of staff. These became both rites of sensemaking, used to help staff understand the need for and implications of change, and rites of challenge, legitimizing questions about the current way of doing things.

- *Language*: Hospital porters, cleaners and catering staff were given the new title of ward assistants. In the early days of change, as the imposition of the NHS internal market on 1 April 1991 approached, the CEO used crisis language, such as 'go under' and 'not survive' to encourage recognition of the need for change.

- *Stories*: Stories were not consciously used by the CEO himself, but they did play a role. Stories were told by others about the CEO and his energetic style, since it symbolized to them that there was a new openness and that ideas were welcomed.

- *Structures*: The 12 leading consultants from each directorate were made the majority group on the senior management executive to indicate that the consultants would continue to carry weight. A group of 12 staff drawn from across levels was used to aid communication between staff and the executive, but this also indicated that managers wanted to hear staff views.

(Adapted from: Ian Brooks, 'Leadership of a cultural change process', *Leadership and Organization Development Journal*, 17, 5, 1996, pp. 31–7.)

cessful if they are used as one-off interventions, and more likely to be effective if there is a consistent and ongoing use of many different symbolic levers throughout the transition. Attention also needs to be paid to the removal of behaviours, events and language that symbolically suggest no change to the way of doing things within the organization.

6.4.2   *Symbolic activity and transition management*

To consider how symbolic activity can help individuals through the transition curve, and therefore unfreeze, move and sustain the change process, it is necessary to consider:

- How symbolic activity can be used to *challenge* the status quo to achieve a realization of the need for change.
- How symbolic activity can be used to legitimize *questioning*.
- How symbolic activity can be used to indicate what is *expected* of employees in the changed environment.
- How symbolic activity can be used to help employees develop a new and united *identity*.

Chapter 5 has already discussed the use of symbolism during unfreezing. Symbolic breaks with the past, through senior manager behaviours, or events, or the removal of status symbols, can be used to indicate that things are to be done differently in the future, and to legitimize questioning and challenging the status quo. The use of ritual can also be particularly helpful here – see Table 6.1 for a list of the different types of rituals.

Rituals (rites) can be defined as 'a formal action normally repeated in a standardized way' (11), that have become embedded into the way of life in an organization. It is possible to encourage people to challenge and question, and also to indicate new desired ways of working, by removing or changing old rituals, and putting in place new rituals. Rites of passage, degradation, enhancement, renewal, conflict reduction and integration help to varying degrees to unfreeze, move and sustain organizations (12). As such, different rituals may have different impacts throughout the unfreeze, move and sustain process (see Figure 6.5).

During the *unfreeze* phase:

- *Challenge* rituals, such as the publication of details of declining performance or increasing competition, can be important as they can be used to trigger a recognition of the need for change. They can also be used to create and mandate dissatisfaction with the current way of doing things, be it by new executives doing things in a different way, or competitive benchmarking. The behaviour, dress and language of the CEO of GH Hospital at away-days (Illustration 6.2) constitute rites of challenge.

Table 6.1   *Organizational rituals and culture change*

Types of ritual (rite)	Role	Examples
Rites of passage	Consolidate and promote social roles and interaction Confirm transition	Induction programmes Training programmes New offices/logos
Rites of enhancement	Recognize effort benefiting organization Similarly motivate others	Award ceremonies Promotions Published successes
Rites of renewal	Reassure that something is being done Focus attention on issues	Appointment of consultants Project teams/task forces
Rites of integration	Encourage commitment to shared identity Reassert norms	Christmas parties Uniforms Lunchtime drinks
Rites of conflict reduction	Reduce conflict and aggression	Negotiating committees Internal appeal systems Union management committees
Rites of degradation	Publicly acknowledge problems Dissolve/weaken social or political roles	Firing top executives Demotion or 'passing over' Limit scope of previously powerful groups
Rites of sensemaking	Sharing of interpretations of, and making sense of, what is happening	Rumours Stories Gossip Surveys to evaluate new practices
Rites of challenge	'Throwing down the gauntlet' Indicate old way no longer the best	New Executives' different behaviour/dress Deteriorating company performance Removal of old ways of doing things Redundancies
Rites of counter challenge	Resistance to new ways of doing things	Grumbling, anti-change graffiti Working to rule, sabotage, absence from change meetings

Source: Adapted from *Exploring Corporate Strategy*, 5th edition, G. Johnson and K. Scholes, 1999, Hemel Hempstead: Prentice Hall.

- *Degradation* rituals, such as removing and replacing top executives, or discontinuing old practices, can be used to generate questioning about the validity of the old ways of doing things.
- Since challenge and degradation will also create a lot of uncertainty, it is likely that there will be many *sensemaking* rituals, much specu-

	Change process	Symbolic acts	Effect
Unfreeze	Shock/Denial	*Challenge*	Legitimize questioning
		Degradation	Show old ways gone
	Awareness	*Sensemaking*	Help understanding
Move	Acceptance	Decreasing *Challenge*,	Legitimize questioning
		Increasing *Degradation*,	Provide new role models
	Testing	*Counter-challenge* and	Provide new identity
		Conflict-reduction,	Tackle resistance
	Search	Increasing *Enhancement*,	
		integration, renewal	
		and passage	
Sustain	Integration	*Enhancement*	Reinforce new role models
		Integration	Reinforce new identity
		Renewal	Assess and reinforce progress

Figure 6.5   *The use of ritual during change*

lation, gossip, sharing of information and rumours, during the unfreeze phase.

During the *move* phase:

- *Challenge* and *degradation* rituals are likely to continue to be important as individuals are continually encouraged to discontinue old ways of doing things and adopt new ways of behaving.
- The greatest levels of resistance, and therefore rites of *counter-challenge*, may be encountered in this phase as individuals have to actually undertake change. It may, therefore, be necessary to use ongoing *degradation* rituals to diminish old social identities, possibly by using shock tactics such as redundancies and demotions in crisis driven change.
- Rites of *conflict reduction*, including consultations and negotiations with unions or staff groups, and dealing with staff grievances, may be necessary to overcome resistance.
- Rites of *enhancement*, *passage*, and *integration* are likely to become important, as it becomes necessary to establish new role models of how things should be done, and to foster a new organizational identity. This is the time when individuals will be testing out new behaviours and searching for new meanings.
- Rites of *enhancement* could involve the giving of public rewards to individuals performing well according to the terms of new organizational performance criteria (see Illustrations 6.1 and 6.2), or the public praise of such individuals in newsletters. When TSB, the bank, started its quality programme in 1991 to improve customer service, cut costs and improve staff morale, it provided recognition for quality

successes in newsletters and recognition events. Individuals or teams nominated by colleagues were given Q-shaped silver or gold pins and invited to local and national recognition events, hosted by Peter Ellwood, the chief executive (13).

- Rites of *integration* encourage a common organizational identity, and could include a wide variety of social events or meetings.

The *sustain* phase is about reinforcing change, as such; the rituals likely to be of use are those to do with *enhancement, integration* and *renewal*. The rites of integration and enhancement may be the continuation of those introduced during the move phase. These rituals may become part of the new organizational culture. For example, at Finelist, a UK vehicle-parts supplier, the rites of integration include an annual roadshow on business developments, followed by question sessions with a senior manager for staff in groups of six, and monthly newsletters and videos. Rites of enhancement include monthly gold and silver staff awards for customer service, which consist of a letter and phone call from the chairman, with a gold pin presented by a senior manager in front of colleagues. There is an annual lunch for all winners at which the 'supreme winner' is awarded a prize of a holiday (14). Rites of *challenge* and *degradation* should only be relevant if there are still individuals resisting change

6.5   *Linking communication to design choices*

The above sections detail some of the different ways of communicating, and some of the issues to take into account when designing a communication strategy as part of any transition. In general, in any change process, the more communication with staff by a variety of different means, the better. Furthermore, there is always a need for certain types of communication like progress information. However, there is a need to match the communication strategy to the context of the changes and the design choices already made. The key issue here is to understand the role of communication in the design choices made so far. For example:

- If the change style selected is *communication* and *education*, then the communication strategy needs to be designed to have many seminars and/or training and education interventions up-front that are about creating an awareness of the need for change, an understanding of what needs to change, and providing staff with the skills to undertake change.
- If the change style is to be *collaborative* or *participative*, communication seminars and workshops throughout the change process have to be designed to allow for collaboration and participation. In collaborative change approaches, particularly those that are also bottom-up,

collaboration could also extend to the design of the communication strategy.

- If the change style is to be more *directive* or *coercive*, particularly since these change styles by their nature are top-down, and may be associated with a lack of time, then much of the communication may be more one-way with less of an emphasis on participation. Dramatic symbolic gestures are more likely to be used to support directive and coercive change styles.

- If the change levers selected include *communication, education* and *personal development*, perhaps to effect a value change, then such activity needs to be built into both the unfreeze stage and the move stage to help staff understand what is expected of them, and to enable them to change.

- If the change levers selected include *symbolic activity*, as they should if there is an intent to effect either behavioural change or ultimately value change, then those communicating the changes, and those in a prominent managerial role, need to be seen to support the espoused messages of change by their behaviours, actions and language. Conscious thought should also be given to how symbolic activity can be built into the communication strategy at all stages of the transition process.

- All unfreezing tactics (see Chapter 5) involve communication in one form or another, be it verbal, written or symbolic. Decisions about the unfreezing tactics will need to be built into a communication strategy.

- Time and capacity, particularly money and managerial resources, can affect the communication strategy. It may be that these factors mitigate against an extensive communication strategy. This is likely to be true for organizations in crisis. In such situations communication may be primarily by decisive symbolic actions, such as those undertaken by Ralph Halpern at Burtons (Chapter 3, Illustration 3.3), or those at Apple (Chapter 5, section 5.5.4, Drastic measures and shock tactics). Face-to-face communication is likely to be limited and more tell than sell.

6.6   Managing resistance and politics

6.6.1   Managing resistance

Resistance management is the term used to cover a number of techniques for diagnosing and managing resistance to change. It ties into the discussion in Chapters 3 and 4 on stakeholder analysis. Once the various stakeholders or groups of stakeholders have been identified, it is then necessary to consider who might resist change, and why, during the transition phase. Only then is it possible to consider the various tactics that should be employed to overcome possible resistance.

The transition curve discussed in Chapter 5 shows that change is an emotional and difficult process for most individuals. Resistance should always be expected and should not necessarily be perceived in a negative light. It is possible that initial resistance is a natural response to change for most individuals, and that the resistance needs to be worked through before change recipients can start to accept change and adapt. Resistance should not be assumed to be age-based either. There are a number of different models, lists and categories of reasons why individuals are likely to resist change (15). Figure 6.6 shows one such categorization.

Once potential areas of resistance have been identified, it is necessary to consider the appropriate tactics to overcome the resistance anticipated among the different stakeholders (16). Resistance can be overcome by a range of tactics (17) that are very similar to the range

---

Resistance may be due to:

Self-interest and politics: Issues to do with personal loss and cost of undertaking personal change, such as loss of turf, loss of status, loss of promotional prospects, separation from long-standing colleagues, or even a less convenient journey to work.

Psychological reasons: Issues such as fear of the unknown, fear of failure, concern about ability to develop needed skills, or a low ability to cope with change.

Emotional reasons: May include lack of energy and motivation, denial of need for change, or demoralization. Also uncertainty about impact of change on individuals, such as job security and earnings levels.

Change approach: Lack of participation, involvement and communication.

Recipient perceptions: To do with lack of understanding about why change is needed and its implications. May include different assessments about what should be done and the likely outcomes of proposed changes. A lack of trust may result from previous change experiences in which promises were not kept.

Cultural bias: Entrenched ways of thinking (selective perception), and 'we have always done it this way' attitudes and habits. Conflict between proposed changes and existing values and beliefs.

Historical organizational factors: Traditional relationships between managers and the unions and the workforce, or traditions of rivalry between functions or departments.

Figure 6.6   Resistance to change

Education and communication: Could include sharing information such as communication of reasons for change, what will and will not change, who will be affected, benefits and timetables. Could also include promoting a vision. Helps overcome negative recipient perceptions, and emotional and psychological fears of change.

Participation and involvement: Managers and staff can be included in task forces, working parties, focus groups, quality circles, or just involved through some sort of consultative process. If staff are involved and feel they have contributed to the design of the changes they are less likely to resist them. Can reduce resistance arising from the change approach, and can help reduce concerns about the impact of change and the ability to cope.

Facilitation and support: This could include the creation of peer support networks and groups, counselling for those experiencing difficulties or stress, access to external and internal consultants for advice and help, or simply the availability of a line manager who staff can talk to. Support can also include training in needed new technical and business skills. Such support may be critical for some staff who are fearful of the impact of change.

Negotiation and agreement: Tactic common in a unionized organization. It involves discussion with employees or their representatives to resolve areas of dispute about the changes, such as remuneration, hours of work, levels of employment, and terms and conditions. It may involve giving incentives to gain acceptance of change, such as guaranteed levels of pensions for those taking early retirement, or additional payment for more demanding duties and greater flexibility. Can help overcome resistance due to self-interest.

Manipulation and co-option: This involves attempts to influence others in a more covert manner, perhaps by the way information is presented. It could include inviting an influential manager who could be obstructive to join a working party since the manager would be more likely to be supportive of recommendations she or he has contributed to. However, if individuals perceive themselves as being manipulated they are likely to react negatively to this tactic.

Explicit/implicit coercion: Individuals are forced to accept change, by either explicit or implicit threats, such as the loss of employment. The threat may not be direct, it may be that transferring one or two individuals, or even making them redundant, sends an implicit message to others that their jobs could also be at risk. This sort of tactic is only likely to be successful if rapid change is essential, as people understandably resent such tactics.

Figure 6.7   Tactics for managing resistance to change

of change management styles discussed earlier in Chapters 2, 4, and 5 (see Figure 6.7). The difference here is that the approach taken with one or two individuals to overcome their resistance may need to be different to the general approach taken with other employees.

Much resistance will not be overt. Some staff will hide their resistance and instead this resistance will manifest itself later in the change process by foot dragging, or poor performance or productivity from the staff concerned. In extreme circumstances some staff may even practise sabotage. Other staff may just spread negative stories about those leading the change effort and the potential impacts of the changes. Therefore, some resistance will have to be tackled as and when it is encountered.

A lack of readiness for change should not be confused with resistance. If people have been prepared for change, and understand what is expected of them, they are less likely to exhibit resistance. For the majority of staff, therefore, most effort in the early days of change should be devoted to strategies designed to create a readiness for change. This includes use of techniques such as education and communication. However, there may be staff that may never be able to cope with the changes whatever assistance they get. Those that continue to resist change well into the move phase may be the staff the organization should choose to let go. It may even be that the persistent resistors are the ones selected for redundancy, since this also sends symbolic messages.

6.6.2 Managing politics

Change needs to take into account the informal as well as the formal processes within organizations. A common problem encountered when implementing strategic change is a failure to take into account the balance of power, how the political system operates, and who externally has influence over the process. Yet, power affects outcomes. Therefore, as *Exploring Corporate Strategy* (Chapter 11) points out, political activity is a relevant change management activity for any manager involved in change. Implementation games such as diverting resources, financial or human, away from change projects; using bureaucratic, organizational procedures to slow down the acceptance of change proposals; limiting communication of change goals and tasks; damaging the change agent's credibility; or agreeing to change proposals but not doing anything to advance them (17) are common place in organizations.

Methods for analyzing the political systems within organizations, and likely stakeholder reactions, include stakeholder analysis and resistance management, and the use of social network analysis (18). Social network analysis, or sociograms, is a useful technique for understanding the political landscape within an organization. Sociograms are diagrams which reveal the patterns of influence and trust that exist within organizations, which may be very different to the patterns that formal organization charts suggest exist. This is due to the influence of informal networks, both work and social.

Illustration 6.3 describes how sociograms were used to diagnose the problems preventing a new structure from working, which had been put in place in a business services organization by a new CEO. As the illustration describes, the previous patterns of trust and influ-

Change in action

Illustration 6.3

The case of Business Services plc

The newly appointed CEO of Business Services plc, wanted to move from a traditional regional sales-based structure, in which all regional sales directors reported directly to the CEO, to a key account management system in a matrix structure. Her predecessor had achieved significant sales growth over the past six years, but success had brought problems and so a restructuring was now required. The new CEO first strengthened her Board by appointing a marketing director and an HR director, both of whom she had worked with before. The new key account management strategy and structure was presented to all of the directors and everyone agreed to the plan. The regional sales directors became key account managers with responsibility for particular business sectors.

The former regional sales directors found it difficult to understand what was required of them as account managers in a matrix structure. Finance argued constantly with marketing over how to assess performance, and sales

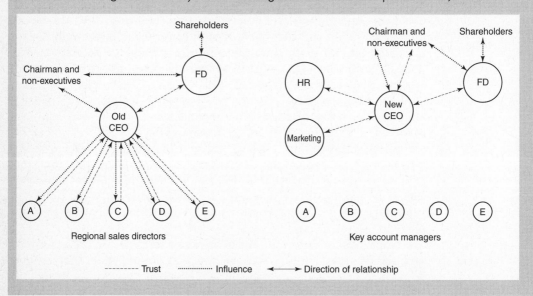

ence in the organization, and the way they operated, were disrupted by the new structure and the new CEO's way of working. The CEO had to change her approach to match the political landscape of the organization, in order to build sufficient trust to make the new structure work, and in turn rebalance the informal relationships at work within the organization.

Sociograms are developed by interviewing people about their networks – their formal and informal work and social relationships (18). They can be used to understand who influences and trusts whom

Illustration 6.3 continued

teams on the ground did not cooperate. The institutional shareholders expressed their concern to the Finance Director (FD) while the Chairman and Non-Executives began pressing the CEO to take action. Dismissal and replacement of the former sales directors was not an option, partly because it was felt that the market would react badly to such a move, as would customers. The CEO also realized that her job was on the line.

The CEO employed an ex-colleague to conduct a sociogram analysis of the organization. From conversations with the CEO, about who in her team had worked together before, who met informally and who she trusted, or mistrusted, and similar interviews with the rest of her team, including the former sales directors, the consultant constructed the sociograms shown in Figures 1 and 2. In the old structure, the CEO and the FD had trusted each other and could influence, and were in turn influenced by, the Chairman, the non-executive directors and the shareholders. All the regional sales directors trusted the old CEO and were influenced by him, although they did not trust each other. In the new structure, the CEO trusted and was trusted by the Marketing and HR directors, and she also trusted her FD. The new FD did not trust the CEO, but was influenced directly by the Chairman and the non-executive directors who did trust the new CEO. The key account managers were isolated, although they were starting to talk to each other which was some basis for moving forwards.

This analysis revealed that the former sales directors had seen the new structure as taking away their status but had not aired their concerns in front of the others. This was because the former CEO had tried to keep the sales directors from forming a united front. No one under the former CEO ever argued at meetings, but rather lobbied for change independently, often at the local golf club. The new CEO did not play golf and so individuals had not been able to air their problems. Furthermore, the CEO believed in getting a team on board quickly, and preferred not to have one-to-ones with individuals because they were divisive.

As a result of this analysis, the CEO changed her implementation strategy, and began holding one-to-ones with the old directors. An off-site top team meeting was subsequently held at which differences were aired and a revised structure agreed.

(Written by Phil Davies, Cranfield School of Management, 1997.)

within an organization, both to gain an understanding of the networks that may be used to subvert change, and to identify the individuals who have the informal power to build support for change. Sociograms can also be used to reveal individuals within the organization who might carry a lot of formal power, but have an insufficient level of influence to help develop support for change.

6.6.3 Linking resistance management and politics to design choices

Resistance management and politics are needed in all change processes. The reality of change is that it involves resistance and it involves politics. However, yet again there is a need to match the tactics to the change context. The choices as to the type of resistance management tactics to use are a little like those to do with change style. If there is a lack of time, then more coercive and manipulative resistance management tactics may have to be used, and if there is a crisis they may also be perceived as more legitimate. However, if there is more time, then communication, education, participation and negotiation may be better approaches. On the other hand, resistance management is also about tackling individual resistance. It may be that for more senior staff, if some individuals are not behaving as required in the new environment and are therefore obstructing the change process in some way, they have to be treated differently and on an individual basis.

6.7 Building new human resource management systems

Human resource management (HRM) policies and processes are one influence on individual and group behaviour within an organization. They can be used both to move the organization through change and also to reinforce and sustain the newly formed organization once the change is over. The main components of a human resource system are shown in Figure 6.8 and include:

- *Recruitment and selection*: designing jobs, and attracting, selecting and appointing staff into the organization.
- *Appraisal*: measuring, monitoring and assessing staff performance, assessing staff for either reward or future training or development, and defining future performance objectives.
- *Reward*: rewarding individuals or teams for contribution, and motivating them to stay and/or perform.
- *Development*: training and developing staff for either improved future performance or as part of a general career development.

The following examines both the need for linkages between these different components of the HRM system if it is to operate as a set of uniform practices, policies and activities, and the role of each of these HRM systems in change.

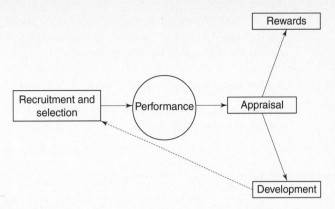

Figure 6.8   The human resource cycle
(Source: *M.A. Devanna, C.J. Fombrun and N.M. Tichy, 'A Framework for Strategic Human Resource Management', in N.M. Tichy and M.A. Devanna,* Strategic Human Resource Management, *1984, New York: John Wiley)*

6.7.1   Linkages between the components

In order for the components of the HRM system to work effectively as change levers the organization has to ensure three forms of linkage: temporal, vertical and horizontal (19):

- *Temporal linkages* ensure that the human resource policies and processes change over time as the business strategy evolves.
- *Vertical linkages* ensure that the human resource policies and processes are congruent and reflective of the business strategy and the business goals within that strategy. There is little point in having a business strategy which can only be achieved through the development of a team culture if the compensation and benefits system rewards individual performance rather than team performance.
- *Horizontal linkages* ensure that the human resource policies and processes are congruent with each other. Do the criteria by which people are selected bear some resemblance to the criteria by which they are appraised for performance? To extend the example given above, if the business strategy needs a team-based culture, then the criteria used in selecting staff, and appraising staff and rewarding staff, should all be linked into team-performance so that each activity complements the others.

Competencies are often used as a mechanism to achieve horizontal linkage. A common set of competencies are established for an organization. Different combinations or clusters of competencies are then put against specific jobs. For a specific job the same competencies can be used as selection and appraisal criteria, and for assessing rewards and determining development needs. One retail bank introduced new competency-based selection procedures across its retail bank network in an attempt to achieve consistency in criteria and standards for selection and promotion.

6.7.2   Recruitment and selection

Recruitment and selection are two separate stages in the overall process of bringing new people into an organization:

- *Recruitment* is concerned with looking for people whom the organization might wish to employ. It is to do with advertising vacancies and attracting people to apply to the organization.
- *Selection* is the process by which an individual or individuals are chosen for appointment from the pool of individuals who have either applied through the recruitment process or been recommended for a position.

   Recruitment is the process that produces candidates. Selection is the sorting of the candidates, possibly through interviewing and profiling questionnaires, to identify the final appointments. There are several ways that recruitment and selection can be used to support change interventions. During the *unfreeze* phase one of the most common mechanisms used to indicate the need for change is redundancy. However, tactics can be more subtle:

- Organizations can change the *selection criteria*. Selection criteria may include past experience, personal skills, qualifications, knowledge areas, attitudes, and so on. If the organization is seeking to achieve a cultural change, for example, these criteria can be altered to reflect the new norms and values that an organization is hoping to embrace. ASDA (see Chapter 3, Illustration 3.4) actively started to recruit staff who liked to serve customers.
- New selection criteria also enable the use of degradation and challenge rituals. For example, setting new selection criteria for certain positions may mean that staff with appropriate qualifications need to be brought in from outside the organization to fill vacancies previously filled through internal promotion. This also indicates to existing staff that they no longer have the appropriate skills.
- Staff can be made to *re-apply* to the organization for a job. If selection criteria have also been changed, or less jobs made available in the new structure, this may mean that some staff are offered redundancy rather than a job. When Heather Rabbats, the new chief executive of the London Borough of Lambeth, initiated change in the local authority in the mid-1990s, she not only replaced all the chief officers, she also reselected all staff for their jobs leading to job losses of 1,300. Incompetence among staff was a problem, so *all* employees had to take competence tests devised to relate to the jobs they actually did. Those

who failed were made redundant, border line cases were retrained, moved or demoted (20).

- Organizations can change the *type* of people recruited. Organizations may choose to make redundant certain types of staff, but take on a different type of staff. Ericsson Australia (see Chapter 5, Illustration 5.3) made staff from the manufacturing side of the organization redundant as part of their move to create a customer-focused organization, but took on staff in services and marketing. Organizations may also decide to start to *recruit* and/or *promote* from a pool of potential candidates previously ignored. Challenging existing perceptions of who fills which jobs can both symbolically and practically aid a change process. For example, intended changes at Shell (see Chapter 1) included a diversification of the senior management group to include more women and greater ethnic diversity.

During the *move* phase, the tactics may be similar to the unfreeze phase. Selection criteria may be altered to allow for an ongoing reduction of staff by identification of those staff not able to perform against the competencies now required by the organization. Job redesign may also be used. Job redesign is concerned with the actual structure of a job. Change may involve changes to certain working practices within the organization – perhaps the way cars are assembled, or telephone enquiries are dealt with. This in turn may affect the number of staff needed and the sort of people who will fill them. It could also lead to the introduction of a move to flexible working, or annualized hours, where staff work more hours at one time of the year than at others to meet the fluctuating level of customer orders.

During the *sustain* phase, the recruitment and selection interventions are likely to be concerned with interventions aimed at longer-term change within the make-up of a workforce, rather than short-term change to the staff an organization already has:

- Organizations may change the *way* people are recruited. For years UK life insurance companies recruited from among the best 'A' level school leavers. The life insurance industry ran a strong internal labour market, with good internal training processes, which enabled the school leavers to rise to the top managerial levels within an organization. As the industry changed, with new entrants coming into the marketplace and the advent of new technology, the internal labour market broke down, and the majority of staff recruited in as clerical workers were much more likely to stay within the clerical ranks for much of their lives. It was then necessary for the industry to change its recruitment practices. It could not continue to take the brightest and the best from the school leavers while being unable to fulfil their career expectations. Equally, it made more sense economically to seek to recruit less qualified people who would cost less for the clerical jobs.

- Organizations may change the *selection mechanisms* (interviews, assessment centres, psychometric tests) for both new recruits and for the promotion of existing staff, although some organizations may choose to do this in the move phase. Such moves can also be symbolic sending messages about which practices are now valued in comparison to the old ways of doing things. In the mid-1990s KPMG changed the way future partners were selected. Managers had traditionally been promoted to partner through the patronage and recommendation of an existing partner. Assessment centres were introduced to determine which of the prospective candidates for partnership had the appropriate profile, and who would therefore be put forward for partnership. Candidates that failed the assessment centre would not be accepted for partnership even if the candidate's sponsoring partner continued to push the candidate forward.

6.7.3   Appraisal

Appraisal is the assessment of an individual's past performance, often against objectives previously set, and the establishment of future performance objectives; it may also include the identification of development or training needs and/or the determination of rewards or bonuses.

The most common way of using appraisal systems to help deliver change is to change either the criteria or the objectives against which staff are assessed. Criteria may be changed by reshaping the skills, competencies or behaviours against which staff are assessed, and objectives may be changed by reshaping what staff have to achieve. For example, to aid a shift in priorities for lecturers at a university from teaching to research, the objectives in the appraisal system may be altered to include getting research published in academic journals. Whereas at UBS, the Union Bank of Switzerland UK Group, the appraisal mechanism for their IT staff was altered more in terms of criteria or competencies. To support a re-engineering of their London-based IT function, a competency framework was put together which specified the competencies required for each type of staff assignment, and maintained a competency profile for each member of staff. The new appraisal and performance review mechanism was supported by this competency framework. Individual performance standards for each member of staff, as specified in a job guide, were to be reviewed formally three times a year. This information was also to be used to update an individual's competency profile as appropriate, and to build personal development plans that would lead to the development of competencies that match the future requirements of the company (21).

However, there are other symbolic changes that can be made to an appraisal mechanism to aid unfreezing and movement. 360-degree appraisals can be introduced whereby staff also appraise their managers as well as the other way round. This was done at WH Smith News (Chapter 4, Illustration 4.1) to help unfreeze the deferential culture. The frequency with which managers have to appraise their staff could also be changed. It may be specified that managers are expected informally to keep in touch with their staff throughout the year to assess how they are coping with change, so that the formal annual appraisal is merely a summary of what is already known. This suggests a change in role for the manager, to one more to do with coaching and counselling.

6.7.4   Reward

Reward covers the whole compensation and benefits area and is a common change lever to help obtain changes in staff behaviour and performance. Reward is concerned with both rewarding people for past performance and motivating them for future performance, it also acts as a means of retaining staff. However, reward is a very broad category and people can be rewarded in many different ways. Reward can encompass being sent on training courses as a bonus for particular performance. It might include extra holidays, payment for college fees, access to childcare, and company cars. All of these forms of reward can be used to help recruit and retain staff with a range of different needs, but also be used to motivate people to embrace change.

To understand how to use a reward system effectively within an organization a change agent needs to understand the different motivations of staff groups. For some groups, such as sales representatives, financial rewards are a critical motivator. For others, financial reward is not a primary motivator, for example, nurses, most academics, and people working within the voluntary sector. Furthermore, if the recruitment policies have been changed to start tapping into a previously neglected type of staff, such as mothers returning to work, a different range of rewards may need to be offered to retain these staff. Such employees may value flexibility over financial reward. This may also require a shift in the company policy towards a 'cafeteria' benefits system, such as that operated by Price Waterhouse, whereby staff can pick and mix from a range of benefits, such as extra holiday, childcare vouchers, company car, pension and shopping vouchers, to top up their basic salary. Different types of staff can then have salary packages that are best for them.

Given the links between reward and motivation, it is easy to see how compensation and benefits can promote change, both through the transition phase and beyond. In the unfreeze phase, changes to the reward system, as with changes to the other HRM systems, are likely to be symbolic, and may include:

- Pay freezes, pay cuts such as at Pearl Assurance (see Chapter 3, Illustration 3.2), or the non-payment of the usual annual bonuses.
- The alteration of non-financial rewards. Subsidies for canteens or health clubs could be stopped as part of a cost-cutting drive. Staff clubs could be closed.
- The criteria against which bonuses are paid could be altered. If previously performance-related pay was determined by how many individual sales were achieved over a short period of time, a shift towards relationship marketing might suggest that the reward system should be altered to reflect the ability to sustain longer-term customer relationships. This is as true for senior managers as it is for more junior staff.

During the move phase, the reward system is more likely to be used to encourage change-related behaviours – through both financial and non-financial means. Again, these rewards may be symbolic, giving messages to staff about what they have to do to help with the change process – or perhaps even to keep their job. For example:

- Staff may be rewarded for simply supporting the changes. For instance, line managers can be given bonuses for spending time counselling their staff through change or implementing change-related initiatives. The same can apply to non-managerial staff. Chapter 5, section 5.3.2, discusses the change process undertaken at SKF. Here, managers were given bonuses for implementing initiatives that supported the vision of 'Trouble Free Operations'. There was also a service initiative programme which offered prizes to all staff for ideas on implementing trouble free operations.
- Other rewards may include writing about staff who are deemed to be doing the right things in newsletters to portray them as role models to others, or publicly giving staff who make the sorts of change wanted recognition through the use of rites of enhancement as discussed above.
- Staff could also be rewarded by other means, such as training and development courses. Those staff who are doing the right things may receive sponsorship for something like an MBA course, or be sent on a high-profile management development programme at a top business school.

Sustaining change is more to do with maintaining and retaining changed behaviours into the longer term. Changes to reward systems in this phase of change are more likely to be permanent changes to the overall framework of rewards. It is at this point that an organization may implement, for example, a new cafeteria benefits system, or embed symbolic rewards into the permanent way of working in an organization. At Richer Sounds, the hi-fi retailer, each time a staff member is rated as excellent on the customer questionnaire that accompanies each sales docket, they receive £5. Employees are also rewarded for contributing to the company suggestion scheme. Team effort is rewarded separately. The three winning branches in the monthly customer service competition gain the use of a company car for the next month – a Bentley or an XJS (22). Such reward mechanisms could be used as a permanent part of the reward system by any organization wishing to support a shift to improved levels of customer service into the longer term.

6.7.5 Development

Change may involve staff acquiring new skills, new knowledge, new working practices, or new behaviours, attitudes or values. Development and training is the mechanism used to help achieve this. Training seeks a specific outcome in terms of skills or behaviours. Development is more challenging and broader in remit. It may include experiential learning, which can encompass outdoor development courses, or it can be classroom based. Education is even broader in its aim, seeking to open a delegate's or student's mind to new ways of thinking. The key to success is to choose the right delivery channel for the type of change design chosen, and the level of people who are the recipients of the learning process. Senior management react less well to training and better to education, whereas staff requiring new skills need training.

There are many mechanisms for delivering development and training:

- *Off-site interventions*: This can involve courses on specific skills or knowledge areas such as IT, or qualifications in banking.
- *General management programmes* (either in the form of degree-based courses such as MBAs, or executive development courses that examine all the management functions): Organizations can also have customized general management programmes designed to suit their own needs. For example, in the early 1990s, the NHS decided to fund a number of hospital consultants to attend management development programmes at business schools, to improve the level of management within the NHS. However, some Regional Health Authorities chose to devise their own tailor-made programmes.
- *In house training*: This can take the form of courses or job-based learning.
- *In-house computer-based training*: Employees can have direct access to new knowledge and skills, without using the training manager or their manager's training budget as an intermediary. For example, Hyatt International, the hotel group, uses CD-Roms as the basis for staff training.

These different interventions can be used to different effect to

help unfreeze, move and sustain an organization. Personal development is very powerful during the unfreeze phase, since it is concerned
with helping an individual to grow and change at an individual level.
It is about challenging the way individuals see things. As such, it is a
type of intervention that is valuable in circumstances where value
change is required of individuals. British Airways, for example, used a
personal development programme as part of the unfreezing process for
the culture change in the 1980s. The programme, Putting People First,
was used to help staff develop a recognition of what customer service
was about. Personal development can also be used to aid unfreezing
when a type of behavioural change is needed which in turn requires
individuals to recognize the degree of change this requires from them
personally (see the Glaxo case study, Chapter 4, Illustration 4.5).

Personal development programmes designed to aid unfreezing
are likely to be in-house programmes designed with the intent of
putting many staff through them simultaneously to achieve a critical
mass of support for change. However, if the need is to unfreeze particular senior managers, then these people may be sent on open management development programmes. Of course, if the unfreezing style
selected is communication and education, then the unfreeze interventions may be more about education than personal development.

During the move phase, both training and development will be
needed to help staff develop either new skills, behaviours or attitudes.
If change is about delivering new skills, the interventions will be more
to do with training, whereas if the emphasis is on value-based change,
more personal development interventions will be needed. Again,
courses are likely to be designed specifically for the organization if a
critical mass of people need to attend. Coaching and counselling by
outside facilitators, a more intensive form of private, individual personal development, may be provided for more senior managers to help
them develop the new attitudes or behaviours required of them or to
provide them with the change skills they need to help their staff
through change. Following the collapse of a tunnel during the construction of the Heathrow Express railway from central London to
Heathrow Airport, the companies working on the project decided to
develop a cooperative approach to get the project back on track. One of
the interventions put in place to achieve this change from the more
traditional adversarial culture found in the construction industry was
coaching, to encourage the development of a single team among the
senior managers (23).

If training and development initiatives are to be used as change
levers they must be chosen with the change outcomes in mind. So, for
example, if an organization decides that for it to succeed at change all
its senior and middle managers need to understand the change process
and how to help their staff through change, then the course designed

would need to fit this objective. This means that the contractor of the course for the organization needs to be able to evaluate the objectives of every available course and assess their fit with the requirement. It also means that the participants need to be able to link the content of any change-related training to the desired outcomes of the organizational change programme.

Sustain interventions will be more to do with putting in place training to ensure the ongoing development by staff at all levels of the sorts of competencies the organization requires for it to remain competitive in the longer-term. Things such as new induction courses for new recruits could also be put in place at this point. Training and development initiatives will need to be supported by corresponding changes to the appraisal system, to ensure people are put on appropriate training courses and assessed against whether or not they are able to use the skills and competencies they are supposed to have acquired.

Another important sustain intervention is career development. Any organization undertaking change needs to make suitable adjustments to its career planning processes, to build the organizational leaders and competencies required for the future. It is very short sighted for the current senior managers to anticipate that the behaviours or knowledge that got them to the top should also apply to the next generation of leaders. Career development may be delivered by a series of planned project assignments or job promotions aimed at giving the individual the range of experiences deemed necessary for future leaders, and/or management development programmes such as MBA courses. It may also incorporate activities such as coaching and mentoring, whereby more junior managers are assigned a more senior manager to act as their mentor on personal and career development.

6.8   Linking HRM systems and design choices

As with all other levers and mechanisms it is important to link the use of the HRM interventions to the design choices already made. For example:

- If the change target is outputs, then changes to rewards and performance objectives within the appraisal system are likely to be particularly helpful. Chapter 2 gives the example of city traders to illustrate this when discussing outputs as the change target.
- If the change target is behaviours, then a range of HRM interventions will be needed including training and development to help effect the changes to skills and behaviours, and changes to appraisal criteria and rewards to support the new behaviour. These rewards may be symbolic as were the rewards given at TSB (see above, section 6.4.2)

during its quality programme. Development interventions may also be needed as at Glaxo (Chapter 4, Illustration 4.5) if the behavioural shift also requires an accompanying recognition of the types of personal change needed to support the changes in behaviours.

- If the change target is values, then as the discussion on training and development makes clear, many longer-term development-related initiatives will be required aimed at altering the way individuals think about their work and their customers.
- If the change start point is to be bottom-up, rewards and promotion could be used to encourage participation on an ad hoc basis. This would also be a symbolic intervention, indicating that those staff that get on and are valued are those that are contributing to the change process. More permanent changes to reward systems would only be instituted in the longer term to sustain the changes that had evolved.
- If the change start point is top-down, then things such as performance objectives and rewards may be imposed to force in change, particularly when accompanied by a focus on behaviours to force change in quickly.

Other factors may also influence the decisions about which HRM interventions to use. Capacity, in terms of cash and employee time for change is an issue as Chapters 3 and 4 have already explained. Organizations can be so over-stretched because of the changes they are trying to implement that they cannot release staff, or allow them the time, for the training that has been set up. There is little point in investing in an initiative whilst having no capacity to deliver it. Training and development programmes can also involve significant investment in terms of time and finance. When TSB launched the quality programme mentioned above (see section 6.4.2), the training of all bank staff took two years and the equivalent of 150-man years. The training cost £7 million, plus £12 million in staff time (12). Again, there is little point in designing a change process that requires these types of interventions, or extensive and expensive personal development interventions, if there is not the money for it.

6.9   Summary

The purpose of this chapter has been to describe in some detail the use of particular levers and mechanisms to aid the transition process and help effect the required changes, namely:

- Communication is particularly important during all phases of the transition. During the unfreeze phase, communication needs to be designed to create readiness; during the move phase communication needs to provide explanation; and as change progresses, communication also needs to provide update information for staff. It is always necessary to focus on matching the communication to the needs of the audience.

- Symbolic activity is important as an alternative form of communication during change. Rituals can be used to help facilitate the unfreeze, move and sustain change process by legitimizing questioning and challenging in the early stages of change, and promoting new role models and social identities as change progresses.
- Resistance management, and understanding the political landscape of an organization and how to work within it, are other legitimate change interventions.
- Finally, but by no means least, HRM systems are a key change lever. Recruitment and selection, reward systems, appraisal mechanisms, and training and development are all interventions that need to be used to encourage individuals to adopt the new skills, behaviours, attitudes or values required as part of the changes.

This chapter completes the analysis of how to design the transition process, although it is also starting to address considerations of how to manage the transition. As Chapter 7 will explain, given the dynamic and at times unexpected nature of the transition state, communication and political skills are key attributes required of change agents if they are to negotiate the rocky terrain of change implementation successfully.

Notes and references

(1) For a discussion of some of the principles of communication see S.R. Axley, 'Managerial and Organizational Communication in Terms of the Conduit Metaphor', *Academy of Management Review,* 9, 3, 1984, pp. 428–37.

(2) For an examination of the some of the factors that contribute to effective communication see L.R. Smeltzer, 'An Analysis of Strategies for Announcing Organization-Wide Change', *Group and Organization Studies,* 16, 1, 1991, pp. 5–24.

(3) See J.D. Duck, 'Managing Change: The Art of Balancing', *Harvard Business Review*, November–December 1993, pp. 109–18.

(4) See A. Barnetson, 'What does it take to build a "Communicating Culture"', *Focus on Change Management*, October 1996, pp. 13–17.

(5) See R. Corzine, 'Communicating the Message: Shell gets its own TV shows', *The Financial Times*, 31 March 1998, p. 20.

(6) Various authors discuss the need for communication to be relevant to the needs of the audience. See for example, S.M. Klein, 'A Communication Strategy for the Implementation of Participative Work Systems', *International Journal of Management,* 10, 3, 1993, pp. 392–401. Also B. Bertsch and R. Williams, 'How Multinational CEOs Make Change Programmes Stick', *Long Range Planning,* 27, 5, 1994, pp. 12–24.

(7) For a discussion of the need for personal visions see Downing and

Hunt, *International Journal of Human Resource Management*, 1, 1990.

(8) See Klein as in note 6 above for the role of supervisors in communication.

(9) See G. Duncan, 'Managing a Merger: Getting employees on board at Glaxo Wellcome', *Focus on Change Management*, July–August 1996, pp. 21–6.

(10) See D. O'Brien and J. Wainwright, 'Winning as a team of teams – transforming the mindset of the organization at National & Provincial Building Society', *Business Change & Re-engineering*, 1, 3, winter 1993, pp. 19–25.

(11) For more information on organizational rituals and the use of ritual in change see D. Sims, S. Fineman and Y. Gabriel, *Organizing and Organizations: An Introduction*, 1993, London: Sage; H.M. Trice and J. Beyer, 'Studying Organizational Cultures through Rites and Ceremonies', *Academy of Management Review*, 9, 4, 1984, pp. 653–69; A.D. Brown, 'Transformational Leadership in Tackling Technical Change', *Journal of General Management*, 19, 4, 1994, pp. 1–12.

(12) See n. 11.

(13) See F. Gee, S. Dutta and J. Manzoni, *Transforming TSB Group (D): The Second Wave (1992–1995)*, 1996, INSEAD, case number 697-043-1.

(14) See 'The Enterprise Network', *The Sunday Times*, 22 March 1988, p. 9.

(15) For one categorization of reasons individuals are likely to resist change, and the categorization of tactics for overcoming resistance used here, see J.P. Kotter and L.A. Schlesinger, 'Choosing Strategies for Change', *Harvard Business Review*, February–March 1979, pp. 106–14.

(16) A simple technique for helping to clarify what resistance management strategies to deploy for which stakeholders is to use the concept of a commitment chart. R. Beckhard and R.T. Harris, *Organizational Transitions*, 2nd edition, 1987, Addison-Wesley.

(17) See D. Buchanan and D. Boddy, *The Expertise of the Change Agent: Public Performance and Backstage Activity*, 1992, Hemel Hempstead: Prentice-Hall.

(18) For a discussion of social network analysis and sociograms see S. Wasserman and K. Faust, *Social Network Analysis*, 1994, Cambridge: Cambridge University Press.

(19) See L. Gratton, V. Hope Hailey *et al.*, *Strategic Human Resource Management*, 1999, Oxford: Oxford University Press.

(20) See G. Golzen, 'Tackling Mission Impossible', *Human Resources*, September–October 1996, pp. 22–9.

(21) See B. Timms and R. Finn, 'Banking on a wise investment in HR', *People Management*, 22 February 1996, pp. 32–5.

(22) See G. Golzen, 'Richer Sounds Right', *Human Resources*, March–April 1998, pp. 28–33.

(23) See M. Coles, 'Culture shock pays off', *The Sunday Times*, 21 June 1998, p. 28.

7

Managing the transition: monitoring and resourcing

7.1 Introduction

The last two chapters explained how to design the actual change implementation, the transition state, and also discussed how to sequence the selected levers and mechanisms throughout the transition. This chapter builds on this, by focusing on the management of the transition state. It considers:

- The design of change outcomes and monitoring mechanisms to evaluate the progress and success of the change process.
- The different roles that need to be managed during the transition state and the issues for the individuals who fulfil them, with a focus on change agency, middle managers and change recipients.

The chapter opens with a consideration of the nature of the transition period itself. An understanding of what change is like once implementation gets underway is important for a fuller appreciation of the types of monitoring mechanisms required and the types of skills required by those responsible for managing the transition.

7.2 Managing the transition

It would be all too easy to assume from what has been said so far that the key to managing any transition is good up-front planning. It is true that the more planning and forethought given to the transition state, the better the chances of success, which is why the previous chapters devote so much attention to it. However, as Chapter 1 pointed out, it would be wrong to believe that implementation will unfold neatly in a linear fashion in accordance with carefully laid plans. The transition is better characterized as an emergent process full of surprises, with unpredictable and uncertain outcomes. Words like 'frustrating', 'chaotic', and 'difficult' are often used by managers to describe their experiences.

A good analogy is to think of the old slot machines that used to be found in entertainment arcades for children. A penny dropped in a slot at the top could take many routes. The 'prize' a child would get out of the machine would depend on the route the penny took. Leading change is a similar experience. Managers can drop interventions in at the top of the organization, but the resulting outcome, in terms of the changes in behaviours or attitudes it produces, can be surprising and disappointing. Outcomes achieved are not always as intended. Change is about managing individual expectations and interpretations, not just structures and systems. Change agents need to work to align the interpretations of individuals with their change vision. This does not involve the use of just verbal and written communication, but also the use of symbolic activity, education, training, and possibly personal development, all discussed in the previous chapter.

The nature of the implementation process also has implications for its management, one of which is that some type of specific transition management is needed to resolve problems as they arise, and keep the change process on track. It also involves recognizing that the very nature of change, and the way individuals react to change, makes misinterpretation and unexpected outcomes not only likely to happen, but very probable. It is therefore necessary to attempt to monitor change progress from the recipients' perspective. These issues are discussed in more detail in the rest of the chapter.

7.3   *Designing change outcomes and monitoring mechanisms*

7.3.1   *Designing change outcomes and measures*

As with any management intervention it is wise to establish some measures of success for the change process based on the desired change outcomes. Change outcomes describe the behaviours required of people and the types of outputs they are expected to produce in the future. They spell out how the behaviours of staff need to change on a day-to-day basis. Change outcomes are also measurable aspects of change. They are therefore important because they enable the change agent to devise ways of assessing whether the desired behaviours and outputs are occurring.

Illustration 7.1 describes two examples of setting change outcomes – one in an organization needing to grow by internal product development rather than by acquisition, and the other for an organization wanting to introduce better customer services. Both these examples are of organizations that require their staff to undertake behavioural change. Therefore, the outcomes set are more qualitative requiring means of assessment and measurement such as staff and customer surveys and interviews.

If an organization is in crisis, however, and needs to effect a rapid reconstruction, then the desired change outcomes are more likely to be financial measures. These outcomes may be to do with the types of

Change in action

Illustration 7.1

Setting outcomes

From growth by acquisition to growth by internal product and service development

An organization with a policy of growth by acquisition realized that it was no longer viable to maintain the organization's growth rate in this way. A policy of growth by internal development of new products and services was introduced. This required an overall outcome of more innovative staff behaviour. Changes introduced to help achieve this included job role flexibility with much less job demarcation, restructuring around teams and experimentation. To assess whether the overall desired outcome was being achieved, additional behavioural outcomes set included team as opposed to individual working, a tolerance of mistakes, more risk taking, the generation of new product ideas, and new patterns of selling to push new products and services. The degree to which all of these behaviours were developing could be assessed through staff surveys.

Introducing better customer service into a telesales organization

A telesales organization wished to achieve an overall change outcome of a better level of customer service. This required a number of behaviour changes from staff, such as being more polite and friendly to customers, showing more initiative in the way they tackled customer problems, and taking more responsibility for resolving problems. Interventions put in place included training courses, newsletters circulating examples of good customer service and staff initiatives, and forums which allowed staff to exchange ideas on the ways to resolve common problems. Whether or not the new behaviours were occurring could be assessed by both staff and customer surveys. However, the softer measures were supported by some prescribed outputs that could be measured directly, such as standards for rapidity of response to phone calls, letters and faxes.

measures derived from an annual report, such as profit margins, levels of debt or stock levels. The desired outcomes might also include hard measures to do with internal efficiency, such as cost reduction, which in turn may be associated with targets for staff reductions, levels of waste and cycle times. Hoerner used such measures when putting in place his reconstruction of the Burton Group (Chapter 3, Illustration 3.3).

Other outcomes and measures can be set to indicate the impact of change on the workforce, such as labour turnover, absenteeism and levels of commitment. These outcomes may seem generally desirable, but even low labour turnover is not a good outcome in all cases. In some mature corporations, with a historical legacy of strong internal labour markets, staff cuts might become inevitable in the longer term. In that instance higher labour turnover among certain groups of staff with skills less relevant to the future of the organization might be a welcome outcome. Furthermore, following change, indicators like absenteeism may improve not because staff are more motivated or happier, but because they are scared for their jobs. Once other employment becomes available, they may leave. The critical component is the appropriate measures for this change – each change process determines its own outcomes.

The results from the performance management systems or staff appraisals can be used to assess the achievement of change outcomes. If new criteria for staff assessment or managerial competencies have been brought in, how well are staff performing against these? How many staff are demonstrating changed behaviours as a result of training or development interventions? As for the telesales organization (Illustration 7.1), these measures may need to be supported by more prescriptive outcomes, such as staff answering the phone more promptly, customer satisfaction indices, or throughput indices for daily work activity.

Other techniques for collecting information on progress against change outcomes include attitude surveys, customer surveys, interviews and questionnaires, as well as data on control measures such as how quickly the phone is answered. The data from these different mechanisms can be cross-compared to determine aspects such as the degree of innovatory behaviour and risk taking within the organization, levels of staff satisfaction, and the extent to which people are rewarded for new ideas. The findings can also be cross-compared to the HRM systems to see how well these systems are supporting the achievement of the desired outcomes (1).

The emphasis so far placed on softer measures, to do with understanding the well-being of the workforce and monitoring whether or not staff behaviours are changing as required, is not meant to imply that other harder and more quantifiable measures are not also needed. Of course, it is important to set objective targets that people can work towards, such as reducing cycle times, levels of rejects or defects, or improving levels of customer service, or the time to answer enquiries, within a certain time period. There is evidence that results-driven programmes, which focus on achieving specific, measurable, operational improvements within a short time frame, in order to help achieve specific organizational goals, can yield considerable benefits (2). The achievement of such goals will also provide visible early wins (see Chapter 5) in the change process.

Furthermore, it is important that any set of measures put in place support the change process by encouraging staff to work towards the company's change vision and goals, as well as providing an overall view of business performance. A technique for achieving this that has become popular since the early 1990s is the balanced scorecard (3). The balanced scorecard uses four sets of measures:

- financial measures to assess how the company looks to shareholders;
- customer performance measures to assess how the company is performing in the eyes of the customer;
- internal operational measures to assess how well the company is doing on the business processes that impact on customer service;
- measures of innovation and learning to assess if the company is continuing to improve.

The emphasis here has been placed on more qualitative measures because as this text has already stressed, unless individuals change, then the organization will not achieve its new strategy. Furthermore, simplistic measures such as levels of absence may be measuring levels of fear rather than levels of motivation, and may be masking problems.

7.3.2 Monitoring progress

Transition management is about ensuring that what is planned happens, but also about detecting and managing the unexpected. There are many well-known project management techniques that can help with developing detailed plans and schedules, monitoring progress against the plans, and developing resource requirements and implications (4). Similarly, budgeting techniques will be required to prepare budgets and monitor costs. However, monitoring progress is also about responding to people issues and understanding how recipients of change are reacting. This requires communication with people. This is particularly true when trying to drive in more transformational change which involves a radically different way of working to the past, which is possibly also associated with changes to organizational assumptions and beliefs. If despite the best efforts of the change agent(s) staff do not understand what is expected of them, appropriate new behaviours and beliefs will not develop.

The senior managers, the ones leading change, may be the last to find out about the things that are not progressing according to plan. Bad news does not travel upwards well. This means it requires explicit effort to collate information on how change is progressing from the perspective of the recipients. Various techniques can be used to monitor and evaluate the progress of implementation:

- *Focus groups and workshops*: Groups of people from across different organizational levels, departments and functions can be drawn together to discuss the change process. Participants can be asked to discuss both what is going well and why, and what is going badly and why. They may also be able to contribute ideas on how problems can be solved, and perhaps help each other with problems they are encountering. Workshops can become a way of sharing learning as well as monitoring change.

- *Management by walking about and open door policies*: Senior managers can make a point of being visible, and available for staff to talk to. They can visit departments and offices and discuss the progress of change with staff.
- *Team briefing*: Many organizations use team briefing to keep staff appraised of progress. Team briefings usually take the form of monthly meetings with a departmental manager or supervisor, at which organization-wide news is discussed, with a particular emphasis on issues that affect the staff attending the briefing. These meetings can be made two-way so that comments staff make are collated and passed back upwards (see Illustration 7.2).
- *Question and answer sessions*: Managers can host informal question and answer sessions for staff. These may take the form of informal staff/management meetings, such as breakfast or lunchtime meetings (see Illustration 7.2).
- *External consultants to monitor progress*: External consultants can be engaged to run focus groups or workshops, or conduct staff surveys. Staff may be more prepared to be open and honest about what they say in front of an outsider, particularly if guaranteed some level of anonymity.
- *Staff representatives who collate feedback*: Staff representatives can be nominated to collate feedback. They may be the attendees of the focus groups or workshops. Illustration 6.2 of change in the National Health Service (NHS) Trust discusses such an arrangement under symbolic structures.
- *Staff suggestion schemes* can be used to gather feedback on things that need changing or could be done better.
- *Confidential 'hot lines'* or internal mail mechanisms (see Illustration 7.2).
- *Attitude surveys* and other questionnaires.

Context-sensitivity is an issue for monitoring mechanisms as well. It is unlikely that people who are feeling unsure about what the future holds, and nervous about 'who's next' for redundancy, will tell an MD on a walkabout what is going badly. To be open about the way they are feeling, and what they see as the obstructions to change, those on the receiving end of the changes may initially need to be afforded some degree of anonymity before they will speak openly. Once it can be seen that there is no comeback for honesty, then it may be

Change in action

Illustration 7.2

> ### Examples of feedback mechanisms
>
> #### Team briefings
>
> The Royal Bank of Scotland launched Project Columbus, a review of the bank's structure and procedures, in 1992. The communication strategy utilized team briefings to collate feedback. Team leaders giving the briefings had to pass on questions they could not answer to a more senior manager who could provide answers. Answers had to be given at subsequent team briefings. In the nine months after the scheme launch in 1994, 750 questions were referred to and answered above the level of regional managers, and four times as many questions were answered by lower level managers (6).
>
> #### Informal meetings and internal mail mechanisms
>
> Allstate Insurance in the USA launched a 'reinvention' effort in 1994. Two monitoring mechanisms put in place included 'town meetings' and 'kiosks'. Town meetings were taken by the chairman or president and could be attended by all employees who could ask any questions they liked. Early reluctance to ask questions disappeared as the chairman and president proved themselves willing to answer honestly whatever questions were asked. The kiosks were a type of bulletin board on which employees could 'post' their comments. Many of the comments were not complimentary, but all were circulated to all senior managers each week, providing a regular stream of unfiltered feedback (6). Glaxo Wellcome used a similar kiosk mechanism when they underwent their merger in 1995. The most frequently asked questions were answered through a response that went to all employees (6).

possible to develop more open lines of two-way communication. For people to give feedback there also needs to be visible action on feedback, or staff will feel that their managers are not seriously interested in their opinions, so why bother.

7.4 Role management

The nature of the transition state and the impact of change on individuals requires special attention to the nature of change agency, and the roles of middle managers and change recipients during change.

7.4.1 Change agency

Chapter 1 has already discussed a number of skills required of change agents. These skills include the ability to *analyze* the change context, to *judge* the key contextual features of the change context and there-fore design an appropriate change approach, to take *action* to achieve implementation, to handle *complexity,* to be *sensitive* about the impact of change, and to be *aware* of the potential impact of one's own prefer-ences on the design choices made. Change agents also require good *influencing* skills because of the political nature of their role. However, change implementation is a complicated and difficult task. Transition management once change gets underway involves coordination of all the planned activities, but also the management and resolution of any unexpected problems. It involves:

- ensuring that what is planned happens, but also anticipating, detect-ing and dealing with the unexpected;
- providing continuity between formulation and implementation to ensure consistency in the way plans are turned into practice;
- overseeing the changes, which includes the coordination of the myriad change projects and change-related activities;
- monitoring change progress against plans.

Whoever is leading the change process may also take responsi-bility for transition management. However, the more fundamental the transition, the more time-consuming transition management is as a task. If change is being led by an individual, such as the MD or CEO, the individual may find that even if all his or her operational respon-sibilities are delegated, just being visible and championing the change takes up most of the time. Therefore, the bigger and more complex the change, the more likely it is that a transition management team will be needed to support the main change agent(s).

Similarly, middle and senior managers with operational respon-sibilities may also have insufficient time to fully address transition management responsibilities. Therefore, although creating a manage-ment team out of the hierarchy, or selecting representatives from the main stakeholder groups within the organization, or even assigning responsibility for transition management to the line managers, are all possibilities, in large-scale change it is more likely that the transition management team will be most effective if it is staffed with individuals whose sole responsibility is transition management. This team of additional change agents will need to be a powerful group and, there-fore, either accepted by the organizational power structure or given backing by the chief executive for what they do (6).

The individuals within the transition management team will also need to be well trained. The individuals will need to:

- understand the business;
- understand and buy-in to the change vision and goals;
- understand the mechanisms, tools and techniques of change manage-ment;

- have good people skills, be sensitive to people issues, and be well respected within the organization.

In major change projects, it is also more important that individuals managing the project have *process* rather than *technical* skills (see Figure 7.1). Process skills are to do with managerial and interpersonal skills, such as communication, consultation, team building, managing politics, and being able to motivate others and demonstrate enthusiasm. Technical skills are more to do with being able to use control techniques such as planning, budgeting, resourcing and scheduling, or the techniques and technology required by the change project, such as information systems. This does not mean that planning and scheduling tasks are not necessary, but that transition management involves more than traditional project management skills, particularly if it is accepted that managing change involves working with individuals and their interpretations.

	Strategic change	Operational change
	Rapid change, quick results	Slow change, slow results
	Significant resource commitment	Few extra resources needed
	Fickle support	Solid support
	Complex interdependencies	Few interdependencies
	Multiple 'ripples'	Self-contained
	Conflicting perceptions	Shared views
	Multipurpose changes	Single-function systems
	Unstable goals	Stable goals
	Confused responsibilities for process and outcomes	Clear 'ownership' of process and outcomes
Agenda	• Process • Control • Content	• Content • Control • Process
Skills	• Managerial and interpersonal • Business 'awareness' and political capabilities	• Technical • Traditional project management capabilities

Figure 7.1   *Change skills*
(Source: Adapted from D. Buchanan and D. Boddy, The Expertise of the Change Agent: Public Performance and Backstage Activity, *1992, Hemel Hempstead: Prentice Hall)*

7.4.2   Middle managers

Traditionally, middle managers were viewed as change implementors (7): the people in the organization responsible for taking the change plan and making it happen by translating it into actions. Middle manager tasks were more to do with monitoring and control (8). Middle managers are also often characterized as resistant to change, providing powerful obstructions to changes that counter their own self-interests (9).

However, most managers fulfil a complex and demanding role in change. They have to:

- undertake personal change themselves;
- implement the needed changes in their departments or teams;
- help and lead their staff through personal change;
- and in the meanwhile, keep the business going.

Thus, for much of the time managers are simultaneously change recipients and change implementors. They fulfil a role more accurately described by the term *change relayers* since they are responsible for absorbing change and passing it on. In effect, each manager of a team has to be a change agent in her or his own right. Managers need:

- *verbal communication skills* to fulfil their role of selling the need for change to their staff;
- *team building skills* to build a team from a group of staff who may not have worked together before;
- *coaching* and *counselling skills* to help members of their team cope with change;
- *negotiating skills* to help resolve problems encountered during the development of new working practices.

The traditional role often given to middle managers, one primarily to do with putting new working practices in place, is expanded by the need to spend an extensive amount of time furthering both their own understanding of change and that of their staff. If the demands of the relayer role on managers are not recognized by the designers of the change process, the outcome will be that this unanticipated role places an overhead on the time of middle managers when they themselves are having to undergo a lot of change. This can lead to a lack of time for important, although less tangible, change-related activities, such as communication with staff, team building, counselling and coaching.

The notion of middle managers as change relayers presents an alternative to the view of middle managers as a source of resistance. It suggests that it is not just getting support from middle managers for the changes that is important, they also need to have sufficient interpersonal skills and the time to fulfil their relayer role if they are not to become blockages to change. If designers of change still conceive of them in purely operational terms and automatically expect them to be sources of resistance, the designers may fail to recognize the pivotal role middle managers play in change, and to equip them with the necessary skills and support.

However, research also shows that middle manager involvement is important in the formulation of strategic decisions. This is not just because involvement in the thinking increases their levels of commitment and strategic understanding. Figure 7.2 shows that middle managers have four strategic roles, only one of which is *implementing strategy* (8). The other three are:

- *Championing* strategic alternatives, which involves middle managers in bringing innovations they have nurtured in their own department to senior manager's attention.
- *Synthesizing*, which is to do with middle managers collating information on external opportunities and threats and passing it on to senior managers.
- Middle manager *facilitation*, which involves middle managers in coaching and encouraging their staff to pursue new ideas and experimentation.

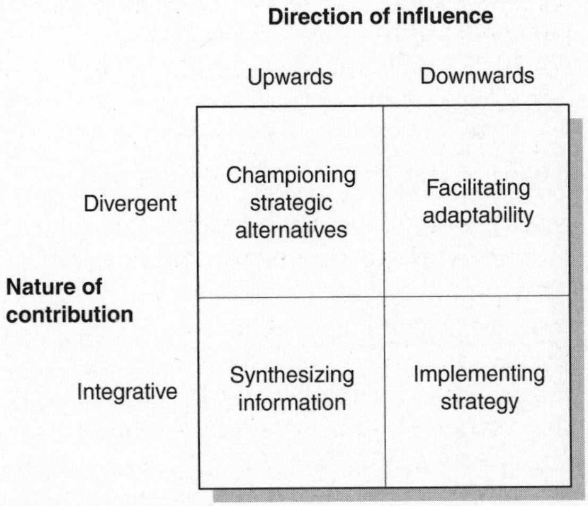

Direction of influence

	Upwards	Downwards
Divergent	Championing strategic alternatives	Facilitating adaptability
Integrative	Synthesizing information	Implementing strategy

Nature of contribution

Figure 7.2   *Middle manager change roles*
(Source: Reprinted with permission of Academy of Management, P.O. Box 3020, Briar Cliff Manor, NY 10510–8020, S.W. Floyd and B. Wooldridge, Dinosaurs or Dynamos? Recognizing Middle Management's Role, 1994, Vol. 8, No. 4. Reproduced with permission of the publisher via Copyright Clearance Center, Inc.)

As such, middle managers can play a role in developing new organizational capabilities and improving an organization's competitive advantage. More important, however, is ensuring that middle managers have the skills to make the strategic contributions that they should be capable of providing. This links back to the discussion on change capabilities in Chapters 3 and 4, to issues of training and development discussed in Chapter 6, and the need for influencing and political skills.

7.4.3   Recipients

Change recipients are those individuals on the receiving end of change, those that must adopt and adapt to change (7). Chapter 6 discusses the transition curve, and makes it clear that change is traumatic for everyone. As such, this text has already discussed some of

Change in action

Illustration 7.3

Survivors' syndrome

Survivors' syndrome describes the individual reactions to changes happening within organizations, often as a consequence of downsizing, reorganization and restructuring. The emotional responses of survivors are not unlike those experiencing redundancy, and can range from shock, anger and anxiety, to animosity towards management. Survivors are often concerned and guilty about their colleagues who have been made redundant, but also relieved that they still have a job. Survivors can also experience fear about their future security. The reactions and behaviours of survivors after change are not only potentially detrimental to the individual, but may have a detrimental impact on organizational performance and adverse effects on bottom line results.

Survivors' syndrome is also characterized by a variety of behavioural outcomes:

Reaction or emotions	Behaviours
shock	decreased motivation
anger	decreased morale
scepticism	increased stress
guilt	increased work effort
fear	decreased work effort
insecurity	increased loyalty to peers
anxiety	focus on personal goals
excitement	career insecurity

These reactions are often precipitated by increased work pressure. Survivors may be expected to work harder, over longer hours, to fulfil the tasks of

the issues about recipients and change, and how managers need to help both their staff and themselves through the transition curve.

Another issue affecting change recipients that has received far more recognition recently is that of survivors' syndrome. Following a change process in which there has been a loss of jobs and a change in working circumstances, those staff left often struggle to cope. Their feelings can lead to lower morale and therefore stress and lower staff performance if not tackled and managed. Illustration 7.3 discusses survivors' syndrome in more detail.

There are interventions that can be used to address survivors' syndrome, by equipping survivors to cope with personal change, and providing the skills for future survival (10):

- *Strategic interventions*, such as the creation of a new corporate culture which is compatible with the new business strategy, can help create a

Illustration 7.3 continued

departed colleagues. Technological changes and business process re-engineering bring new working practices and different ways of working together. Job security often decreases after layoffs as employees may perceive the threat of additional cuts in the workforce. For many survivors this means a lack of clarity and mission which feeds insecurity and uncertainty about future prospects within the company. Survivors also face the dismay of losing the peers who have formed the social fabric of their work life and often experience a loss of direction in their own career or future with the company. This can result in decreased confidence and commitment, and a lack of trust and loyalty to the organization, whilst for others these circumstances may provide an exciting opportunity to forge a new role.

The extent to which remaining employees exhibit the 'symptoms' of survivors' syndrome is mediated by both organizational and individual variables. These include the rationale for redundancy espoused by the company, the individual's position and role in the organization, their attitudes towards work, their self-esteem and personal coping mechanisms. The handling of redundancies is also an important factor. Survivors are concerned with the detail of the layoff procedure, for example, how the notice was communicated, what decision rule was used to choose people for redundancy, whether good services were provided for those leaving – including severance pay, counselling and the continuation of benefits. Such factors influence the perceived fairness of the layoffs, the perceived threat of further redundancies and the ability to cope with change, which in turn determine how survivors react when colleagues leave.

(Extracted from N. Doherty, 'Downsizing', in S. Tyson (ed.), *The Practice of Human Resource Strategy*, 1997, London: Pitman Publishing.)

clear vision of the future and help employees to become active agents in supporting and achieving the new vision.

- *Technostructural interventions*, such as participation, communication, problem solving and employee involvement, can provide information to survivors about their future role within the company, and support systems to help them achieve this.
- *Human resource management interventions* can address the rebuilding of the employment relationship after major change.
- *Human process interventions* can also help. These include team-building activities to facilitate open communication and rebuild trust, morale and commitment; counselling and support to facilitate the personal change required; and stress management to manage work role conflict, feelings of job insecurity, and role and career confusion.

The overall message from work such as that on survivors' syndrome is that unless the human factor in change is recognized, and managed appropriately and sympathetically, the reactions of the employees, on whom the organization ultimately depends for its performance, can nullify the effects of change, leading to poorer organizational results and profits than anticipated following change.

7.5   Summary

This chapter completes the discussion of the design and management of the transition state. Its aim has been to explain how the nature of the transition state places particular demands on those leading change, which in turn has implications for change agency skills, and monitoring and measuring mechanisms.

This text has stressed throughout that successful change is reliant on the development of a context-specific approach. There is no approach that can be applied irrespective of context. Furthermore, change implementation is a highly complex task involving a number of decisions about how change should be approached in the particular context in question. The overall process that a change agent is juggling during the transition looks something like that depicted in Figure 7.3.

Leadership or change agency requires first of all a diagnosis of the change context and judgement about the best approach to take. Then based on the selected approach, it is necessary to manage both the organizational change path *and* the individual transitions that will ultimately underpin the organizational transformation. The complexity of this process is increased by the need to conduct many additional tasks in parallel with the transition design and management. These tasks include working at all times through various communication mechanisms to keep individual understanding of the need for change and the goals of change aligned with the overall vision.

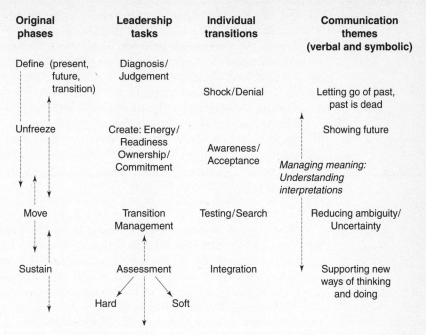

Original phases	Leadership tasks	Individual transitions	Communication themes (verbal and symbolic)
Define (present, future, transition)	Diagnosis/ Judgement		
		Shock/Denial	Letting go of past, past is dead
Unfreeze	Create: Energy/ Readiness Ownership/ Commitment	Awareness/ Acceptance	Showing future
			Managing meaning: Understanding interpretations
Move	Transition Management	Testing/Search	Reducing ambiguity/ Uncertainty
Sustain	Assessment	Integration	Supporting new ways of thinking and doing
	Hard Soft		

Figure 7.3   Putting it all together

The subsequent, and final, chapter revisits the change flow chart presented in Chapter 1, to help the reader put together the various steps in the development of a context-sensitive approach to the implementation and management of strategic change.

Notes and references

(1) See L. Gratton, V. Hope Hailey *et al.*, *Strategic Human Resource Management,* 1999, Oxford: Oxford University Press.

(2) See R.H. Schaffer and H.A. Thomson, 'Successful Change Programs Begin with Results', *Harvard Business Review*, January–February 1992, pp. 80–9.

(3) For more information on the balanced scorecard see three *Harvard Business Review* articles by R.S. Kaplan and D.P. Norton – 'The Balanced Scorecard – Measures that Drive Performance', January–February 1992, pp. 71–9; 'Putting the Balanced Scorecard to Work', September–October 1993, pp. 134–47; 'Using the Balanced Scorecard as a Strategic Management System', January–February 1996, pp. 75–85.

(4) For more information on project management techniques see G. Reiss, *Project Management Demystified,* 1992, London: E&F Spon, or J.R. Turner, *The Handbook of Project Based Management,* 1993, London: McGraw-Hill.

(5) For Royal Bank of Scotland example see 'Loud and Clear: Internal Communication at the Royal Bank of Scotland', *IRS Employment Trends 595*, November 1995, pp. 6–10. For Allstate example see R.E. Gorman and P. Overstreet-Miller, 'Why Change Efforts Fail to Connect with Employees', *Focus on Change Management*, June 1996, pp. 3–11. For Glaxo example see G. Duncan, 'Managing a Merger: Getting Employees on Board at Glaxo Wellcome', *Focus on Change Management*, July–August 1996, pp. 21–6.

(6) Some of the issues involved in transition management and putting together a transition management team are discussed by J.D. Duck, 'Managing Change: The Art of Balancing', *Harvard Business Review*, November–December 1993, pp. 109–18.

(7) For a description of the three change roles of strategist, implementor and recipient see R.M. Kanter, B.A. Stein and T. Jick, *The Challenge of Organizational Change*, 1992, The Free Press.

(8) The various roles that middle managers can play in change and the implications of this for the middle manager skill set and job roles are discussed briefly in S.W. Floyd and B. Wooldridge, 'Dinosaurs or Dynamos? Recognizing Middle Management's Strategic Role', *Academy of Management Executive*, 8, 4, 1994, pp. 47–57. For more detail see S.W. Floyd and B. Wooldridge, *The Strategic Middle Manager: How to Create and Sustain Competitive Advantage*, 1996, San-Francisco: Jossey-Bass.

(9) See, for example, W.D. Guth and I.C. MacMillan, 'Strategy Implementation versus Middle Management Self-interest', *Strategic Management Journal*, 7, 1986, pp. 313–27.

(10) See K. Buch and J. Aldridge, 'Downsizing Challenges and OD Interventions: A Matching Strategy', *Journal of Managerial Psychology*, 5, 4, 1990, pp. 32–7.

8

Concluding comments

8.1 Introduction

This text argues that successful change is reliant on the development of a context-sensitive approach to change. A diagnostic framework, the change kaleidoscope, has been presented. The kaleidoscope enables change agents to assess the change context in which they are operating, judge which are the key contextual features of this context, and therefore make appropriate design decisions to create a context sensitive change approach. This chapter summarizes the main arguments put forward by revisiting the change flow chart presented in Chapter 1. It also discusses the limitations of the models proposed. In conclusion some thoughts are presented about the role of change agents in the twenty-first century.

8.2 The change flow chart

Chapter 1 presents a change flow chart (see Figure 8.1) to explain the different stages in the development of a context-sensitive approach to change. As Chapter 1 explains, stages 1 to 3, analyzing the competitive position, determining the type of change needed and identifying the desired future state, are discussed in detail in this book's sister text *Exploring Corporate Strategy* and are not revisited here.

Stages 4 to 6, analyzing the change context, identifying the critical contextual features and determining the appropriate design choices, form the first half of this book and use the change kaleidoscope. Chapter 2 examines the choices that a change agent must make when designing a change process. The choices include the *change path*, the *change start point*, the *change style*, the *change target*, the *change roles* and the range of *change levers*. However, the key argument in Chapter 2 is that it is impossible to choose from this menu of choices without understanding the context of the organization. The change context and how to assess it is therefore examined in detail in Chapters 3 and 4.

Chapters 3 and 4 examine the change context through the change kaleidoscope. The concept behind this model is that every organizational change is unique. Therefore, in each change situation the configuration of contextual features will also be unique like fingerprints.

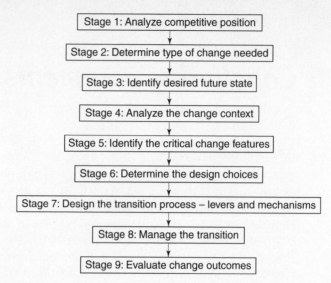

Figure 8.1   The change flow chart

However, there are questions which can be asked about any change context which remain constant. These questions include the amount of *time* available for change, the *scope* of the change required, the degree of *diversity* within the organization, the staff's *readiness* for change, the change *capability* and *capacity* to undertake change within the organization, the *power* relations and what needs to be *preserved* within the organization. Chapter 3 explores each of these contextual features in detail, and examines the implications for the design choices of each feature. Chapter 4 puts the change kaleidoscope into practice. Five case studies of companies undergoing different forms of change are analyzed. This chapter also illustrates the criticality of different features in different change situations.

Chapters 5, 6 and 7 consider the design, implementation and management of the transition phase of change – the final stages in the change flow chart. Too often change management stops after the design choices have been made, or worse still at the point of strategy development. These three chapters reveal the complexity of change management in action. They illustrate to the reader the different stages of transition, and the relationship between organizational transitions and the personal transitions of individuals. They also describe the different levers and mechanisms that can be used to support each stage of transition, and suggest methods of evaluating change through outcome measures.

8.3 The complexity of change

This book has sought to both reveal and address the complexity of change. Some texts either ignore the complexity of the process or reduce its management to ten-step plans. This has not been the purpose of the book. However, equally impractical are the texts which reveal the complexity of change management to the reader through clever analysis without seeking to help the practitioner or student through that analytical maze. This book has tried to honour the idea of management as both an intellectual and analytical pursuit, but simultaneously present it as an activity which is practical and requires action.

The models presented in the book therefore seek to provide universally applicable questions not answers. They ask questions about the features of change contexts which if ignored by change agents may become barriers to change in the longer term. Readers may like to see the models as mapping devices which help to hone their judgement in change situations. They are not predictive – they cannot take the place of judgement. They merely seek to inform judgement. Furthermore, the models have their limitations. They are not dynamic and organizations may need to use them in an iterative way. In addition, they can only capture the complexity of change if the reader grasps the way the contextual features of any change situation interconnect, and the uniqueness of these interconnections within each new change scenario.

8.4 In summary: change agency in the twenty-first century

The ability to manage change is fast becoming a mainstream competence for managers. It is no longer an optional extra in the managerial toolkit. This is driven by the pace and nature of organizational change, rather than any fashion pushed by business schools or consultancies. The pace and nature of change is also determining the composition of change competence. Change is so rapid and so constant that it is rendering obsolete universalistic formulae to many management problems. Best questions become the key tools rather than best practice.

For that reason change agents require many strengths. They need intellectual rigour to ask penetrating questions and dig deep into an organization's life in order to understand it. To do that they need a curiosity and a maturity at the same time. They need curiosity to make them ask the peculiar questions that would be missed otherwise: they need maturity to recognize that change is difficult because organizations and their staff are complicated to understand. They also need maturity to appreciate the subtle interconnections that exist within organizations, and a sensitivity to understand the implications of change on the lives of employees and the wider society. Yet, at the end of the day, these sensitive, mature analysts have also got to make judgements, take action and manage the consequences of those actions with as much skill as was needed for the analysis and design.

Appendix 1
The Cultural Web

A1.1 Introduction

The cultural web shown in Figure A1.1 provides organizational members with a way of auditing their organization's culture, and the barriers to change presented by the existing culture. All of this is discussed in some detail in *Exploring Corporate Strategy* (Chapters 2, 5 and 11), to which the reader should refer if a fuller understanding of these issues is required. It is also possible to use the web to build an outline vision for a desired new organization. This is referred to as re-webbing (1). A comparison of the new and old webs gives managers a good feel for the extent of change to be undertaken.

The purpose of this appendix is to provide a reminder of the principles of the cultural web for those who have read *Exploring Corporate*

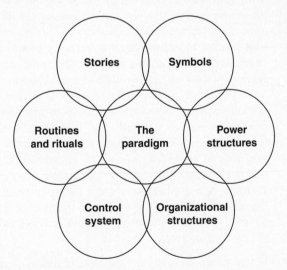

Figure A1.1   The cultural web of an organization
(Source: *Adapted from G. Johnson, 'Mapping and Re-Mapping Organisational Culture', in V. Ambrosini, G. Johnson and K. Scholes,* Exploring Techniques of Analysis and Evaluation in Strategic Management, *1998, Hemel Hempstead: Prentice Hall)*

Strategy and an introduction to the web for those who have not done so.

A1.2   *A definition of culture*

Culture is often defined as 'the way we do things around here'. However, this definition implies that the visible action and behaviour of an organization's members *is* the organization's culture. Behaviours are certainly part of culture, but not the only aspect of it. They represent the tip of the iceberg, the visible manifestation of culture. Beneath the day-to-day language, behaviour and actions of the members of an organization lie a set of basic assumptions and beliefs that are driving the behaviour. Therefore, culture here is defined as 'the deeper level of basic assumptions and beliefs that are shared by members of an organization, that operate unconsciously and define in a basic 'taken for granted' fashion an organization's view of itself and its environment' (2).

A1.3   *The cultural web*

The cultural web reflects this cultural definition in the way it is constructed. The assumptions and beliefs are held in the paradigm, and are hedged around and connected to everyday visible behaviour by the other aspects of the web surrounding the paradigm, namely tangible aspects of the organization such as structures and control systems, but also harder to define aspects such as formal and informal power structures, symbols, stories and myths, and routines and rituals. Table A1.1 provides an explanation for all the elements of the web.

Figure A1.2 shows a completed web for Andersen Consulting, one of the world's largest consultancy companies. The assumptions in the *paradigm* are to do with the fact that Andersen has 'one firm, one voice' internationally, which means that the firm has a common style and way of operating across all countries. The common way of operating is encapsulated in the 'Andersen Way' which is instilled into all recruits, since Andersen until recently primarily recruited their staff from university and developed them through the Andersen training courses. Finally, the organization is a partnership. The other aspects of the web include:

- Many *routines* support the Andersen Way and 'One firm, one voice'. There is much emphasis on training to teach staff the Andersen Way of doing things in all aspects of their work. These courses are taken by Andersen people – the more senior staff teaching more junior staff about the Andersen Way. Promotion is on merit leading to an up or out system. Staff development is also important. Each junior staff member

Table A1.1   *Elements of the cultural web*

- The *paradigm* is the set of assumptions about the organization which is held in common and taken for granted in the organization.
- The *routine* ways that members of the organization behave towards each other, and that link different parts of the organization. These are the 'way we do things around here' which at their best lubricate the working of the organization, and may provide a distinctive and beneficial organizational competency. However they can also represent a taken-for-grantedness about how things should happen which is extremely difficult to change and highly protective of core assumptions in the paradigm.
- The *rituals* of organizational life, such as training programmes, promotion and assessment point to what is important in the organization, reinforce 'the way we do things around here' and signal what is especially valued.
- The *stories* told by members of the organization to each other, to outsiders, to new recruits and so on, embed the present in its organizational history and flag up important events and personalities, as well as mavericks who 'deviate from the norm'.
- Other *symbolic* aspects of organizations such as logos, offices, cars and titles; or the type of language and terminology commonly used: these symbols become a short-hand representation of the nature of the organization.
- The formalized *control systems*, measurements and reward systems that monitor and therefore emphasize what is important in the organization, and focus attention and activity.
- *Power structures* are also likely to be associated with the key constructs of the paradigm. The most powerful managerial groupings in the organization are likely to be the ones most associated with core assumptions and beliefs about what is important.
- In turn the formal *organizational structure*, or the more informal ways in which the organizations work are likely to reflect power structures and, again, delineate important relationships and emphasize what is important in the organization.

Source: Adapted from 'Mapping and Re-mapping Organisational Culture', G. Johnson, in *Exploring Techniques of Analysis and Evaluation in Strategic Management*, V. Ambrosini, G. Johnson and K. Scholes (eds), 1998, Hemel Hempstead, Prentice Hall.

has a counsellor. To maintain upwards feedback to the partners, there are regular partner/manager dinners.

- *Control systems* also support the Andersen Way, with standardized training, teaching staff standardized procedures and methodologies. The training is supported by extensive manuals. To ensure each country releases staff to act as faculty on training courses, they are assigned a training budget for faculty that they have to meet.
- The *structure* follows a complex matrix structure across industry sectors and skill groupings.
- Most *power* resides with the partners.

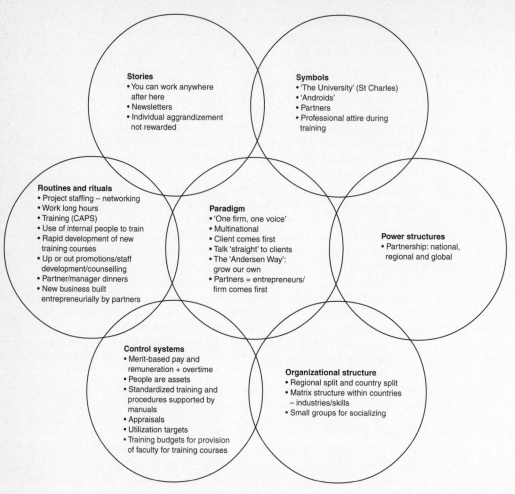

Figure A1.2   *Andersen Consulting prior to business integration*
(Source: *Adapted from Mary Ackenhussen and Sumuntra Ghoshal,* Andersen Consulting (Europe): Entering the Business of Business Integration, *1992*)

- *Symbols* emphasize the training. The main training centre at St Charles, Illinois is known as 'The University', and professional clothes are worn during training courses to emphasize the importance of the training. The strong Andersen culture is recognized internally and externally to the firm by the term 'Andersen Androids'. Partners are also symbolic of the firm's structure and way of working.
- One of the key *stories* recognizing the strength of the training and staff development at Andersen's is that after working at Andersen you can work anywhere else. There are newsletters spreading information about what the firm is doing. It is also recognized that individual aggrandizement is not a thing that Andersen Consulting values.

A1.4   *Completing a cultural web*

When completing a cultural web, fill in the outside circles first. Remember to consider not just the formal structures, but also the informal structures and power networks. In particular concentrate on the softer aspects, such as language and ritual. Once the outside circles are complete, consider what these circles say about the organization. Try and work out what the organization cares about most. Customers? Costs? Staff? Consider how the organization functions. Is it complacent, arrogant, entrepreneurial, bureaucratic, fast to respond, slow to respond and so on? Use these thoughts to complete the paradigm.

To complete a desired web for the future organization, fill in the paradigm first, then think about what is needed in each of the outer circles to support this. For instance, it is no good putting 'market led' into the paradigm if there is then nothing about customers or understanding markets in the outer circles.

A1.5   *Conclusion*

This appendix is only intended to provide a brief review of the key aspects of the cultural web. However, once the cultural web has been completed, it is possible to use it to address a number of questions. These include issues such as:

- To what extent does the existing culture support or hinder the desired changes that need to be made?
- To what extent does the existing culture need to be changed if the desired changes are to be implemented?
- To what extent does the existing culture underpin existing organizational competencies that need to be retained?

The main text of this book builds on this list of questions. In Chapters 3 and 4, it discusses how to use the cultural web to help identify the scope of change to be undertaken, the degree to which existing aspects of the culture need to be preserved or destroyed, and the degree of cultural homogeneity across the organization. In Chapters 5 and 6, the text discusses how to use the web to diagnose barriers to change, and how to use the new web to develop some of the levers and mechanisms that can be used to help deliver the needed changes.

Notes and references

(1)   For more information on webbing and re-webbing, also refer to G. Johnson, 'Mapping and Re-mapping Organisational Culture', in V. Ambrosini, G. Johnson, and K. Scholes (eds), *Exploring Techniques*

of Analysis and Evaluation in Strategic Management, 1998, Hemel Hempstead: Prentice Hall.

(2)   Edgar Schein gives this definition of culture in *Organisational Culture and Leadership,* 1985, Jossey Bass, p. 6.

Appendix 2
The People Process Model

A2.1 Introduction

The People Process Model (1) has been developed by Lynda Gratton and assesses the strength of strategic linkage between human resource management processes and business strategy. Therefore, since the model can assess the links between strategy and employee behaviour it is also useful for measuring *change capability*. If an organization has a visible ability in narrowing the gap between what an intended business strategy wants to achieve and how employees direct their everyday behaviour then strategic implementation becomes a rhetoric not a reality. Correspondingly, if that strategic linkage is strong, then an organization's capability in implementing strategic change processes will be greater than in companies where there is no apparent link between employee behaviour and business strategy.

A2.2 The People Process Model

The model works by grouping human resource management processes into three clusters: achieving short-term business objectives; assessing the long-term; and embedding transformational processes (see Figure A2.1). The model argues that by being constantly attentive to both short-term and long-term people management requirements, an organization can:

- assess what its human resource needs are for the future;
- assess these needs against its current short-term abilities;
- implement a series of transformational interventions to narrow the gap between future requirements and present capabilities.

The transformation cluster examines the activities of leadership development, transformation of the workforce and organizational transformation. These measures alone assess change capability within an organization. However, a further indication of change capability is gained by assessing the extent to which these three change activities

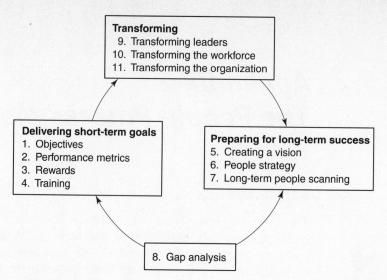

Figure A2.1   *The People Process Model*

are also linked to the activities in the short-term and long-term clusters. If they are linked then the organization is capable of constantly realigning employee behaviour on an incremental basis.

The cluster of human resource processes concerned with achieving short-term business objectives are standard activities within a performance management system. They include objectives, performance criteria or the measures against which performance is assessed, identification and delivery of training and development and determination of rewards. The key question that the model poses is the extent to which these activities are strongly aligned with business objectives. Can an individual link her/his individual performance objectives with the objectives of the organization's overall business strategy? Do reward, training and development appear to reinforce behaviour that is consistent with business objectives? Are the measures used within the performance appraisal scheme reflective of business objectives?

The long-term processes are concerned with the creation of a long-term human resources strategy and the amount of external labour market scanning that is carried out. This cluster of activities is similar to the activity of scenario planning within general business strategy. This model asks how much equivalent scenario planning is carried out for people management issues.

The model also allows for organizations to be rated in each of these activities along a scale of 1 to 5, where 1 = low linkage and 5 = high linkage.

A2.3 Summary

This text uses the People Process Model to help assess the contextual feature of change capability within the change kaleidoscope. The purpose of this appendix has been to explain how to complete the model. Chapters 3 and 4 give more detail on how it can help organizations to assess change capability.

Note

(1)   For more detail on the People Process Model see L. Gratton, V. Hope Hailey *et al.*, *Strategic Human Resource Management*, 1999, Oxford: Oxford University Press.

Appendix 3
Stakeholder analysis

A3.1 Introduction

Stakeholder analysis is covered in detail in Chapter 5 of *Exploring Corporate Strategy*. The purpose of stakeholder analysis is to identify those key individuals or groups of individuals who have an interest in an organization's performance and may be able to influence it in some way. As such, stakeholders include not only employees, managers, shareholders and unions, but also bankers, customers, suppliers and, potentially, the wider community.

When undertaking change, it is important to understand how much power these different stakeholders have to either facilitate or hinder change and whether or not they view the proposed changes favourably. Those that have power and support change need to be encouraged to support and back the changes. Those who have power but do not view change favourably either need to be convinced of the wisdom of the changes or worked round in some way. In particular, any change agent needs to understand the relative position of the most powerful people in the organization to the proposed changes, and how much power they have in comparison with the change agent, as the degree of support and opposition will affect the approach the change agent needs to take. This is discussed in some detail in Chapters 3 and 4. The purpose of this appendix is to explain how to conduct a stakeholder analysis.

A3.2 Stakeholder analysis

The technique presented in this appendix is the one proposed by Grundy (1), which is an adaptation from Piercy (2). It builds on the approach presented in *Exploring Corporate Strategy* which proposes the use of the power/interest matrix, in which the stakeholders are plotted on a grid in terms of their level of power to influence and their level of interest in the particular event or change under consideration. Here instead the matrix used is an influence/attitude matrix (see Figure A3.1). Stakeholders are plotted on the grid in terms of their attitude to the proposed changes, and the degree of influence they have on the organization. The degree of influence involves both a stakeholder's level of power *and* its degree of interest in the organization and what it does. For example, a stakeholder may be potentially powerful, but if she or he is also disinterested in the particular changes, then she or he will exercise a low influence. Just as with the power/interest matrix, once stakeholders are positioned on the matrix it is then possible to consider how to reposition them to gain the support needed for the proposed changes.

A3.3   Constructing a stakeholder analysis

Stakeholder analysis is best carried out by following a process. The steps in stakeholder analysis include the following (1):

1. Identify the key stakeholders given the current stage of implementation. Internal stakeholders are often the most influential and important during change and should therefore be considered first. However, this is not always the case as some strategic changes can impact greatly on customers and therefore make shareholders nervous. The stakeholder identification also needs to be as broad as possible, encompassing not only those who have decision-making power, but also those who will be affected in some way by the changes.

2. Decide if the stakeholders have high, medium or low influence on the issue in question.

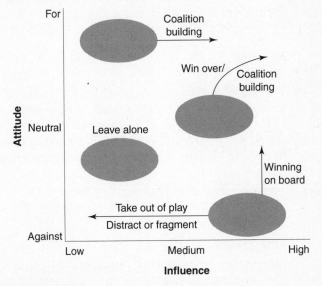

Figure A3.1   *Stakeholder analysis*
(Source: Reprinted from Tony Grundy, 'Strategy Implementation and Project Management', International Journal of Project Management, 16, 1, 1998, pp. 43–50. With permission from Elsevier Science)

3. Decide if, at the time the assessment is being made, the stakeholders are for the proposed changes, against them, or neutral.
4. Position the stakeholders on the grid to assess the extent to which the change agent can exercise her or his power to direct change.
5. If the change agent cannot direct change, or directing change would be inappropriate for some reason, maybe because it would risk alienating key stakeholders, or possibly losing key members of staff, then it is necessary to consider a different change style and approach.

Various strategies can be considered for tackling obstructive stakeholders. As shown in Figure A3.1, obstructive stakeholders can be won over or removed from the game in some way. Obstructive stakeholders may be converted into supporters of the changes if they are involved in a more collaborative or participative change approach, and are able to contribute their ideas. Alternatively, it may be necessary to use more manipulative or coercive means on powerful and obstructive stakeholders. This may involve ensuring they do not lose out as a result of the changes in a way they fear they might. If the change agent has enough power, very antagonistic stakeholders could be allowed to leave the organization, or moved to a position where they have less power to obstruct the changes.

A parallel approach may be to build the power and influence of those who do favour the changes. Those who are for the changes, but weak in power, can possibly be brought together into a coalition to make them more powerful. It may also be possible to use stakeholders who are in favour of the changes to win over those who are antagonistic.

A3.4   Conclusion

The main purpose of stakeholder analysis, as it is presented in this text, is to enable change agents to determine the relative position of key stakeholders to the proposed changes, and therefore how this affects the approach to change they need to take. The analysis can also be used to identify what barriers to change are presented by the stakeholders. It therefore provides a starting point to enable any change agent to develop a strategy for tackling those stakeholders who have the power to exert a negative influence on the change process.

References

(1) See T. Grundy, 'Accelerating Strategy Change: The Internal Stakeholder Dimension', *Strategic Change*, 6, 1997, pp. 49–56.
(2) See N. Piercy, 'Diagnosing and Solving Implementation Problems in Strategic Planning', *Journal of General Management*, 15, 1, 1989.

Index